A Gospel Journey
through Lent and Easter

From Ashes to Fire

*Other Books of Peter Varengo
published by Coventry Press*

We want to see Jesus

You are the kingdom

A Gospel Journey
through Lent and Easter

From Ashes to Fire

Peter Varengo

COVENTRY
PRESS

Published in Australia by
Coventry Press
33 Scoresby Road
Bayswater VIC 3153

ISBN 9781922589514

Copyright © Peter Varengo 2024

All rights reserved. Other than for the purposes and subject to the conditions prescribed under the *Copyright Act*, no part of this publication may be reproduced, stored in a retrieval system, or transmitted in any form or by any means, electronic, mechanical, photocopying, recording or otherwise, without the prior permission of the publisher.

Scripture quotations are from the *New Revised Standard Version Bible*, copyright 1989, Division of Christian Education of the National Council of the Churches of Christ in the United States of America. Used by permission. All rights reserved.

Catalogue-in-Publication entry is available from the National Library of Australia
http://catalogue.nla.gov.au

Cover design by Ian James – www.jgd.com.au
Text design by Coventry Press
Set in EB Garamond

Printed in Australia

Contents

The Word is the Message	
An Introduction	7
Ashes for Life	
Matthew 4:1-11	12
Tabor and Beyond: The Journey of Life	
Matthew 17:1-9	24
God in his Temple	
John 2:13-25	36
No Walls by the Well	
John 4:3-42	48
A Matter of Relationships	
Luke 15:1-3, 11-32	64
A Drama of Misery and Mercy	
John 8:1-11	79
Sight and Blindness – A Faith Intersection	
John 9:1-41	91
Signs of Death – Instrument of Life	
John 3:14-21	98
Life through Death	
John 11:1-45	108
Triumph and Execution	
(Holy Week)	
Luke 22:39-71; 23:1-56	114
Oneness in Love and Service	
Matthew 26:26-29 / John 13:1-17	123
Together at the Breaking of Bread	
(Holy Thursday)	
Matthew 26:26-30 / Luke 24:29-32 / John 6:53-57	130

The Cross – The Place of Encounter with God (Good Friday) John 18:1 to 19:42	148
Expectant Stillness (Holy Saturday) Genesis 1:1-5	162
The Impossible is Real The impossible becomes possible...	171
Resurrection: A Journey into Self-Discovery (Emmaus) Luke 24:13-35	186
Peace: the Gift of a Wounded and Risen Christ (Thomas) John 20:19-29	203
A Shepherd God John 10:1-30	217
Vine: Obsessive Possessiveness (Self) John 15:3-16	237
Goodbyes Among Friends John 15:14-15	251
Presence in Absence (Ascension) Mark 16:15-20 / Matthew 28:1-10	260
The Energy of God in our Hands (The Spirit) Acts 2:1-12	276
Love is his Name (Trinity) John 3:16-18	291
Food for the Poor from the Poor The Body and Blood of the Lord John 6:51-58 / Luke 9:11-17	298

The Word is the Message

An Introduction

'WORDS, WORDS, WORDS. *They have a plentiful lack of wit*', would muse Hamlet to Polonius. Entrapped by a tsunami of sounds and words spoken, sung, read, or just assumed or muttered to ourselves, we can become de-sensitised to reality, blissfully or tragically unaware of life and death hemming us on all sides. That is when encouragement or compassion, war or peace, affection or condemnations, excitement or shattering pain have lost all significance. This very superabundance of communication creates distance, heightening anonymity and estrangement even between people sitting at the same table, while interfacing each other across a telephone screen, without meaning or relevance of the message transmitted. But there is an escape. Our consciousness automatically shuts down until that instant of uneasy emptiness full of silence strikes us uncomfortably while we jog down the street or stand by the kitchen sink. Yes, paradoxically we are jolted into reality when struck by the 'sounds of silence' of Simon and Garfunkel's happy memory.

In this world of communication overload and of 'unheard and unheeded words', if communication is to become life-giving, we need to make a deliberate decision for 'listening'. Listening means to awaken in ourselves an awareness of the reality around us; and it demands that we focus our minds away from hearing words and onto the message that speaks to us through this reality. However, such a shift of focus depends on the hearer becoming a listener, allowing the superabundance of words to envelop us and turning into a challenge both at personal and communal level. This demands a conscious conversion from hearer to listener, allowing the superabundance of words to become a message challenging the listener to become the mature person one is meant to be. Alternatively, the word is dead, losing its very nature and transforming power, reduced to nothing beyond a meaningless amorphous sound offering a 'plentiful lack of anything'.

This is the technique underlying the Word of God adopted by the Master-Communicator. By tapping into the life experience of his contemporaries, Jesus draws the attention of his audience to hearing the words and then to listening to the message. Unfortunately, just as the over-profusion of words can choke our existence, when we fail to listen to the Word of God, as believers we can become equally anesthetised to God's presence.

In the Christian economy, the Word is never dead or empty but ever-present and life-giving, taking on a uniquely powerful and personal significance. God could not find a more apt way of communicating life and love to us than becoming personified in 'the Word', not as an amorphous sound or the result of some electronic or wizardry, but as a living and life-giving reality embracing the whole human experience The Word incarnates the very presence of God in human affairs, an active life-giving presence and life-giving power embodied in the very nature of the human psyche and story (John 1). Because of the absorption of this Word into our story, only the listener will be able to discover their own self as well as experience the God immersed in that personal self. The Word of God shuns any theoretical and abstract dissertation, but it delves deeply into the language of personal experiences embracing us in every insignificant skerrick of existence. We can neither escape its challenging message or deny its appeal by separating word and life or by ignoring the absolute interconnectedness between hearing and listening.

As the parable of the Sower warns us, even this 'living Word' can become empty and meaningless. Choked by the plethora of concerns and lacking any personal appropriation, the Word of God becomes disempowered of all its potential to bear fruit. If we are to become true disciples of the Master-Proclaimer, we need to become listeners, or our faith will dissipate into some amorphous sound uttered through a superficial ritual. Whether in liturgy, biblical reflection, or personal prayer, the Word of God is not about information but about transformation, never about some historical reportage of long ago, but for us and about us. calling out to us or through the multi-faceted encounters that dot our day every today.

By confronting us with our reality and delving to the very core of our being, Scripture narrative is meant to express and nourish the lived and living human-divine relationship with our God and with each other, a relationship called fullness of life energised by the Spirit. Only by listening and appropriating the word we hear, will we be able to discover our own self and experience God immersed in that personal self – not in a one-way monologue reminding God of our personal agenda, but in the listening within the silent depth of the heart, as Benedict invited us to do centuries ago, and then incarnating that message in our own life journey.

What is in contention, however, is the human readiness to receive and nourish that word in such a way that it will grow into abundant fruitfulness and energy for life. In the Gospel narrative of 'The Sower' (Matthew 13:1-9), we encounter an extravagant and careless God, who is never silent, nor does he desist from speaking his Word with generosity and largess whatever the human condition may be. The Sower is reckless and in his eagerness to disperse the goodness and life-giving power of the seed, scatters randomly and almost wastefully in large handfuls, without concern for the suitability of the soil to receive it and nurture it. In his eagerness to spread his generous goodness as widely as possible, no one is excluded, no human situation is ignored, and 'The Sower' takes no notice of stones, footpaths, or thorns. Surely, he must have realised that the rocky ground and the thistles would inevitably stifle growth and waste the goodness of the seed! That may well be the logical, rational, and economy-savvy look at our reality, focusing specifically on returns in kind and with substantial interest.

But that is not the perspective of the Sower of the Gospel, the Absolute Giver who wants everyone to have access to his gifts and the full potential for life. That is the God Jesus came to reveal; a God who knows no bounds or limitations when it comes to communicating his love and life with human beings. Life may be rocky and thorny, we may be dry, unreceptive or unresponsive, and we may ignore his gifts of life or be totally unaware of his presence. Yet, nothing will stop God from freely lavishing his goodness with extravagant generosity, regardless of our condition.

In this perspective, listening and responding to this 'wasteful' lavishness is the diamond drill of biblical communication, particularly in our liturgical gatherings as much as our daily experiences where the Word is scattered within the rocky soil of our life.

When the seed falls on a rich soil of perception, awareness and attitudes, Jesus promised a hundredfold fruitfulness but that is conditional to us embracing 'The Word' of God as a dynamic continuum of hearing-listening-and-reliving. As if in a mirror, WE are those thousands fed by Jesus out of nothing (John 6:1-15). We encounter blind Bartimaeus ignored by most and yet trusting as we sit by the side of the road, maybe seeing the bird pecking away the good seed of our life journey (Mark 10:46-52).

We crouch in the dust, gripped with terror and we breathe judgment and justification, facing execution (John 8:1-11). We are executioner and bystanders on Golgotha, confronting both despair and forgiveness (Matthew 27:46; Luke 23:34). We are Myriam, distraught and desperate, called by name into joy and ecstasy just when she is seeking a dead body in an empty tomb (John 20:11-18). Like the disciples of Emmaus, we may not expect or recognise the Lord, but he falls in step with us along the road to reassure us and enter the intimacy of our home (Luke 24:13-34). This is our experience; this is our story, and our God is right there in the midst of it all.

These are not casual repetitious accounts of long ago or ritualised performances today, but imperatives urging us to listen

and then to relive the message encapsulated in the Word – not as passive hearers but as active listeners and actors committed to making those narratives the blueprint of God's life-giving presence engulfing us within the soil of our human journey and energising us into life in spite of death from the deadness of Lenten Ashes to the conflagration of Easter Fire.

Ashes for Life

Matthew 4:1-11

THE GOSPEL READINGS throughout this Lenten season put before us a sequence of events or Jesus-encounters within the context of a journey. Jesus is the journeyman, his sights firmly set on Jerusalem – the place of final condemnation and death, but also the place of ultimate fulfilment in Resurrection. However, the progression of incidents that dot this journey towards life beyond death, and in spite of death, is neither casual nor random. Each episode challenges reader and listener to become a traveller, confronting specific situations in one's life that make for continuous growth in faith as a personal and communal relationship with God and commitment to the Kingdom. Jesus' journey is our journey, and the encounters along the road to Jerusalem are the inevitable challenges that make for authentic and mature discipleship.

Remembering Grandma

The beginning of Lent invariably awakens my memory of Grandma, now more than sixty years resting in the Easter of God. I believe that Grandma had a special relationship with Lent that she would bring into play in the most unconventional and surprising situations. Though our safety refuge from Dad's stern looks and sharp voice, whenever as grandchildren do we would try to push the boundaries of legitimacy or patience, Grandma would repeatedly bring Lent into play with her peculiar reproach; 'Stop being my Lenten penance'. Likewise, if we struggled to keep up with her short, brisk steps, she would turn around and call out that we were 'as long and as slow as Lent'. So, as children, we concluded that Lent was something unpleasant lasting a long time and upset Grandma.

On reflection, as I grew older, I discovered that unfortunately even today many of us would readily relate to this kind of belief through a false spirituality of self-denial and self-denigration expressed and justified by the traditional triad of prayer, penance and good works.

Doing versus Being

Lent is not the season of 'self-satisfying spiritual masochism' warming the heart, trying to convince ourselves that a little suffering for its own sake is good for us, or when we engage in some personally satisfying devotion 'to please God'. At the very first announcement on Ash Wednesday, the prophet Joel strongly condemned such practice aimed at self-justification in preference to a radical change of heart (Joel 2:12-13). Lent points to Easter, the new life beyond and in spite of Good Friday and death; and life is a journey and a process rather than a performance. Consequently Lent must be a radical process that incarnates life in spite of death in the reality of who we are. More that fulfilling a keeping a tradition of *doing something*, Lent must be a *commitment to incarnate* in ourselves new attitudes and perspectives that make for life and eliminate death in us and in the world around us by focusing not on ourselves but on God. The exterior or personal act of penance-prayer-and-work-of-charity is an outer sign pointing to an inner disposition of emptiness, docility, and trust in God.

An act of penance without that inner disposition of letting go unconditionally into God may feed our egos without necessarily leading to that conversion of heart and mind which Lent is meant to install and Easter is meant to celebrate in our world and in our very self. The physical hunger that fasting may engender must be a sign of our hunger for God, or it is nothing beyond lip service to an idol, satisfying our own ego and advancing claims on God. *The external act of doing is a sign that must project us into a spiritual reality of being* that speaks of a relationship with God and with each other as intense as the hunger of a starving man, and as deep as the yearnings of a woman trapped in loneliness and doubt in a desert place.

Such incarnation is neither automatic nor pre-programed through a personal performance but will inevitably demand a commitment and a struggle to journey through Good Friday by letting go of anything and everything that in some way hinders our growth towards the fullness of life with God. That is the meaning of penance and repentance.

'*Repent*' is the catch cry launched and resonating throughout this liturgical season of Lent as we begin our journey towards the new life of Easter exploding through the desolation and devastation of the cross. To achieve this, Lent *must be a journey of change, of review, and of renewal by undertaking an honest self-appraisal and thereby gaining both insight and energy towards re-establishing our authentic relationship with God.*

Any form of human growth and spiritual journey can only take place by moving on from an infantile faith focused on doing to the maturity of faith expressed on being, in relation to self, others, and God. From this standpoint, rather than the expression of an inevitable and painful change brought on by letting go, Lent is a critical invitation to grow from within by changing perception and revitalising our relationship with God and with each other. All this will inevitably demand some form of diminishment of self and of jealously guarded securities, but this diminishment is for the fullness of life and not for the sake of some self-righteous and self-satisfying ritual practice.

As believers, we need to be prepared to constantly review and renew the values that we hold dear, and jettison most of them as we grow and face ever new situations, so that they can energise us. We need to question the attitudes expressed through our rapport with each other. We need to be open in our religious expressions and never be satisfied with an inertia or a droning routine that satisfy our ego but stifle any sense of God's presence. Most of all, we need to challenge constantly our underlying understanding of both God and self – a God longing to be part of our personal history and of a self, yearning and seeking fulfilment through the humdrum of each day and in the whole of history.

Ashes: the Paradox of Change

Few of us would identify ashes as elements of change and transformation into new vitality and growth. Yet, paradoxically, local experience reveals that within a few days following a forest fire annihilating any semblance of life, nature quickly responds to the catastrophe by putting on an unexpected green tinge of newness and freshness. Somehow those very ashes that spoke of total and universal destruction become the signs and energy of a new vitality over that unredeemable death-like blackness that reigned supreme.

Here again Grandma's homemade and down to earth wisdom comes into play as she would surprise us by gathering cold ashes from the hearth and spray them on her beloved roses. I still remember her faint smile of self-satisfaction as she would instruct us that in this way, by seeping into the soil, those elements of destruction would become energy fertilising her colourful and scented garden as well as her favourite vegetables. By breaking the hard husks imprisoning the energy and vitality in the kennel of the seed, those very results of destruction and death would thus release energy of transformation into beauty and life. That is the call and the commitment that Christian Tradition confronts us on the very first day of Lent – break in order to release life out of death, Good Friday into Easter.

By the sign of ashes placed on our heads on the very first day of Lent, we are invited to challenge ourselves honesty and sincerely as Jesus did in his self-confrontation at the very beginning of his public life at John's baptism in the Jordan and in the loneliness and hunger of the desert. As we look ahead to the celebration of life through death in the Resurrection of Jesus at Easter, we are endowed with the sign of ashes and invited to commit ourselves to a complete transformation from what is death-dealing in us and around us into a new vitality and fullness of life. Lent unconditionally enjoins on us the absolute need to seek what may hinder us from reaching our full growth into our human and God-empowered fullness of life engendered and celebrated at Easter through the cross of Good Friday.

That is the call that resonates throughout the Christian Liturgy and Tradition on Ash Wednesday, but to achieve this self-awareness, we need a double process. We need to make space to allow our traditional Lenten triad of prayer, fasting, and almsgiving to transform hearts and minds. At the same time, as the Lenten Sunday liturgical narratives put to us, we need to harness energy and courage to undertake a journey of trust into the unknown future while remembering the glimpses of God in our past.

As believers, this search raises questions both of giving and of taking in terms of:

What is there in my life that needs regenerating?
What is there in me that hinders the releasing of the full vitality and energy God has placed within the kernel of my life?
What is there in me that prevents the greening of new life in those around me and in the world?

Lent calls to growth, a growth incarnated through letting go of anything that hinders or slows down the journey of faith (*fast*); secondly, through letting God reach deeply into the recesses of our heart and letting God do the talking (*prayer*); and finally by allowing ourselves to be thrown into total dependency on God and on each other (*almsgiving*).

The liturgical catchcry at this time of year is self-denial and penance expressed through fasting, prayer and almsgiving; and for centuries Christians have identified this dynamic trio as the instruments of purification and as the genesis of new life eventually blossoming out on Easter Sunday. Most of all, this is the time-honoured tradition sinking its roots deep in biblical times as *a sign of our commitment to let go of ourselves into God and of allowing God into the very fabric of our life and story.* However, the tradition – while being a powerful spiritual stimulus – also hides its traps as it can easily become a yearly practice for its own sake, to be resumed with monotonous regularity next year and for many years on, without meaning and with even less impact on our faith growth.

It is relatively easy to fast and to 'do penance' when it gives us the satisfaction of having kept Lent, but it is much more difficult to accept that God calls me, takes me as I am, journeys with me every step of the way, and then sends me to the other(s) to share my life with them, as they are.

As we embark on our Lenten journey, our focus must *shift from doing* something to *being and becoming* someone. Our concern must move from the practice of a performance or 'penance' that makes us feel good and worthwhile for having ticked a box, to making a decision to be and to become who we are meant to be in our relationship with God and the world.

In this context, we cannot overlook the fundamental call of Lent that *authentic penance has little to do with doing and everything to do with being.* What are our priorities, our ambitions, our energies? Indeed, who is and where is our God, right now and throughout our life journey? What are the energies, gifts and talents that I can harness to enliven my faith and my personal relationship with God and with others? What is there that hinders me from finding God, or hinders God from entering my life? What needs to change in my life in relation to self, others and God? What do I need to let go and/or take up in a different way? These are not pious or academic questions. They are the sort of questions that underlie every Lenten journey, and give meaning to the external 'penance', which otherwise would ultimately engender a sense of self-satisfaction, rather than an honest encounter with God.

Encounter and Identity in the Desert

Liturgically, the first two months of the calendar year can be called an insert in a fast-moving narrative, compacting thirty years of Jesus of Nazareth's earthly life into a few lines. Following immediately upon the infancy description of Christmas, the Gospel narrative suddenly confronts us with a mature, grown-up Jesus engaged in two personal but very significant incidents of self-disclosure. At first, he mingles unknown and unnoticed by the river Jordan among the adult crowds seeking baptism by John the Baptist, and soon after we find him struggling in the desert of loneliness, hunger and temptation. Although our post-Christmas and pre-Lent liturgical sequence disconnects these two incidents by a long hiatus of weeks, both events represent an important unity of self-revelation in the overall narrative. While marking the beginning of Jesus' active ministry, they enable us to plumb the depths of the revelation that they share and the challenge that they set to the believer, by positing the same question of Jesus and of the believing disciple: *Who are you really? Do you know?*

By identifying with the crowds at the Baptism in the Jordan (Matthew 3:13-17), Jesus proclaims his total immersion within the specific cultural and religious situation as the place of encounter with God. In that event, the Father anoints Jesus of Nazareth with the fullness of divinity by calling him 'The Beloved', thus linking human and divine in a unique bond. Humanity is now beloved, and God becomes totally enmeshed in our human story in the reality of time and place. At the same time, in the desert event which all the three Synoptics (Matthew 4:1-1; Mark 1:12-13; Luke 4:1-13) introduce immediately after John's baptism, Jesus embraces the fullness of human experience with its heavy freight of struggle and suffering and eventually death, making our humanity part of God's story of divine presence. Jesus is both the Beloved integrally caught up in the divine, and the one so caught up in our human story that our humanity becomes the place of God's active presence in the world.

In answer to our question of our identity and destiny as to who we are and are meant to be, on the blueprint of Jesus' first human self-disclosure, our answer must be the same as Jesus': as human beings we are 'the Beloved' caught up in the life-giving presence of God and destined for fullness of life, while struggling and wandering through the desert of temptations, doubts, human weakness and failure (John 10:10). What Lent really asks of us is to reverse a negative, self-centred, and practice-driven perspective by looking at this time of year as an invitation to journey and to grow more deeply into God and with God. This is the death-life-death vision imaged by the ashes and the liturgy of Lent and the challenge addressed to us as we undertake the journey of renewal and transformation.

Lent begins with Jesus in the desert (Matthew 4:1-11; Mark 1:12-13; Luke 4:1-13. While Matthew and Luke will focus on both the setting and on Jesus' handling of the situation (Matthew 4:1-11; Luke 4:1-13), in his typical sharp and concise style, Mark does not tell us what Jesus is doing in the desert; he simply highlights the *being* by focusing exclusively on the situation of struggle that Jesus lives through. Mark's narrative lacks details, thus reflecting the starkness of the desert setting, and he has none of the details of temptations and struggle described by the other two Synoptics. However, Mark introduces a strong sense of urgency, telling us that 'the Spirit *immediately* drove Jesus into the wilderness Before launching into a frantic mission of healing and liberation (*doing*), Jesus is driven into a situation of wilderness, where he is to confront demons and wild animals (*being*).

There is a sudden and crucial turn in Jesus' life as he sets out on the mission the Father has given him, and the same urgency must belong to his followers. What Lent really asks of us is the urgency of focusing on who we are with God at the core of our being and by reversing the more negative, self-centred, and practice-driven performance, and heed the invitation to journey, and to grow more deeply into God, and with God. This is the kind of reversal that Jesus had to confront in the desert. He had to come to terms with the question of who he was, before finally abandoning himself to the mission set out for him as the Beloved of Abba, sent to reveal and realise the presence of God in the reality of unfolding history.

Tempted as we all are, in the desert of loneliness and hunger, Jesus confronted his crises and he had to decide where his priorities lay, choosing between his natural tendencies and God's plan for him. He has to let go of something in order to be faithful to the Father who sent him, lived in him, and operated through him.

In this crisis situation, Jesus could easily have taken the easy way out and abused his divine powers to prioritise his personal human needs of food, security and control, instead of remaining open to the call of God in his life. Instead, he stood up against any obsessive passiveness with regards to the good gifts bestowed on the earth by God.

Confronted with the challenge of his own personal needs and ambition to reveal himself as the wonder-worker to attract attention and make an impact by safely throwing himself off the pinnacle of the temple, he chose to be the human instrument of God and let his life speak of the presence of God by rejecting the advances of self-centeredness and chose trust by placing his life in the hands of God.

None of us wants to admit to living in constant uncertainty, in total dependency on others, with chronic insecurity as our life companion. Driven by the natural tendency to seek power and gain control of oneself and of others at all costs, Jesus – on the mountain where he could claim absolute control and possession – rebelled vehemently against that insatiable human hunger for power and control, be it over our lives, our futures, or our self-imposed destinies, and embraced total insecurity and abandonment into the hands of the Father.

Decisions in the Desert

In the foreboding desert environment, Jesus struggles vehemently in the desert of temptation, loneliness and depravation, as he tries to come to terms with the prospect of uncertainty and the challenges of the unknown journey set out for him by the Father (Luke 4:1-13. Matthew 4:1-11, Mark 1:12-13) while setting up a dilemma for the disciple, inviting us to seek the focus of existence and of decision to be a truer disciple. The resolution of the dilemma will demand a painful either/or decision between God and self. Facing the unknown in the desert of temptation, Jesus rejected unequivocally exclusive compulsion with material goods (bread), obsession with self-importance and personal ambitions (pinnacle of the temple) and said 'No' to control and power (mountain).

Lent is a call to live through the experience of emptiness and dependency, abandonment, alertness, and of trust borne of deep attitudes of mind and heart, alert and actively in tune with the presence of God. In the desert of loneliness and hunger, Jesus must decide where his priorities lie in terms of obsessive passiveness with regards to the good gifts bestowed on the earth by God. On the pinnacle of the temple, it would have been easy to turn on the stunt of a deceitful side-show charlatan to draw attention to himself and satisfy that almost natural thirst for adulation and popularity that puts self at the centre of all reality. Finally, as human beings, we have an insatiable hunger for control, whether over our lives, our futures, or our self-imposed destinies.

Deep down, none of us wants to admit to living in constant uncertainly, in total dependency on others and ultimately on God, and with chronic insecurity as our life companions. That was precisely the future and the mission that the Father had entrusted to Jesus and, as for all of us, his humanity rebelled vehemently against this absolute lack of control. Yes, we all want to control our lives, but ultimately, we know that we will never be able to do that without resorting to violence or some destructive behaviour that ultimately negates life itself.

The immediate aftermath of a forest fire is a desert of ashes, and from the perspective of a Lenten journey, the only fitting rejoinder for us is to have the courage to create the desert within us and all around us. In that foreboding environment, I can face my own self and my values and come to terms with my personal demons. Stripped of all security and support systems, the desert one becomes attuned to the encounter with God, with self, and with others, demanding reassessment and conversion, focusing entirely on God at the core of one's being and shedding the baggage that may hinder both the search and the encounter in any way.

One of the most antagonistic energies of our culture is the obsession with doing and with having. Our self-worth is often measured by production, competition and social-climbing; and sometimes we stop at nothing to achieve our ambitious designs. We become so driven by our achievements, our personal success stories and by our me-centred outlook on life, that there is no room left in our soul for anything or anybody else, be it values, people, social awareness, or even spiritual strivings, and least of all for God. As a prelude to his ministerial journey, Jesus said no to any exclusive compulsion with material goods, to obsession with self-importance and personal ambitions, and unequivocally rejected control and power.

How do we respond to the compulsion to use, to have, and to grasp for the sake of our own personal satisfaction? Within the web of relationships entangling our day, how do we relate to each other at home, at work, or just down the street? Are control and self-seeking the energy of our lives, or are we motivated by love, compassion, and understanding?

All of us are challenged to confront ourselves with the same critical questions, and to seek our own life-giving response. These were the wild animals Jesus as a man had to struggle with in the desert in trying to come to terms with the challenges that hindered the full expression of his identity, before finally abandoning himself in faithfulness and trust to the mission set out for him as the Beloved of Abba. These are also the wild animal-like obsessions that threaten constantly our true self and prevent God from energising us into who we are meant to be.

Conclusion

Lent leads to Easter as the definitive sign of God's active, life-giving presence in our human story even through the struggles and misunderstandings of the Good Fridays of our daily life and experience. In 2018, Pope Francis spelt the following Lenten program of spiritual renewal.

> *Fast from complaints and contemplate simplicity.*
> *Fast from pressures and be prayerful.*
> *Fast from bitterness and fill your hearts with joy.*
> *Fast from selfishness and be compassionate to others.*
> *Fast from grudges and be reconciled.*
> *Fast from words and be.*
> *Fast from pessimism and be filled with hope.*
> *Fast from worries and have trust in God.*
> *Fast from hurting words and say kind words.*
> *Fast from anger and be filled with patience.*

Tabor and Beyond: The Journey of Life

Matthew 17:1-9

AS WE MOVE into the high liturgical and personal drama of Holy Week and Easter, we are confronted with the primal and ultimate call of the Lenten journey: we are challenged to change. As uncomfortable as the call may turn out to be in real terms, it is unavoidable if we want to grow into people who not only believe and celebrate Easter, but live their whole life as Easter People, because this is who we are meant to be.

Luke the evangelist shapes much of his narrative around Jesus' journey to Jerusalem, the place of fulfilment through death and resurrection, and this journey becomes the epitome of the disciples' journey of Lent towards life through and in spite of death.

From Fishermen to Mountain Climbers

It was not the first time that Peter, James and John had reason to believe that they were Jesus' favourites. Throughout the Gospel narrative, this trio of names occurs with frequent regularity as the official witnesses to some particularly significant moments in Jesus' journey to Jerusalem, such as the occasion of the climb of Mount Tabor which all the three Synoptics record (Matthew 17:1-8, Mark 9:2-8, Luke 9:28-36 as well as 2 Peter 1:16-18).

Yet, for the puzzled reader, the sudden and unexpected invitation to take a stroll up a mountain conjures up anything but a feeling of favouritism. That isolated rocky outcrop – rising stark and solitary in the middle of the Galilean plain – is barren and steep, uninviting, and challenging to someone more at ease with casting for fish or mending nets on a rocking and familiar boat. Peter and company knew fish and fishing and they could readily face even a treacherous gale out on the lake. The invitation to trudge their way up the mountain must have sounded preposterous to the trio of fishermen. Why risk life and limb to venture on an unfamiliar track that revealed no life and held only dangers, while at the same time uncovering painful weaknesses and inadequacies? Besides, the fertile plains of Galilee were home, reassuring the trio of both familiarity and security.

Not an unfamiliar story really, resonating with much of our experience. Often, we are called to incarnate the three fishermen turned mountain climbers, as we are called unexpectedly out of our well laid plans, of our securities and of our clearly marked limits, and being thrust into total insecurity, not knowing why we should leave what to us seems to be life-giving in order to venture into the unknown and unwanted and sometimes meaningless life-situations. Yet, to claim and live by faith often begins with letting our God take us out of our tried and true, in order to face unplanned and unexpected life insecurities. We have to let go of personal plans and begin to trust this God who may well invite us to where we would rather not go. We feel safe within the boundaries that we have set ourselves over the years, and we know our limitations and our strengths.

The disciples thought they knew who Jesus was and how God worked, but to discover the full reality of the God they claimed to know and feel comfortable with, they had to climb the mountain instead of sailing fishing boats on the lake.

Journeys necessarily imply movement; change of position and of perspective, and constant reassessment of where one is and of where one is going. By contrast, holding on to one's position and/or perception because it is comfortable and offers security denies any possibility of growth and of reaching fulfilment. There is no arrival unless there is a departure or a journeying on. This is precisely the first step towards the fundamental call of Lent: conversion

Conversion: A Journey for Change

Like the ascent to Tabor, conversion demands a movement from a position of comfort into one of personal 'dis-comfort', from 'I know' and personal agenda into the liminality of stepping on unfamiliar ground and up a steep and insecure track, precisely when 'we know' and we feel perfectly at home with the gentle ebb and flow of our well-worn boat.

The disciples thought they knew who Jesus was and how God worked, but to discover the full reality of the God they claimed to know and feel comfortable with, they had to climb the mountain instead of sailing fishing boats on the lake.

If we are to undertake the life-long journey of insecurity called conversion and grow into fullness of life in discipleship, we must first acknowledge our endemic unconfessed sin of self-security and comfort within the plain of daily life and of feverish activity. Over the years on the plain of sameness of misguided self-knowledge, self-styled boundaries of limitations and strengths, we are in control, and we readily become conscious of our own self, fathom where we can go and assess what we can do. However, as we journey through the years, we must leave the plain of security, and climb the harsh mountains of age, tiredness, and insecurity, with no guarantee that we will be able to bear the challenges and maybe with no support system to strengthen or enlighten us. Unless we embrace the insecurity of the passing of years, we will never grow into adulthood, regardless of our chronological age. To claim discipleship, we must convert from attachment to our life to abandonment to God's plan for our life. even a life carrying a heavy load of sinfulness and brokenness. To move into the experience of God, we must first confess to our sin of comfort and personal security and abandon ourselves, yes, our sins and fears included, into God's plan for our individual lives.

Being versus Doing

Security can take many different forms, not the least of which is that sense of personal purification achieved through a ritual that has become repetitious and mechanical, or a routine liturgical performance such as a routine confession of a long list of sins. that satisfies our ego but leaves no imprint on the rest of our life because we do not let it challenge us. The ancient Lenten tradition of *fast, prayer and works of charity* is not a call to perform a yearly repetitious routine of religious practices but a demand by the ancient prophets to allow ourselves to be lured into the desert – of letting go of our own self by being thrown into total dependency on God (fasting) and there heed the invitation to 'let God reach deeply into the recesses of our heart' (prayer) and let God do the talking, just a lover speaks to the heart of the loved one (Hosea 2:16).

I am going to lure her, and lead her out into the wilderness, and speak to her heart
(Hosea 2:16).

That is the true meaning of penance: leading us to focus entirely on God at the core of our being, through shedding obsessions and self-satisfaction One of the many obsessions of our time investing the totality of our culture and our psyche is the obsession of performance by doing and of having. All too often, our self-esteem and our social acceptance is very much dependent on our activity and performance. We need to perform and to produce and be seen to produce, if we are deemed to be worthwhile at every level of our existence investing as much the material as our spiritual and psychological strivings. But penance – in its most authentic biblical meaning – has little to do with doing and all to do with being.

A symbol is only real and authentic in relation to the reality it signifies. If there is no reality behind the symbol, the symbol is empty, pretentious and deceitful. At the same time, if the symbol is not visible or understandable, the reality will remain abstract and unintelligible. Our 'giving up or giving in' to poverty at social and community level will be authentic and believable only when it emerges from and leads to a total commitment and availability to God as the place of encounter with God, as Peter, James and John discovered by abandoning a well-known fishing boat and trusting simply on the words of Jesus to climb an unknown and unwanted mountain.

Conversion is that radical turnaround from self, to look at God and allow God to transform us into the people we are meant to be, a look that begins as an awareness of the *Presence* and *Priority of God* in our life that we call *Prayer*. By claiming to follow Jesus on the journey to fulfilment, we need to confront ourselves with the same questions and to seek our own life-centred responses. For us, that challenge means to question our tendency (1) to take the easy way out for our exclusive satisfaction or comfort, (2) to focus entirely on our own personal needs and ambition, and (3) to seek power and control at all costs.

The physical *hunger* and the exterior or personal act of 'penance' must be a commitment to embark on our Lenten journey towards *being and becoming who we are and are meant to be*, totally dependent on a God passionately in love with our human story and stopping at nothing, not even at the cost of crucifixion, until perfect love and intimacy are attained. That was the fire and the call of Hosea in yearning and searching for his wife, unfaithful though she had been (Hosea 2).

Penance and self-denial have nothing to do with self-satisfying masochism, nor are they just nice traditions warming the heart. Rather, they are the expressions of that inevitable and painful change brought on by letting go of whatever holds us back from becoming authentic disciples, and hinder God from making us who we are to be. Often, the desert demands struggle and pain as the revelation of God inevitably activates, as we are stripped naked of all props, alibi and securities. Only by losing all control can we achieve the fullness of life, even if this call to lose everything may at times seem too much to bear.

By focusing on *essential practicality and simple life-style*. To undertake the desert experience, we need to be *alert to the whisper of God* (cf. 1 Kings 19:11-14), a whisper certainly not of our own making, but from God's own initiative. We need to be still, fully *attuned to what God wants* – when, how or where God wants it for each of us – and carry the bare necessities, ruthlessly jettisoning anything that will slow our pace or deplete our energy. All our senses on full alert, the desert travellers must be totally attuned to the slightest whisper of the breeze, or the unfamiliar, almost imperceptible sound. '*Be still and know that I am God*' is the desert call of aloneness with God (*prayer*), and when we have the courage to venture into the desert and *sit still and alone* with our God. Like for the frightened disciples on Tabor, God will touch us in the silent depth of our being and challenge us to change our comfortable perspective on life and to *discover and wonder at the beauty in simplicity* of who we really are and who God is in and for each of us individually, in all of us, and all around us.

On Tabor, the confused and uncertain disciples come to a personal understanding of who God is for us and who we are for God by focusing on those glimpses of God rushing into our lives and letting this God transform us into the glory of our true selves, in spite of our mistakes. When we have the courage to disengage ourselves from the familiar plain of our comfortable selves in order to set out on the unfamiliar and risky track of self-discovery, of change, of re-assessment, of re-evaluating and re-directing, and follow a beckoning God enlightened by faith and energised by trust, then we will truly experience transfiguration. Then, even in our brokenness, we will be able to journey into the fullness of life (Easter). Our decision to follow Jesus on the journey will lead to healing and fullness of life, only after we have acknowledged our chronic and endemic brokenness.

Glimpses of God

The three-hundred-and-sixty degrees vista from the top of the mountain is stunning, and somehow it relieves the anxiety and the tiredness of the climb. Along the journey of our personal development we may be tempted to possess these moments of excitement – of utter clarity and peace – seeking a to crystallise these experiences forever, ignoring everything and everybody else, and most of all ignoring the fundamental call to change. But that is not possible, because the inner journey into life does not allow for stability, possession, mediocrity, apathy, or self-seeking, and the disciples must confront the situation in which they find themselves and give their personal answer to the call of God. In an effort to incarnate a personal spirituality of self-denial, we often overlook the small but powerful moments of presence, peace and deep joy that reveal the face of our God in and throughout our lives: that unwanted situation has somehow been resolved, that weakness has revealed inexplicable strength, the need has been met, and fear has dissipated into joy.

The events on the mountain quickly become a roller coaster of unexpected experiences, touching deeply into personal identity, and arousing powerful emotions. This moving out of the tried and true of their familiar surroundings is meant to open the minds and hearts of the disciples to new and unexpected glimpses of self-awareness and of who Jesus is. 'Glimpses' is the operative word that will eventually make all the difference to the roller coaster of our personal and/or communal story. By engaging both memory and commitment with honesty and sincerity, we can readily discover that our journey has often been signposted by questions, doubts, mistakes, and confusion, mingled with moments of utter clarity and of an exhilarating sense of God's presence: the smile of a child, the peacefulness of an elderly parent, the inner joy that follows an encounter with someone whom life had kept distant from us for a long time, the warmth of a sunny day shared with a cuppa and a friend. These are the glimpses that speak of a God who, after journeying with us up the mountain, stands by us in our tiredness and struggles, brokenness and fragility, in spite of heavy personal baggage.

But the roller coaster continues. We wish we could freeze these glimpses in time, and so feel God-with-us forever and no longer worry about the hazards of life's journey, but that is not the reality of our life journey. The memory of these glimpses affirmed by the Father's acknowledgment of Jesus addressed to us, *This is my Son, my Chosen*' (Luke 9:35) must become the energy that leads us on when clouds gather around us and within us. When we stand by the bedside of a dying parent, when relationships become strained and children stray, when solitude turns into loneliness and loneliness becomes the only life companion, we need to remember that Jesus touched those desperate and fearful disciples, reassuring them that he was still with them inviting them to continue the journey with him.

Typically, Peter is no longer concerned about his fishing nets or even about security or shelter for himself. He just wants to possess the experience of God for his own satisfaction for ever. Three tents would do it, bottling up God as a private idol to manipulate for our own personal advantage, while sheltering the real person from their memories of the past and their concerns about the future. However, such realisation is neither automatic nor easy to accept in real terms. It may actually engender pain, challenge our hope and self-esteem, and we may still question the possibility of healing ever becoming a reality in our lives. In a way, the disciples are not even allowed to bathe in the glory and excitement of Tabor where they had a glimpse of the presence of God in the person of Jesus and a foretaste of their own destiny. But precisely when they wanted to capture and preserve this experience of God for themselves, uniquely and forever, darkness and cloud descended upon them, enveloping them in fear and confusion. We cannot capture God as a lightning rod against human weakness or brokenness, but we can and must look on God as the one enveloping us totally, as we are.

Paradoxically, that is the moment of ultimate revelation of who Jesus is and who we are in him. While the Father proclaims Jesus as the Beloved, those words are not addressed to Jesus alone. Enveloped by the presence of God, fearful and confused though the disciples may be, those words of affirmation are addressed to them and to us as well, defining their and our identity as Beloved. In the one glimpse, the disciple not only discovers who Jesus is but we too, through Jesus, are identified as beloved in the mind and heart of God.

We need to recall these glimpses of God as the experiences of Jesus touching those desperate and fearful disciples, reassuring them that he was still with them, and inviting them to continue the journey with him down the mountain.

Coming Down the Mountain – Reality Re-energised

Called out of their normality and led into an unknown future where they experience glimpses of God, the disciples cannot stay there; have to go down that mountain . The disciples would have liked to freeze in time to experience of belovedness and of being touched by God on the mountain and hold on to it for the rest of their lives, but very quickly they have to let go of that exhilarating encounter, set their sights on Jerusalem, and re-enter the commonality of every day. They have just had the greatest mystical experience of God's presence in their lives and in the same breath the ecstasy turns into the nightmare of an uncertain and obscure future. Jesus invites them to go down the mountain, a journey to the plain of commonality ahead full of questions and hearing only foreboding words of suffering and death awaiting them. It sounds like a cruel contradiction, but their 'transfiguration' will only be realised through the reality of each day by holding on to the memory of having been touched and healed by Jesus in the cloud of fear and confusion. Healed and reassured by his presence in that normality of daily life, they will not be transformed into 'other-worldly human beings' but 'transfigured', precisely given a new perception and a new understanding of their relationship with their God.

Jesus makes this point clear, as if to stress precisely that even in the midst of loss, betrayal and death, we need to remember the glimpses of God in our lives, and thereby rediscover healing, and hope and courage to journey on in spite of whatever demands life may make of us. They must confront and live through the reality ahead of them, uncertain and unwanted though this future may be. As they come down from that mountain and re-enter the daily commonality of their lives, they are to remember and to be energised by God's companionship. Most of all they are to remember that glimpse when things do not make sense, when they will be once again lost and scandalised as they see Jesus, in whom they had placed all their trust, hanging as a criminal on a cross.

We have all been on that mountain and in that cloud, and Tabor asks us to move with trust and courage out of self-styled comfort and 'I-know' attitudes into real life with the uncertain and unfulfilled reality of what lies ahead, simply on the assurance that the Lord is there, beckoning and journeying with us up and down the roller coaster of life.

Throughout the event on Tabor, while the disciples are invited to witness the power and presence of God through Jesus, the focus of the event is not about the disciples' turmoil, but about Jesus revealing himself in their midst as the very presence of God. Here is a healing and reassuring presence in their darkness and fears, first inviting them to follow him in the apparently meaningless climb up that unwelcoming rocky outcrop, and then down the mountain again and plunging into the normal daily reality of their lives.

Touched by God and reassured of his presence in the dark and fearsome moments of one's experience, the believer cannot remain on that mountain of unreality and of emotional high, as Peter would have wanted by suggesting making three tents and bottle up the experience of God for one's private and exclusive safe-keeping and consumption. Like the Master, the disciples are on a journey, and they must come down from the mountain of God-energised revelation and move on once more.

To follow Jesus does not immunise us from anxiety, struggle, doubts, fear and confusion. Indeed, the greater the letting go of our own selves into God, the heavier the freight of negativity seems to weigh us down, because ultimately ecstasy or nightmare depend on one's perspective and point of reference. On our journey, we will often feel afraid and disheartened at our own brokenness, and we may cry in anguish for deliverance through the struggles and the unaccepted shadows of our daily life.

Jesus' words to his companions on their descent to the reality of their lives speak of an uncertain future and even of death. In the same breath, however, Jesus also speaks of Resurrection, though they fail to understand what it all means. On the strength of the glimpses of God we have experienced in diverse ways, like the disciples, we too just have to trust this Jesus. Although we may have to walk into insecurities and even death, the final outcome of our journey can only be life to the full, because God is life, and ultimate glorious fulfilment; and he is forever journeying with us through it all to lead us to fulfilment and life beyond and in spite of death. The experience of being touched by God on Mount Tabor will never negate our humanity nor deny our earthiness and fragility. God will never eliminate our humanity, and the experience of being touched by God on Mount Tabor will never negate nor deny our earthiness and fragility. On the contrary, by physically entering our human brokenness and fragility through Good Friday into Easter Sunday, God sublimates humanity into the very realm of divinity.

Conclusion

To those who want to achieve salvation or a personal life project, Jesus proposes a future not of our own making, but one to which God himself calls us, a God who journeys and struggles with us, touching us in our darkness and in our fears. In all the confusion and turmoil, however, there is but one security and one alone: Jesus, who has called us out of our comfort zone, is now journeying with us, dragging us out of the cloud of guilt and fear. Jesus is right in the midst of our tiredness, of our meaninglessness and of our weakness. Is it too much to accept that our God is caught up wholly and vitally in our brokenness and in our sinfulness? Like the disciples, we may only have a fleeting glimpse of Jesus' glory, but we will never experience healing, unless we accept this fleeting glimpse of God's presence while we are enveloped in dark clouds of guilt, shame, and memories that we would rather forget.

The believing disciple must now bring that new energy of divine glimpses into the reality of their daily experience, face their personal future totally immersed in a world of saints and demons, carrying the cross of doubt and brokenness, and still wondering what rising from the dead might mean. Most of all, the disciple must journey on, maybe to new fears and more darkness, but strengthened by that one memory of having been on that mountain, having been touched by our God, and of being uniquely precious and beloved in the eyes of a God journeying with us in spite of brokenness and reticence to change.

God in his Temple

John 2:13-25

LIKE IN ANY GOOD DRAMA, as we approach the climax of Holy Week, the tension intensifies. The weekly liturgical readings become more passionate, and the contrast between Jesus and his opponents and eventual executioners, more challenging and overt. Very early in John's Gospel, we encounter a significant event that anticipates the hostility that will underpin all the subsequent narrative. In the sacred area of the temple, Jesus takes on a surprising attitude and behaviour, visibly angry and almost violent in his confrontation with both leaders and temple worshippers alike.

> *The Passover of the Jews was near, and Jesus went up to Jerusalem. In the temple he found people selling cattle, sheep, and doves, and the money-changers seated at their tables. Making a whip of cords, he drove all of them out of the temple, both the sheep and the cattle. He also poured out the coins of the money-changers and overturned their tables. He told those who were selling the doves, 'Take these things out of here! Stop making my Father's house a market-place!' His disciples remembered that it was written, 'Zeal for your house will consume me'. The Jews then said to him, 'What sign can you show us for doing this?' Jesus answered them, 'Destroy this temple, and in three days I will raise it up'. The Jews then said, 'This temple has been under construction for forty-six years, and will you raise it up in three days?' But he was speaking of the temple of his body. After he was raised from the dead, his disciples remembered that he had said this; and they believed the scripture and the word that Jesus had spoken.* (John 2:13-25)

Temple Ritual and Divine Presence

The sanctity of the temple and temple worship was untouchable and unquestionable, and no effigy of any kind could cross its threshold without defiling the holiness of the place and all it represented. Hence, moneychangers would set up outside the gates, and exchange a temple coupon for any currency carrying an effigy of a foreign leader or a religious symbol. In this way, the task of the moneychangers – while a necessary dimension of the temple ritual – would safeguard the sanctity of place and people. Likewise, the sacrifice of animals was central to the temple cult. Whether it was a large animal like a sheep – for those who could afford it – or a small dove for the poor people, these elements for sacrifice would have to be provided and bought before entering the sacred site of the altar of sacrifice. Like in every religious tradition, apparatus and material elements are necessary for the needs of the sacred space and its worship.

And yet, confronted with this 'sacred business' in the 'sacred ground of the temple', Jesus is visibly angry and almost violent in his reaction towards this apparent desecration and to the temple worshippers alike. His words and action must have come as shocking and blasphemous to the champions and guardians of orthodoxy as much as for the simple folks, for whom these customs were the very expressions of their faith. However, within the context of the whole Johannine narrative, constantly contrasting Jesus and 'the Jews' as the fourth evangelist calls his opponents, we need to posit one critical question. Was Jesus attacking the sanctity of the Jewish faith and its traditions, or was he challenging his bystanders – as he often did – in order to push them beyond external and material mediations in their search for God and in their expression of faith?

There is no doubt that the contemporaries of Jesus were deeply religious people, people of faith lived and expressed within a culture totally impregnated with rich prayer, ancient rituals, and deeply significant festivals. The temple was not just the place of worship, but also the focus of all their political, social, economic, cultural and religious expression. Indeed, the temple was the very embodiment of Yahweh's presence with his people from the beginning until the end of time. Unfortunately, such was their devotion that with time the building itself with all its external paraphernalia as well as the cult and rituals to which it gave expression became identified with living and active faith, understood as an expression of relationship with God. In this perspective, roles became reversed and, consequently, the very active and living presence of Yahweh embodied in his temple became conditional to external rituals and to cultic performance. It was not Yahweh who inhabited the temple any longer; but the process of performing rituals by adopting the correct process and uttering the appropriate words would take priority and acknowledge the presence of God. Consequently, their strong faith became a ritual of *doing something* sacred, rather than the rituals *being the channels* of a real, personal, and collective relationship with Yahweh.

On the contrary, Jesus' self-understanding and mission was to reveal the living and active presence of God in the human story as God's self-giving, and through this disturbing criticism, he challenges the human tendency to control God by personal endeavours and manipulations. Clearly, though, this incident and in his own words, *he claimed that here, in his own person, was the real active presence of God with his people, and the temple rituals were only external means signifying and nourishing the relationship with Yahweh*. Jesus is the living temple and the embodiment of God's active and living presence, and consequently *faith consists in recognising and embracing this presence* in a personal and communal relationship of heart and mind with the Father through him. With that poignant allusion to himself, Jesus makes it clear that any faith response must find its fundamental reference to his own physical presence, culminating in the total destruction of the cross as a prelude to the fullness of life in Resurrection (John 2:21-22) to which true faith must lead. Jesus is the only true and authentic sanctuary of God's active and living presence and the place of encounter of God-with-us in this world.

The Discomfort of God

Writing about commitment to the poor as an expression of faith, Catherine De Hueck Doherty raised a fundamental question, pointing precisely to motivation and practice of Christian faith as relationship arising from and energised by an inner conviction of the active presence of God.

> Before we kneel before the Christ in hovels and broken-down tenement buildings, we must be able to kneel before the Christ in our heart. Is he there? This is the question.[1]

Ultimately, the person of faith is the person on a journey from ritual to relationship and from exteriority to inner value-energy, and through this forceful challenge of physically upsetting the moneychangers and the animal sellers, Jesus is confronting his contemporaries precisely with fundamental questions about intentionality and motivation of faith, and the same questions are asked of us today: (1) If we claim faith in our God, what kind of God do we really believe in? (2) What motivates us to respond to this God in faith through our life situations?

Each of us, no doubt, has a personal image of God, a standpoint by which to gauge oneself in relation with this God, and each of us feels comfortable with this image. But, this 'comfort' element is ambivalent, making both for growth and for destruction of the relationship.

Our upbringing, our cultural and religious tradition, our social milieu, indeed our very character and personality – all contribute to create that mental and often idealised picture which mediates that

---

[1] Catherine de Hueck Doherty, *The Gospel without Compromise*, Notre Dame IN: Ave Maria Press, 1979, 100—101.

mysterious human-divine relationship. There is power, meaning, and growth in that personal image, but only to the extent that we are careful not to box our God into little capsules of many 'forms and shapes'. That was the ritualism that Jesus condemned so forcibly in the temple. The little capsules into which we often choose to box our God are psychological ploys by which we exorcise fear and idolise God, and they are many and varied, ranging from a certain infantile spirituality to a routine religious practice or personal devotions, from a 'private' moral code to an uncompromising attitude to openness and change.

In a variety of circumstances and to varied degrees, many of us are guilty of the unconfessed sin of satisfaction in our self-styled securities – a sin which not only colours our image and our living relationship of God, but such that it reflects, often very negatively on our relationships with ourselves and with each other. We should be grateful that God is still one of the few free commodities in our life and we need to stop pretending that we can buy God on our own terms.

We feel comfortable with these psychological capsules because they put us in control by focusing on us doing something that presumably will please God. Unfortunately, when we feel in charge, there is little room for God in our life and in our world, and in these psychological capsules there is only the death of God and self, because no amount of personal effort or of 'banking of good works' will enable us to establish a relationship with God. *God's action is always relational and liberating*, and any enslavement to legalism, ritual, or personally fulfilling spirituality in the end denies the presence of God and stifles God's action.

And so, with an authority that is new and makes people wonder, Jesus breaks the sacred rule of the Sabbath in favour of unlocking the healing and liberating action of God on behalf of those who were broken in mind and body and enslaved by fear and legal bondage (Mark 2:23-28).

As Augustine reminded us many centuries ago, there is a restlessness harbouring deep within the human heart, a restlessness that will be satisfied only by the dynamic fullness of God. But this fullness can come about only to the extent that we are prepared to let God be God on God's own terms. We must stop grasping and creating a God that suits our personal needs and whims. Then, and only then, growth will be possible out of some infantile myth and into a personal commitment to relationship. Then we will truly experience freedom from fear and oppression and selfishness, and we will be able to rejoice and wonder at the unfolding mystery around us and within ourselves. On the contrary, the moment we put up the barricades and take out insurance policies in our faith experience, then we would have stifled the growth process, we would have brought about 'un-creation'.

There is no doubting that the Jews of both the Old and the New Testament were very religious people. Their daily life was punctuated by ancient and precise moments of prayer and religious rituals, and the cyclic rhythm of the seasons was the humus for their liturgical celebrations. Of course, the underlying presupposition is that God can be served and must be worshipped according to strict rules and rituals within a precise time/space framework. This may hold true until the framework becomes a prop, a duty to be performed, a practice to be expedited. Unfortunately, when that happens, then we fall back into the 'security/satisfaction' model which has very little to do with the yearnings of the human heart and the longing of God for intimacy. Likewise, when faith is relegated to faithfulness to a ritual or a process like buying and selling whatever merchandise – yes, even God's grace – then it is not faith at all but business.

Ultimately, the only comfort or satisfaction to which we are honestly entitled in our relationship to God is the satisfaction of standing 'Alone with the Alone',[2] naked before 'The Mysterious One', open to the unfolding Mystery, not knowing what, why, where or when, while those questions burn deeply in our mind and flesh.

The 'God-Abba'

The Word of God is not a reportage of something that happened long ago and far away. The Word of God is for us now and about us, now and so the question is, 'What are our presuppositions about God?' Like the contemporaries of Jesus, for us too it is easy to misconstrue our faith-relationship by pigeon-holing God in ritual practice, in performance of duties, in sacralising days and places like the Sabbath or a Sunday obligation, in imposing and keeping rubrics and laws for their own sake and in operating by categories of punishment, fear and guilt. In such an ethos of externals and of personal make-believe, God truly becomes a faith healer or a wonder worker at best, and, at worst, a puppet manipulated by our whims, from whom we demand satisfaction of every need on our terms. Jesus' proclamation is about a Good News of healing and freedom, and when we operate on our personal preconceptions, we both obliterate Good News and misconstrue our God into an idol of fear and convenience. As for ourselves, we become enslaved by the externals of our own making, devoid of God's presence and action. Indeed, we lose our very self-identity and our relationship with God.

One of the most abused and misused jargons referred to God is the word 'Mystery', If there is incomprehensibility in God, this lies in God's absolute and stubborn determination to reach out to everyone, in spite of the fact that human beings seem hell bent on the contrary. There is nothing inexplicable about God except in the

---

[2] See George A. Maloney, *Alone with the Alone*, Notre Dame IN: Ave Maria Press, 1980.

depth of love relationship and self-giving that Jesus came to reveal in our human story, a revolutionary disclosure so all-embracing that, while the poor and outcasts rejoiced at last, it set Jesus on an inevitable collision course with the authorities.

'*Mystery*' has nothing to do with incomprehensible, syllogistic somersaults or mathematical impossibilities. That would be tantamount to making God a cruel sideshow charlatan who, after plunging his created masterpiece into the swirling white water of a raging torrent, now sits back, sadistically enjoying the plight of me and you groping and grasping desperately at straws in an unsuccessful and doomed attempt at survival.

For too long, 'mystery' has been the door mat under which to sweep the uncomfortable and incomprehensible, while the term 'μυστήριον' refers to nothing short of *a dynamic and saving presence of God, actively engaged in the world, for the salvation of each and every human being, here and now.*

Through the incident in the temple, and indeed throughout his whole life and mission, Jesus is trying to re-establish the correct juxtaposition of values by prioritising God's presence over human expressions, whereby faith lies ultimately in 'letting go' and taking the plunge blind into this *Presence*, a presence so intense and life-giving that it can only be expressed in terms of relationship bonding child to parent. If we are to identify one single reference which stands at the core of Jesus' mission, it is precisely the revelation of a totally new concept of God, a relational idea of God encapsulated in the word: *ABBA*.

The spirituality of the mind and of sensory doing, championed by the Pharisees at the time of Jesus, had generated only fear and sterility, enslaved people and reducing Yahweh to an angry and hungry idol to be placated – though the faithful Jew would have been horrified that such language should be used with reference to Yahweh and to their holy traditions. But Jesus precisely challenged this sacrosanct tradition in order '*to give life, and life to the full*' (John 10:10), by championing a spirituality of the heart.

Only a spirituality of relationship and of the heart can redeem anguish and set people free. Only a *God* known and accepted as *Abba* can foster growth and break down barriers. Whatever a certain spirituality surrounding a mollified sugar and honey Jesus may suggest, the Jewish authorities were perfectly justified in condemning Jesus to death by crucifixion as a revolutionary traitor and blasphemer. By their standards and cultural traditions, not only had he desecrated Yahweh by naming him '*daddy*', but, most of all, he had undermined the very foundations of their political, social and religious system.

'*Abba*' means 'daddy', and along with its feminine gender 'imma' ('mummy'), it forms the very first words which the young child learns to recognise and to call out in life and the rest of our life, conjuring up a powerful flood of memories welling up from the very core of our being, confused and powerful at the same time. We may not always find suitable words to describe the experience, but we all know what the experience feels like.

There is a *sense of eternity, and transformation* there: a presence that needs neither time nor space; a uniqueness which makes that man '*my* daddy' and that woman '*my* mummy' and makes me '*their* child'; a bond which neither death nor life will ever be able to deny or obliterate. Relationship with our mother/father can never be turned on or off at the ticking of a clock or the whims of seasonal changes. Relationship with our life-givers is radical and eternal, and no amount of rigging or infrastructures will either create it or destroy it. In my frailty, I can disown my parents and – at the limit – that man or woman, could even deny me and refuse to accept me as their son. Yet even then, I cannot deny that from that first instant of my life I am *their* son, and they are *my* life-givers father/mother.

The relationship is unique, indestructible and transforming forever. I have no need to think of my father or mother twenty-four hours a day. I just know that though life had kept us physically apart for most of my years, they are and I am. He is 'dad'/'mum' to me when I sleep, when I eat, when I drive, and when I preach. They are 'my life-givers' forever, just as I am their son forever, when I sleep, when I eat, when I drive, and when I preach... in life and in death, for eternity. Sometimes I feel that God must be laughing at us in sheer delight and compassion on observing our desperate but puny efforts to reach out and achieve on our own steam. After all, the first attempts of the child to stand on his own two feet are moments of pure ecstasy for the father; and then daddy puts out his hand and the child wobbles and smiles in return before throwing himself into daddy's arms.

One day, I was fascinated by a simple yet powerful scene at the beach. Junior, not more than three years old, is completely engrossed in building sandcastles. Daddy kills time by throwing a stick into the water for the family dog to retrieve, while – totally caught up in an amorphous mass of sand – Junior takes absolutely no notice of the world around him. He seems blissfully unaware of anyone on that beach. He never once looks up. Daddy takes a stroll twenty yards down the shore to retrieve the wooden stick that 'pooch' got tired of chasing. Not more than twenty yards away! It was then that the word rang out, sharp and crystal clear, twice: 'Daddy! Daddy!' ... Junior never looked up, he never turned his head away from his crumbling sandcastle, and yet he knew; he felt that presence distancing itself, ever so slightly; and the world suddenly became so threatening. He never looked up until 'Daddy' immediately responded by calling Junior to go home.

Convenience versus Conviction

Writing to his first century Christians in Rome and Asia Minor, Paul has no doubts about this unique and totally new presence of Abba, and of its implications in the daily life of the believer.

> *For you did not receive a spirit of slavery to fall back into fear, but you received a spirit of adoption. When we cry, 'Abba! Father!' it is that very Spirit bearing witness with our spirit that we are children of God, and if children, then heirs: heirs of God*

and joint heirs with Christ, if we in fact suffer with him so that we may also be glorified with him. (Romans 8:14-17; Galatians 4:4-7).

In the context of the synagogal encounter (John 2:13-25), two contrasting 'Con' words seem to express our response to this parent-child relationship and the relative faith expressions that Christian tradition invites us to embrace: *Convenience* and *Conviction*. Convenience is the process of using, misusing, and abusing God through external practices for one's own personal agenda and the satisfaction of individual whims. Conviction instead is the acceptance of God deliberately choosing to enter into a personal relationship with each individual. Convenience puts oneself and one's doing in control of God, and, once the proper process is enacted, we can then claim our rights and make demands of God. Conviction, on the other hand, stands with open hands before the God who is present in one's life, without personal security or a blueprint of where this God will take us. *Convenience relies on performance*, while *Conviction seeks, accepts, and enters into a personal relationship with God in control*. Convenience is security and personal safety, while conviction is pure faith and trust in the God one claims to follow and to worship. On which side of the duality do we stand? As a community gathered at worship, where do we stand: as the expression of our faith and energy, or as a personal devotional practice?

Faith in the God Jesus came to reveal does not consist of an accurate and legalistic performance of religious practices aimed at justifying our preconceived ideas of this God, or at tranquilising our conscience. Faith is not encapsulated in a routine Sunday Mass, or some highly personal spirituality disposed of in a suitable time slot, magic formulae hurriedly rattled off as prayers. or in private devotions grasped tightly as a lightning rod against personal mishaps and life's misfortunes. We can only live faith as a relationship with God through our commitment to daily life as the place where God is and where he yearns to be. Refusing to accept this real life-presence is to put the cart before the horse, where God becomes the justification for our agenda. In this way, we turn God into an idol demanding obedience and submission, on the one hand, and on the other condemning ours hearts to fear and our minds to slavery and obsession. Jesus would have none of that, because it ran diametrically counter to the God he came to reveal as the saving '*Abba*'.

Jesus' obsession with '*Abba-God*' is telling us that he is the only real, active, and healing presence in our world and in our personal lives. Is he there? We are sensory beings, and therefore devotion(s) and rituals are necessary for our understanding and expression of faith. However, they do not constitute faith; they are only expressions that may or may not speak to every culture, time, place or individual. As such, they can never exhaust and even less substitute for faith as the individual and collective relationship with God. The focus of our belief is Jesus as the living presence of God, expressed through a variety of cultural media but unique and universal in the appeal to the human heart and in the proclamation and witness of the Good News. With Catherine de Hueck, maybe we should ask the same question of ourselves. In our personal spirituality and in our community celebration of God's active divine presence, where is our God if not at the very core of our being as the energy of who we are and of what we do? That is the question that Jesus put so forcefully to his contemporaries in the dramatic events in the temple and puts to us today and every time we claim faith in God. Who is the God we worship, and where do we encounter this God?

May our faith be truly a living proclamation of the concluding words of every Eucharistic Prayer: 'Through him, in him and with him' challenging us deep down not through external doing but in abiding relationship of being, because that is where God is and where he wants to be found.

No Walls by the Well

John 4:3-42

THE CONTEXT OF THE ENCOUNTER of Jesus with the Samaritan woman within his journey to Jerusalem immediately alerts us to the nature of faith not as a monolithic body of truths leading to a moral code of behaviour, but as an ongoing process of conversion and gradual unfolding, leading to a complete turn-around in one's perspective and relationship with God as the energy of one's life. Jesus gradually dismantles a fortress of walls and taboos that entrap the woman and sets her free, simply by affirming her as a person.

Walls and Taboos

The first strokes of the story which Francis J. Moloney calls '*a story of the possibility of a journey from no faith to partial faith, to full faith*'[3] are simple, ordinary, almost prosaic, but very significant. The scene is almost idyllic. Jesus is tired and the freshness of the well is just what a thirsty man yearns for, and so he takes a rest. The scene is set by a casual encounter between two strangers, both seeking refreshment and energy by an ancient well, and there seems nothing extraordinary in the fact that a woman from the local village should come along to fetch water. It was a matter of routine – as routine as the traveller engaging another person in conversation. However, the ordinariness of the encounter is only apparent, indeed shocking beyond excuses for the contemporaries, hiding deep taboos and

---

[3] Francis J. Moloney, *This is the Gospel of the Lord – Year A*, Homebush: St Paul Publication, 1992, 90-91.

serious condemnation. No self-respecting Jew would dare converse with an unknown woman, and a Samaritan woman at that!

The cultural, religious, and social divide between Jews and Samaritans was deep-seated, embracing every level of private and public life, and the barriers between them carried strong moral implications. The sliver of land wedged between fertile Galilee to the north and the seat of political and social power of Judea to the south, was a land disdained equally by the simple but faithful Galileans and the learned and powerful leaders of Jerusalem. Over its twisted and sometimes tragic history, Samaria had become a cultural and religious potpourri, mixing local gentile customs and cultic mores with the foundational Mosaic tenets, to the point of abandoning the sacred and ancient traditions of Yahweh's people. In Jesus' time, no insult was greater for the faithful Jew than being called 'a Samaritan', and any North-South traveller through Palestine would carefully avoid setting foot on the very soil of Samaria, lest one became morally defiled. There were only two 'safe' routes possible to this traveller. Either one journeyed through the barren desert to the east and beyond the Jordan and then cross the river again once into the Judean hinterland, or conversely seek the same destination by sea, arching into the Mediterranean to the west aboard some leaky fishing boat.

Against this background of cultural and religious barriers and taboos, Jesus seems untouched by any misconceptions and journeys through Samaria, stopping at one of the villages, and after encountering the woman, he actually stays two days with the local town folks of that 'forbidden land'. In this context, the whole story becomes a blatant challenge, not only to his contemporaries, but also for us the readers, centuries later.

From the very beginning, Jesus' request for water and subsequent behaviour raise serious questions of God and of our relationship to our God in faith. The God of Jesus in Samaria is not a static god, sitting aloof on a throne of judgment. Our God is on the move, tired and thirsty, just sitting by the well or seeking companionship in casual encounters and initiating conversation in the midst of daily routine. I am reminded of a disillusioned youngster, full of rebellion and crushed by rejection who once said to me, 'If your god is not in the daily humdrum and the ordinary things I have to live through, where is he?'

It is precisely into this scenario of daily humdrum and ordinary circumstances that the woman moves in for her daily but *unusual* and *unwanted* chore of fetching water. Yes, unwanted and unusual because no self-respecting woman would think of going to the ancient village well to fetch water in the middle of the day, when the heat was at its extreme and everyone else was quietly busy behind doors. Each morning the well would spring alive and become the place of encounter as the women of Sichar would gather to draw their daily supply of water – voices exchanging greetings, sharing news and grief and hope, chatting of chores and children and daily business.

Jacob's well was the hub and the focus of the village life where you would meet to be energised for the day ahead. That was the normal daily routine of the village woman, all home and family. Unless of course you happen to be *that woman* who would much rather avoid encountering anybody, least of all the other women of the village. No, this woman does not want to mix with those village mothers and wives who gather each morning at that well, because in her own mind and heart she really does not belong. Indeed, it is even surprising that she resists an initial urge to avoid encountering that strange man sitting by the well by not turning on her steps and quickly retreating back home again.

Hence, her surprise at being asked for water is both understandable and justified. As a Samaritan, she is trapped within her own cultural heritage, and it is unthinkable and inadmissible that a Jew should ask her for a drink. As we will find out later, as *that woman* with many husbands, she is rejected and despised by her own kin and neighbours, shame, anger, and loneliness her only life companions. As a person worshipping on the mountain the God she does not know, she is the apostate from the true religion, symbolised and incarnated in the ritualistic and legal fortress of the Law and the Jerusalem temple. As a woman and as a Samaritan, she is utterly unacceptable on the grounds of gender, race and religion. She is a non- person whom, paradoxically, Jesus addresses as a person. By breaking down the politically acceptable barriers, he calls forth her self-esteem, her self-awareness and finally her full faith, as the natural response to Jesus' self-revelation in her life by saying to her, '*I who am speaking to you, I am he*' (John 4:26).

God's Initiative and Human Response

An age of achievement-oriented mentality like ours will easily engender the conviction that faith is something that we poor mortals have to obtain through super-human efforts and personal but artificial struggles, in order to ensure a reward and avoid punishment when we die. This kind of faith quickly generates fear and guilt in return, because then God's role is simply to pass judgment on our life, and a severe one at that. Faith then becomes exclusively a matter of our own doing, of personal effort, or ascetical practice expressed through a variety of ingratiating rituals and flavoured by an overdose of self-denigration.

However, the narrative of the encounter between Jesus and the woman at the well, points exactly in the opposite direction. The woman is not seeking either faith or self-identity. She is only interested in fetching water and avoiding publicity, and Jesus simply engages her at that level of reality: a person in need. The encounter of Jesus with this woman is completely *unplanned*, *unexpected* and, as far as the woman is concerned, *unwanted*; and this highlights a foundational premise of faith: our God is not to be found in speculation or ritual cults, or in moral codes. Our God is primarily here and now, unknown but real, in every insignificant moment of our life and in the most unexpected and unwanted experiences and encounters of our journey.

Faith is unequivocally God's initiative, inviting us into a relationship of friendship, and so Jesus takes the initiative by opening the conversation and breaking down the first taboo represented by the distance between human beings on the grounds of gender, religion, culture, or social status. These are the impenetrable walls keeping people apart, often used and misused to justify our faith stance, and consequently creating distance between God and us. Faith is the very antithesis of separateness, and faith in the God of Jesus always begins with a call to accept the presence of God in our life, through our experience of human relationship, yes even while sitting by the well of our tiredness, engaging our loneliness and isolation, or facing taboo and fear-ridden expectations and presuppositions.

> The kingdom of God cannot break into a world which cannot see the presence of God even in the most habitual and familiar people and events.[4]

Having taken the initiative, Jesus does not launch into a theological debate or a moral tirade with the woman. Like most of us caught up in a myriad of personal needs and experiences, the woman's one concern it to fetch water and retreat into her own lonely anonymity. There is neither religious faith nor desire for conversion there, only a basic need, and Jesus respects that by focusing entirely on her need of water. When we reflect on our own journey of faith, most of us will be able to recognise that the catalyst of a significant faith experience has often been some very ordinary particular need, a spark of faith that eventually flared up into a personal, all-transforming decision for God.

However, throughout the gospel narrative, having tapped into the informal and ordinary of daily life, Jesus invariably pushes his hearers beyond the immediate, and projects them into another level, a Kingdom level, challenging the interlocutors to look at the

---

[4] Francis J. Moloney, *This is the Gospel of the Lord*, 1992, 91.

world from a new and more life-giving and God-related perspective. While focusing on the need, Jesus points to a reality beyond the need itself, to the only reality capable of satisfying those needs: the reality of God's active and living presence. Faith calls for readiness and capacity to see beyond the immediate concerns and accept a presence capable of filling graciously and abundantly all the needs of the human heart. Augustine summed it all up in that famous mantra:

> 'You have made us for yourself, O Lord, and our hearts won't rest until the rest in you'.

That is the dynamic of Christian and biblical faith: God taps into our deeper desires, thereby igniting the spark of faith through a new self-awareness and eventually leading to a personal commitment to transformation. As Gerard Hughes comments,

> If we are able to discover what we really want, if we could become conscious of the deepest desire within us, then we should have discovered God's will. God's will is not an impersonal blueprint for living forced on us by a capricious God and contrary to almost every inclination in us. God's will is our freedom; he wants us to discover what we really want and who we really are.[5]

From Religion to Faith

God is always the initiator of the journey of faith by inviting himself into our journey of life beyond personal expectations and presuppositions. However, as Francis J. Moloney suggests, to this point of our story there is no faith response on the part of the woman. At best, this is partial faith where the focus is not a person's relationship with God but only the satisfaction of some personal need according to a personal agenda.

---

[5] Gerard W. Hughes, *God of Surprises*, London: DLT, 1996, 36-62.

> Often, we simply do not hear the word of Jesus because we are too concerned with our own needs. Most of the time, however, we are happy to believe in Jesus. But if we reflect upon the quality of our faith, we will see that, like the Samaritan woman again, we commit ourselves to faith in the Jesus of our expectations. As long as he is our prophet and the messiah we are waiting for, we are comfortable.[6]

The offer of having all her needs of water met gratuitously and forever sows enough doubt in the woman's mind to stimulate her curiosity and to shape the first 'religious' questions beyond the immediate needs. She is certainly not entertaining any desire of a radical conversion, but her comment about the strange one being a prophet carries a suspicious intent, almost an unconscious acknowledgment of being in the presence of someone beyond her immediate experience.

The question of God never leaves us. Unconscious or denied though it may be, the human heart seems unable to obliterate this sense of something more, something greater, something deeper, some One who is all-fulfilling, all-embracing, and yet never possessed. More one grows in self-awareness or engages in the world around, more the sense of the beyond tugs at the chords of our heart, in spite of all attempts at ignoring or suppressing it. The woman externalises this in that word 'prophet', but she is not yet prepared to face the challenge of faith. In a strange twist, she introduces the religious talk, but more as an excuse of her own life-style than an acknowledgment of faith in the presence of God in her life. In her own mind, even if this man is a prophet, he cannot be the Messiah because he does not fit the Messianic expectations of Jerusalem, nor her own understanding of religious belief.

> The particular image we have of God will depend very much on the nature of our upbringing and how we have reacted to it, because our ideas and our felt knowledge derive from

---

[6] Francis J. Moloney, *This is the Gospel of the Lord*, 1992, 91.

experience. If our experience has taught us to think of God as a policeman-like figure, whose predominant interest is in our faults, and if our encounters with him have been mostly in cold churches where we were bored out of our minds with barely audible services and sermons presenting God as he who disapproves of most of the things we like, then we are not likely to want to turn to him, no matter how many people may tell us that (*this*) is necessary.[7]

On a personal note, it fascinates me that when I encounter someone who for the first time discovers that I am a priest, inevitably the conversation reverts invariably to some religious issue that has little or no bearing on the situation at hand. More often than not, it sounds like an attempt at self-justification, an 'apologia pro vita sua' sort of relationship, hiding and revealing at the same time a much deeper reality of doubt, abandonment, or even rejection. In many such encounters, the 'religious' and the whole realm of faith have little or no relevance to the real life of people, but it is a safety screen hiding a personal lifestyle or value system.

In the case of the woman of Samaria, the hidden self-justification lies in the confusing separation of beliefs, moral principles, and ritual practices that divide Jews and Samaritan. While the Jewish people centred their religiosity in the temple of Jerusalem, the Samaritans had built their place of worship on Mount Gerizim on the ruins of an old pagan temple. Not that this posed any serious problem to the woman personally, but at the same time her question reveals a very common understanding of faith expressed in terms of external elements of time and place, sanctioned by taboos, fear and judgment.

There is absolutely no doubt that the contemporaries of Jesus were authentically and deeply religious people within a culture totally impregnated with rich prayer, ancient rituals, and deeply significant festivals. The temple was not just the place of worship but also the focus of all their political, social, economic, cultural

---

[7] Gerard W. Hughes, *God of Surprises*, 1996, 62.

and religious expressions. The temple was the very embodiment of Yahweh's presence with his people from the beginning to the end of time.

However, such was their devotion that both the temple building itself and its elaborate and legal ritual construct became identified with Yahweh. Their strong faith became a ritual of doing something sacred rather than the rituals being channels towards and expressions of a personal and communal relationship with Yahweh. What we overlook in this perspective of faith is the fact that rituals are only external means signifying and nourishing the relationship with God, and Jesus himself, sitting thirsty by a well is the incarnate embodiment of the living temple.

Just two chapters before the incident at Jacob's well, we see a very angry Jesus taking a fierce stance against the ancient temple rituals of buying and selling merchandise needed for the Temple worship (John 2:13-22). When faith is relegated to faithfulness to a ritual or a process of religiously buying and selling God's grace or performing a routine worship with scrupulous accuracy of rubrics and self-imposed devotions or protocols, then it is not faith at all, but only business, magic and taboos.

Unfortunately, sometimes we are not strangers to this misguided concept and praxis of faith by equating faith with the external mediations of religion. In this way, faith becomes a performance. Rituals prayers, times and seasons, even moral laws and traditions are all human expressions and mediations of our faith because, as sensory people, we need to engage the senses in order to reach a full understanding and grasp of reality. Unfortunately, for the Samaritan woman, and indeed often for many of us believers, faith has everything to do with *doing*, and little and nothing to do with *being*, a monolithic compendium of truth, and a painstaking fulfilment of rubrics, a collection of wordy prayers and a plethora of personal devotions. In this perspective, even the sacred moments of sacramentality become part of a process of doing or of 'being done' according to our own schedule and to our own liking. There is no encounter there but only performance, a socialised performance controlled, time-scheduled, and precisely 'done'.

However, faith goes far beyond and much deeper that human sensory stimulation, touching the very depths of the human psyche and inflaming every fibre of the heart. *Biblical faith is relational, and the external expressions must lead to a personal and communal relationship with God and with each other.*

Leaving the Jar Behind

In his response to the woman's semi-religious quest in terms of mediations and practice, Jesus leads her to see *beyond the formal religion and into personal faith*, by focusing on *his own person*, as the indwelling and energy of the real active presence of God with his people.

> *Believe me, woman, a time is coming when you will worship the Father neither on this mountain nor in Jerusalem... A time is coming and has now come when the true worshipers will worship the Father in spirit and truth, for they are the kind of worshipers the Father seeks. God is spirit, and his worshipers must worship in spirit and in truth'. The woman said, 'I know that Messiah' (called Christ) 'is coming. When he comes, he will explain everything to us'. 'Then Jesus declared, 'I who speak to you am he'* (John 4:21, 25-26).

Every journey has its encounters, but every journey has crossroads as well, moments and events that not only demand choices and decisions but also will eventually determine the success or failure of the whole journey. In this narrative, the journey of faith as exemplified by the woman of Samaria is no different, and the moment of decision and choice has now arrived.

Whatever understanding the woman of Samaria may have claimed of the ancient Hebrew Scriptures, those words *'I who speak to you am he'* would not have been new to her. The Jewish faith stood firmly planted on one central concept: the great journey from the slavery of Egypt to the freedom of the Promised Land, and at the very dawn of this archetypal journey, Yahweh not only stood unquestionably as the instigator, the producer, and the hero all at once, but he revealed his name to Moses as 'I AM'. By laying claim to the same name, Jesus leaves no doubt in the woman's mind about his identity: he is the long awaited Messiah. He is the one who will make all things rights and will set the world free; and he is right here, talking to you, sitting by an old well in a desert and abandoned country, asking you for a drink of water for life and survival.

This woman from Sychar sometime called 'a broken woman, a no one, with no name and a nothing in the eyes of society' confronted with her own need, made aware of her personal situation, and challenged in her beliefs and in her personal life, is now told that the answer to her deepest and ultimate yearnings is looking straight in her eye, and talking to her words of encouragement and affirmation.

Now the decision is hers: either trust the Stranger or pick up her jar and maybe a little water for survival and return to her life of isolation, loneliness and rejection. Ultimately, *faith revolves entirely around a decision to accept the presence of a Stranger-God sitting with us wherever and whenever or reject this presence for the sake of personal agenda and walk into doubt, fear, and guilt* for the rest of our days.

The woman of Samaria does not pick up her jar. In a powerful symbolic gesture, the woman *left her water-jar and went back to the city* (John 4:28). That water jar was her only companion, representing everything she had in her life of solitude, escape, fear, guilt and anger. The water jar was the perpetual reminder of who she was, someone locked in her taboos and rejected by discrimination and judgment. However, all that now seems to have vanished, left behind and abandoned like an empty water jar. A jar is meant to hold water, to bring freshness and ensure life, but if it empty it has lost its reason for being. Yes, now that the woman had encountered the Stranger who knew her personally and intimately, her previous life had no meaning beyond lying uselessly in the sand of the past. Until now, the woman was responding to her own agenda, imagining a God of her own making, but in that letting go of her own expectations, she moved into that faith that recognises the living presence of the God in her very self and life.

The journey from no faith to full faith is now complete, personal and life-giving. Now she is free of all her fears and hang-ups, taboos and guilt. Now she can not only face those very people that she would avoid and would condemn her, fearlessly proclaiming the presence of this Jesus who knows her so personally and intimately that 'he told her everything she has done' (John 4:29). Now she can journey on with confidence and peace because she has encountered God face-to-face, sitting with her in solitude and openness, and she trusts him.

I had known the old religious sister over many years, a person of irresistible dynamism, of brilliant creativity, of unparalleled administrative and leadership skills, and of unquestionable control, But now she was in a nursing home, I was told. I must confess that my first reaction had little to do with Christian charity or basic human affirmation. I almost had a sense of pity for the staff caring for her. One day, I decided to pay her a visit and, shown to her room, I was immediately struck by the change in her, a change that was more than physical; yes, a small body too big for the large reclining chair, the whole dominated by an incredibly peace-filled and life-giving smile on the worn out face. Again, my wicked imagination ran loose. 'Miracles do happen', I justified myself, 'but what could possibly have brought on this transformation?' Soon Sister herself, unsolicited, gave me the answer to my unspoken and biased question. In the course of our casual conversation, she commented with pride, 'You see, when I was young, I used to worry about my many things. Now that I am old, I am learning to trust!' Having finally given herself a chance to seek and find God by her bedside, she now trusted fully in that presence, and she was at peace. She had travelled from worry to trust, from partial faith to full faith.

Mission

In the biblical jargon, the word 'salvation' identifies with 'liberation' by opening up to fullness of life, removing fetters and limitations, and setting free from any form of bonding or enslavement. That is what the nameless woman of Samaria now feels has happened to her. Her emotions are so intense that she can neither deny them nor keep them to herself any longer. She cannot hold them to herself, and she cannot but scream to the whole world her newfound freedom and faith. She has to share them with her own townsfolk, precisely those who condemned and rejected her; and the ones she ignored and avoided in the first place are the first to hear and witness her experience. Where escape reigned, now there is total openness, guilt is supplanted by joy, fear becomes reckless courage, suspicion regenerates into trust, and nothingness turns into fullness. *Transformed by the life-giving presence of God in our life, the person of faith is driven irresistibly to share the same life-giving presence.*

Mission is not an optional extra for the person of faith, and faith has nothing to do with privacy, whether this be a personal spirituality, a regular religious practice, or a jealously guarded me-and-God alone type of relationship. *Faith demands action or it is not faith at all.* Jesus' last injunction to his disciples on Mount Tabor before ascending to the Father is unequivocal: '*Go into the world and proclaim the Good News*'. The only way that God's active presence becomes energy for hope, joy, courage and endurance in the real everyday world, is through the active life-giving presence of those who have first experienced it in their own flesh and in their life story. Having travelled from non-faith to full faith themselves, the person of faith now must become co-traveller with all those who need to discover the presence of their God even if sitting by the old well of their personal story and undertaking their personal journey from death to life.

On 17 April 2017, in a letter to his brother bishops of Argentina, Pope Francis warned that if Catholics do not proclaim

Jesus with their lives, then the Church becomes 'not the mother, but the babysitter'.

When believers share their faith, 'the Church becomes a mother church that produces children (and more) children, because we, the children of the Church, we carry that. But when we do not, the Church is not the mother, but the babysitter, that takes care of the baby – to put the baby to sleep. It is a Church dormant... The solution to this is 'to proclaim Christ, to carry the Church – this fruitful motherhood of the Church – forward'.[8]

In Jesus' mission commitment to his disciples, Mark actually lists the fruits that will accompany the mission of faith.

And he said to them, 'Go into all the world and preach the gospel to the whole of creation. The one who believes and is baptised will be saved; but the one who does not believe will be condemned. And these signs will accompany those who believe: by using my name they will cast out demons; they will speak in new tongues; they will take up snakes in their hands, and if they drink any deadly thing, it will not hurt them; they will lay hands on the sick, and they will recover'. (Mark 16:15-18)

In the shadow of his execution in a Nazi concentration camp, Dietrich Bonhoeffer wrote:

I thought I could acquire faith by living a holy life, or something like it. I discovered later, and am still discovering right up to this moment, that it is only by living completely in this world that one learns to have faith. One must completely abandon any attempt to make something of oneself, whether it be a saint, or a converted sinner, or a churchman... By this worldliness I mean living unreservedly in life's duties, problems, successes and failures, experiences and perplexities. In so doing we throw ourselves completely into the arms of God, taking seriously not our own sufferings, but those of

---

[8] Pope Francis, http://www.cathnews.com/article.aspx?aeid=35684

God in the world – watching with Christ at Gethsemane. That, I think, is faith: that is metanoia.[9]

Conclusion

As we sit by the well of our life story, let us imagine the Lord Jesus approaching us. Let us commit ourselves to the faith that listens rather than speaks many words. Jesus clearly tells us that he is the real, active, and healing presence in our world and in our personal lives. Are we prepared to let ourselves be challenged by this revelation? *Is he there?* Before we kneel in front of the God we think we believe in, we must be able to kneel before the God in our heart. Is he there, in our hearts? This is *the* question of faith.

We are sensory beings, and therefore devotion(s) and rituals are necessary. These, however, are not 'the faith' but expressions of faith strongly bound to cultures, times, places or individuals, and they never exhaust or adequately substitute faith as the individual and collective relationship with God. The focus of our belief is Jesus as the living presence of God. That is the challenge that Jesus repeatedly and forcefully addressed to his contemporaries and through this incredible encounter. As we come to worship our God, is he there in our hearts? Where is our God, and who is our God? Before we kneel in front of the God we think we believe in, we must be able to kneel before the God in our heart. *Is he there?* This is *the* question of faith.

Our faith journey must begin with the dismantling the walls of prejudice, taboos, self-denigration, and false gods, and continue to grow through life as a living proclamation of God's active and unrestrained healing presence where we are, as well as where we would rather not be. In the concluding words of every Eucharistic Prayer: *Through him, with him and in him,* not only resonate in

---

[9] Dietrich Bonhoeffer, *Tegel Prison*, 1944, in Greg Dening, *Church Alive – Pilgrimages in Faith 1956-2006*, Sydney, NSW: University of New South Wales, 2006, 77.

our ears, but most of all they must energise us into fullness of life (John 10:10) and fire us into giving life from the depth of our heart. That is where God is and where God wants to be found in spite of preconceptions, fear, taboos, and guilt, and through the most insignificant skerrick of our daily life, as we hear him say to us.

'I am he, the one who is speaking to you' (John 4:26).

A Matter of Relationships

Luke 15:1-3, 11-32

IT COULD BE an everyday occurrence in any of our inner city suburbs, so commonplace it would no longer even rate a mention in the morning papers any longer. Unfortunately, blinded by the plague of street-kids, we are no longer able to see the human drama that brought about the scourge in the first place. That street-kid is the fruit of the life and love of two people with whom he has severed all connections, thus creating a mutual disavowal and rejection. At the same time, in spite of renunciation, somewhere a father and mother, having given life and love, have lost all sense of relationship with their son or daughter. And yet, regardless of the vagaries of time and culture, for eternity that child will always be the son/daughter of that man and that woman, and nothing will negate or obliterate the relationship of life given and received that they share.

Losing sight of that parent/child relationship can only result in shame, guilt, condemnation, judgment, anger, social estrangement and self-pity. Relationship is both the key to the issue and the remedy to its solution. No sociological band aid or psychological palliative will ever heal the rift if we fail to re-establish the proper children/parent relationship. It is only in acknowledging and in re-establishing broken connections that we can bring together people who are apart and heal the rift that separates them.

As Jesus told it long ago, Luke's well known story of the son who leaves home and then returns is precisely a story of relationships, not only mirroring the plight of youth homelessness today, but making a clear statement about the identity of God and the relationship between us and God, and among ourselves. In both cases, it is only in terms of relationship that we can understand our God and heal the brokenness and homelessness that resides deep within our own psyche and our communal story.

The story revolves around three protagonists: a father and his two sons, each character representing a very distinct and specific personality. Most of all, each of them incarnates typical attitudes by which often we relate to God and to each other. Like all the parables throughout the gospel narrative, the story addresses fundamental issues of identity, raising the question of who God is for us, and about the way we respond to God, challenging us about making value choices, incarnating attitudes, and living out our faith commitment as individuals and as a community.

The two sons personify the full range of values, life attitudes, and reactions of the human heart, a heart that is so restless, confused, and reckless when it comes to confronting itself with God, and the two respective positions begin from diametrically opposite stances, run in totally opposite directions, and eventually lead to two equally opposite and unexpected conclusions.

The two personal stories never quite intercept each other until the final critical climax, but, at the same time, the two stories are not irrevocably disjointed. In the middle of the story, that begins with the younger son and ends with the elder of the two, stands the father, the unchanging, non-judgmental fixed centre point that links together individual and collective dramas. As if to give substance and meaning to two brotherly but distant bookends, the father stands as the all-embracing presence and undivided love, and the point of conjunction and of stability between two apparently irreconcilable attitudes. Much more than the drama between a foolhardy and thoughtless young man who eventually discovers and admits to his misdemeanours on the one hand, and on the other, a self-righteous brother who will not accept either mistakes or reconciliation, this is the story of a father whose unchanging love reconciles opposites.

In the face of unfaithfulness and injustice, the father refuses to pass judgment, but rejoices at being recognised as *'father'* even by his ungrateful son, while, at the same time pleading with his older one to look beyond the sinfulness of a wayward brother and to accept him and embrace him precisely as a brother. The father of the story is only interested in re-establishing relationships: a three-way, life-giving relationship between father and two brothers. He is not interested in judgment, sinfulness, unfaithfulness, waywardness, lip service, anger, broken promises, brotherly injustice, or self-righteousness. That is the fundamental revelation about the identity of our God who is seeking nothing else but to be recognised as *'Father'* and bring his two sons to recognise each other as *'brothers'*.

As we know, the Word of God is not about chronology, history, or societal mores. The parables of Jesus are addressed to us and about us, here and now. As I claim discipleship in the Kingdom, the question must be asked: where do I stand? Am I open and trusting in God's love for me, or do I identify more readily, and perhaps more comfortably, with the rebellious son who leaves home to seek a justification by self-styled securities and pleasure? Or am I more alike the older son, whose relationship with the father is based entirely on self-righteousness and on the acquisition of personal merits?

Leaving Home – Self Interest and Rebellion Redeemed

The scene opens with the younger son holding centre stage. Young, idealistic and reckless, he is so trapped in himself and in his own self-interest that he is totally unaware of the pain and injustice engendered by his bold request for his share of the family property. He has neither any feeling for the love and devotion of his father, nor any sense of justice towards his own family; nor does he display any personal concern or responsibility as to how he will dispose of the gifts lavished upon him by a doting father. He simply leaves home and wastes his money.

From a psychological perspective, this younger son typifies the young child for whom the world is his/her personal possession, and the only rationale for his life values is his own self-interest, seeking pleasure, personal security, and unconditional satisfaction. But while this is the natural world-view of a young child, when this kind of self-centeredness and possessive control lingers on as the life-value into adulthood, then we have domination, violence, and dysfunctional personalities.[10]

However, confronted with a crisis, our self-assured young man becomes suddenly aware of the consequences of his recklessness, and his thoughts go back to his household where he belongs, and to his father. No matter how much he has strayed or betrayed his life-giver, that fundamental thrust back to his roots comes to the fore. He remembers who he really is, and all he wants is to go back to where he came from. This is the beginning of reconciliation: *accepting one's mistakes and responding to that fundamental human need that urges us to return to where we really belong.*

This self-acknowledgment is vitally important, but it is only the first step towards re-establishing the relationship. The young man has not yet thought of his father's love and the journey back home towards full reconciliation has only begun. Full re-integration in that relationship with God that Jesus points to demands a life-long ongoing process of growth into self-awareness and decision-making until we come to that fullness of faith that appropriates God's loving presence in our life. whatever shape that life may take. God accepts me and loves me as I am, and not as I would like to be or how I think I should be.

Confronted with his personal destitution, the first reaction is one of self-pity and shame. *He acknowledges his condition,* but his

---

[10] See Brian P. Hall, *Values Shift. A Guide to Personal and Organizational Transformation*, Rockport MA: Twin Lights Publishers, 1994, 133-150.

first concern is still locked within himself. He has not yet come to the full realisation and acceptance of the love of the Father. In a way, he is looking for a solution to his immediate problem, a sort of survival kit, a way out of his miserable situation, or a ritual of purification for his wrongdoings. Consequently, his first reaction is to focus on himself, admit to his wrongdoings, and enumerate his mistakes, in the hope of being re-instated if not into the family circle at least as one of the paid servants. His understanding of the father is certainly not in terms of love but of justice, where wrongdoings have to be paid for and where belonging to the household is a matter of hierarchy and of merit or demerit points.

It makes sense, then, to attempt some sort of bargaining that may help one to keep his/her head out of the mire. In this perspective, we do not have reconciliation and healing, but only a ritual purification that may set my self-styled conscience at peace for a while, but it will never re-establish the father-son relationship that was there in the first place. Conversion is not a matter of bargaining, ritual purity or self-justification, but it is a matter of accepting God who has nothing to do with bargaining or personal merits, and embraces me with unconditional love as I am.

When reconciliation is reduced to a ritual of purification, then we do not really seek to re-establish our relationship with our God, but we settle and/or bargain for some immediate solution, a palliative for a troubled conscience. In that case, we reduce God to a stern and angry judge from whom we can only hope for a lenient sentence, but never quite a full re-instatement into the family home. When reconciliation is reduced only to a ritual practice, then we operate out of self-pity and of fear of punishment, but never out of love of God and from our God. When reconciliation is reduced exclusively to a ritual practice, then we control the process, never allowing God to reveal his true face as a Father full of tenderness and mercy, who rejoices beyond all human expectations, and invites everybody to rejoice with him when he sees the son who had abandoned the family home come back again.

It all revolves around that word *father*. More than in the admission of his foolishness, the solution lies in the recognition and admission of fatherhood, and in that acknowledgment the young man finds the energy to retrace his steps home and accept his relationship with that man who never forgot him, nor gave up hope of him ever coming back. Beyond his self-pity and his fears, there is a father waiting for him, and he recognises him by that very name. '*I will go to my father and say: Father*'. The shift from a justice-image to a life-giver image of his father becomes the decisive spark that will urge him to turn his steps towards home in trust. Only *the acceptance of our God as the Father* revealed by Jesus will heal us of our sins and guilt. Against any personal effort at self-purification, only trust in this Father can bring about true conversion and fullness of life in our brokenness and infidelity. Only the acknowledgment and personal appropriation of a Father-God who waits for our return can bring about total healing and joy.

Waiting at Home – Love

In this perspective, Luke 15 is not about a son who betrays the love of his father, or about another son who refuses to forgive that original betrayal. The real core of the story lies in the patient waiting of the father for the son's return. Past infidelity, ungratefulness, abandonment of home, rejection of family, wastefulness of resources, loose living – none of these seem to come into consideration as far as the father is concerned. He does not even contemplate the possibility that his waiting and hoping will all be futile. He just waits, without ever giving up hope that his son will return home, a waiting based on a rationale that humanly speaking seems totally irrational and even unjust. He is the father, and that young man is his son. That is all that matters.

Such behaviour on the father's part must have come as a shocking disclosure to Jesus' first hearers, creating that kind of dissonance that runs through all the parables. The father's behaviour not only ran counter to the culturally accepted code of behaviour between father and son as well as to their whole social and religious construct dominated by retributive justice. Such un-fatherly behaviour undermined radically their idea of God on which such construct rested. For the Pharisees, the sinner was a person devoid of all dignity, and, consequently, the sinner could only consider himself or herself nothing more than a social and moral outcast, abandoned by God and condemned by humanity.

Through the telling of the parable, Jesus wants to precisely redress this distorted perception in order to restore the sinner's self-image on the one hand and challenge the condemnatory attitude of the leaders on the other. Jesus' intent is to lead his hearers to a new understanding of God and, consequently, to a totally new self-image on the part of the sinner, as well as to a new perception of sin and brokenness. No matter how hardened a sinner a person may be in the eyes of human justice, Jesus invites his hearers to an image based on a personal, living, and the intimate relationship of God with every human being.

Jesus challenges the images of self and of God by presenting a God who loves freely and who accepts to be loved in return only in a relationship of freedom and respect of personal dignity. The God of Jesus of Nazareth is a God who remains forever present and waiting, even in the absence of love or in the rejection on the part of the sinner, in order to offer this sinner the possibility of a radical change and conversion. God's offer of forgiveness is absolute, unconditional and total. It is this new perception of self and of God based on mutual and personal relationship that Jesus is trying to convey to his contemporaries through this story of homecoming. Please God, such disclosure is just as shocking and disturbing for us here today, as we seek reconciliation and forgiveness. While acknowledging personal sinfulness and brokenness, we need to move away from a pathological concern with ourselves that engenders guilt, shame, self-condemnation and fear of punishment. On the contrary, we are invited to re-imagine first of all and then to appropriate our God as the One who is caught up in the same drama of sin and brokenness that we are, never as a judge, but only as a Father, full of tenderness and mercy, gratuitously and unconditionally lavishing love on the sinner-son.

Henri Nouwen puts it beautifully,

> But do I truly want to be so totally forgiven that a completely new way of living becomes possible? Do I trust myself and such a radical reclamation? Do I want to break away from my deep-rooted rebellion against God and surrender myself so absolutely to God's love that a new person can emerge? One of the greatest challenges of the spiritual life is to receive God's forgiveness. There is something in us humans that keeps us clinging to our sins and prevents us from letting God erase our past and offer us a completely new beginning. Sometimes it even seems as though I want to prove to God that my darkness is too great to overcome. While God wants to restore me to the full dignity of sonship, I keep insisting that I will settle for being a hired servant. Receiving forgiveness requires a total willingness to let God be God and do all the healing, restoring, and renewing. As long as I want to do even a part of that myself, I end up with partial solutions, such as becoming a hired servant. As a hired servant, I can still keep my distance, still revolt, reject, strike, run away, or complain about my pay. As the beloved son, I have to claim my full dignity and begin preparing myself to become the father.[11]

The wayward son is quite satisfied with becoming a hired servant. He has not yet understood fully the deep relationship of love that binds him to his Father, and so he begins his well-rehearsed bargaining plea, '*I am no longer worthy...*' Once again, the sinner will attempt to control the process of reconciliation on their terms, by putting forward conditions, even though couched in words and attitudes of shame and guilt. Yes indeed, the Good News probably is too good to be true. Accepting that we are loved and loveable

---

[11] Henri J. .Nouwen, *The Return of the Prodigal Son. A Story of Homecoming*, London: Darton, Longman and Todd, 1992, 53.

in our brokenness is a harsh demand because it deprives us of all control, and we just have to accept love as a gift.

No effort of mine will move God to change his mind about me or his opinion of me. No amount of breast-beating will make me more or less worthy of his love. No list of sins admitted to over and over again, with obsessive accuracy of details, will re-instate me into the household. The only controlling element in my seeking forgiveness is God's unconditional love for me, and I have absolutely no control over that element. I have no choice but to accept that, regardless of how sinful I may be, or I may think I am, I am wrapped in God's love like in a rich new cloak, and gifted by him as with a precious ring that a lover has unexpectedly placed on my finger to show their love for me.

The father is certainly not interested in the son's well-rehearsed speech or his proclamation of a long list of misdemeanours. No one needed reminding about those, least of all his own father. His past behaviour was all too obvious to everyone, but that was now past, and it had no relevance in the present. Healing, reconciliation, and re-instatement into the God's family come when the son finally decides to place his trust in his father's love, believing that this father would accept him back, in spite of his unfaithfulness and sin. On that one surety, and on that alone, he retraces his steps and goes home to his father. Are we prepared to trust that we are loved and embraced in our brokenness and sinfulness, or are we more at ease with many words that will focus only on our sinfulness, thinking that God is a slow learner that needs to be reminded over and over again, of all the wrongs we have done?

Trust is the key. The Father certainly trusted his son in the almost irrational belief that one day that son would come back. And his trustful hope is now rewarded. He is not interested in long catalogues of sins, and he just will not give the son a chance to make his little speech or to wallow in self-pity. He is simply ecstatic for that son *who was dead and has come back to life*, and all he wants is to give full vent to his explosive joy and celebrate life. Nothing else matters.

Staying at Home – Self-Righteousness

By its very nature, celebration implies others, community, friends and family. Not surprisingly, then, we call on these others to join us in our rejoicing, because there cannot be celebration any other way. On the contrary, few things are more hurtful to the human heart than a deliberate rejection of an invitation to a family gathering on the grounds that one does not want 'to meet that person, after all they have said and/or done!' That is precisely the situation that the father, who loves his children unconditionally – no matter what these children may have done – has to face. The older son simply refuses to join in the celebration, because he cannot accept either the return of his wayward brother or the gratuitous love of his father. Unfortunately, there can be no full celebration without the forgiving presence of that older and, in many ways, 'faithful' son. The tragedy of the whole situation is that that son is perfectly correct in his many claims to faithfulness towards his own father and his family. He has done all he had to do, and done it very diligently, if not lovingly, as we can surmise by his reaction.

However, precisely there lies the tragic side of his life-story. He has always operated on a model of subservient obedience and human justice towards his father, and now he cannot accept that his father not only operates out of love, but also that he is actually calling him to operate out of that same love for his brother. In his correct behaviour, the faithful son has become self-righteous, precisely because his behaviour was stimulated not by relationship but by law, not by being-with the father but out of fear of making mistakes, not by acceptance of other people's mistakes but by obsessive legal purity. Consequently, on his side of the ledger, the only conceivable and possible course of action is total and absolute rejection of wrongdoing and condemnation of the sinner.

Unfortunately, in the end, that side of the ledger places him alongside his brother, not because his has to admit to anything wrong in his past life, but because he clings to his own personal rights. Like his brother, but unbeknown to himself, the older son is in desperate need of conversion, beginning with a conversion of his understanding of his father and of God. In his obsession for correct behaviour, he must move away from the slavery of duty and into the freedom of a love relationship.

> The loyal soldier is similar to the 'elder son' in Jesus' parable of the prodigal son. His very loyalty to strict meritocracy, to his own entitlement, to obedience and to loyalty to his father, keeps him from the very 'celebration' that same father has prepared, even though he begs the son to come to the feast (Luke 15:25-32). We have no indication he ever came! What a judgment this is on first-stage religion, and it comes straight from the boss. He makes the same point in his story of the Pharisee and the tax collector (Luke 18:9-14) in which one is loyal and observant and deemed wrong by Jesus, and the other has not obeyed the law – yet is deemed 'at rights with God'. This classic 'reverse theology' is meant to subvert our usual merit-badge thinking. Both the elder son and the Pharisee are good loyal religious soldiers, exactly what most of us in the church were told to be, but Jesus says that both of them missed the major point.[12]

Conversion is not a mere psychological process on the part of the sinner who returns to God. Conversion is a radical transformation of the image of God that both sinner and righteous person alike must undergo in their own lives. The root of sin does not lie so much in wrongdoing, but in the erroneous and self-centred understanding of *Father* and *fatherhood* that both sons carry with them. The younger one, in order to rid himself of his erroneous and oppressive image, takes refuge in the *strategy of pleasure* by rejecting the father and leaving home. The older one

---

[12] Richard Rohr, (2011), *Falling Upwards. A Spirituality of Two Halves of Life*, San Francisco CA: Jossey-Bassey, 2011, 45.

instead, in order to win favours from the same father and to keep him good and on side, seeks the *strategy of duty*, expressed through a servile religiosity and moralistic purity. Both sons, however, miss the fundamental point that Jesus came to reveal, namely that our God is a Father of gratuitous mercy and unconditional kindness, connected to us by a deep and unconditional love relationship. The celebration of homecoming and the joy of being re-embraced by the Father can only come about to the extent that we let go both of guilt born of sin and of presumption born of self-righteousness.

To the end, the father is obsessed with re-establishing proper relationships with both children and between them, not because of what the children have done or not done, but only because they are his children. While the wayward son sought a relationship based on self-assertion and the older one insisted on duty and self-righteousness, the Father operates exclusively on the father-son-brother relationship. In the dialogue with the father who is inviting him to join in the celebration for the return of his brother, the older son, full of indignant condemnation, never acknowledges his sibling as brother or 'my brother', calling him a very distant and derogatory *this son of yours*. By contrast, the father retorts with the language of relationship on which healing and forgiveness rest. 'We have to celebrate and rejoice, because *your brother was dead and has come back to life*' (Luke 15:32).

This page of the Gospel demands, first and foremost, that we convert from an attitude of servile religion to one of celebration in freedom, centred on a self-consciousness of being children of God. God loves us not because we are good and do good deeds, but only because God is Father. There is no need of self-justification, nor is there any place for condemnation of self or of anybody else.

Of course, this is where the parable of the prodigal son becomes most challenging in real terms. Accepting that we are freely loved, now we have no option but to return this love freely and unconditionally to each other, because we all share equally of the undivided love of the Father. We can claim that God is an integral part of our life and rejoice in being forgiven only to the extent that we are prepared to go beyond the brokenness of others, remove all labels and judgments, and accept others as the brothers and sisters that they are. Yes, these may well be the very people who have hurt us and hurt us deeply, those who, by their way of life, do not conform to our expectations, those whose weaknesses and shortcomings have a public face and maybe fill us with embarrassment and shame, those who are likely to continue hurting us. That is precisely the point of the story. The father trusted that his son would come back unconditionally, and his trust was rewarded.

However, now he has no guarantee that, once forgiven, the son/brother will not sin again, nor can we place conditions in reaching out to each other in forgiveness. Have you ever noticed how this narrative – like all the Gospel stories of forgiveness and healing – is open-ended? At the end of the whole saga, there is no conclusion, and we are left wondering if the older son did actually accept the invitation to join in the festivities and to embrace his brother, or whether the younger son, in another moment of folly, did not actually leave home once again in search of other adventures? I really believe that these are not just idle questions. The Father has trusted that his son would come back after all, but there is no guarantee that once forgiven, the sinner will not err again. But that is precisely the point of the story. Regardless of past events or future possibilities, these are the brothers and sisters whom we are called not only to encounter, but to re-embrace and to rejoice with.

The love that heals us becomes true and authentic for each of us individually and all of us collectively, only when it becomes brotherly love towards all, when it awakens a personal responsibility and commitment for the good of all, and when it engenders trust and courage in the face of all human brokenness, particularly the brokenness of those who share our life in the myriad of ways that we experience every day. We must make the first move towards meeting and embracing with trust those who are overburdened with sin, guilt and shame for their mistakes, those who have lost all meaning and self-awareness of brokenness, those who have lost the very sense and taste for life. The call to forgiveness of those around us must be unconditional and universal, or our own forgiveness is void.

Both sons need healing through accepting this call to relationship born of love, or the joy for the return of one will only provoke the distancing of another. As we see in the parable, healing through acceptance and love is both personal and communal.

The Lord's Prayer – Commitment

In the Kingdom perspective as proclaimed by Jesus, the social dimension of reconciliation and forgiveness is unequivocal and non-negotiable. Are we prepared to take seriously the words we pray each day, several times a day, *'Forgive us our sins, as we forgive those who sin against us'*? Have we allowed ourselves to be challenged by what we pray? Are we aware of the commitment we take on each and every time we utter those words, by which we proclaim our readiness to forgive each other with the same measure with which God forgives us, knowing full well that God's measure is measure-less, universal and unconditional?

Either our response to the call to forgive each other is unconditional and universal, without expectations or pre-conceptions on our part, or we will never be forgiven ourselves. As we ask each day for God's forgiveness and healing, let us also ask ourselves whether, in our dealings with each other, we reflect the action of God in our world, as enjoined on us by Jesus Christ, particularly in the way he welcomed sinners, in his trust towards those who had gone astray, and in his ultimate forgiving act on the cross. As we pray the Lord's prayer, we need to begin with a variation to the words we utter and, in all honesty, pray each day that the Lord of healing may touch our hearts and convert us to the kind of attitudes that will lead us to forgive each other as God forgives us.

We will never be truly converted, nor will we ever reflect an authentic image of God and Church in our lives, unless we learn to imitate the forgetfulness of God. Once he has forgiven the sinner, he looks upon this person as a new creation, unencumbered by any handicap or baggage that the past may have laid on them. This is the living witness of Jesus in word and deed, right to the final instant of his earthly life on the cross. This is the challenge thrown at us by the prodigal Father in Jesus' story. This is the commitment we take on each time we dare say, *'Teach us to forgive others, as you forgive us!'*

May the 'Our Father' we pray each day stimulate us beyond words and motivate actions that reach out in forgiveness to the poor, the hopeless, the broken and the misguided, those who are overburdened with sin, guilt, and shame, those who have lost all meaning and self-awareness of brokenness and the very sense and taste for life, because a loving and forgiving God can only be experienced and witnessed through the unconditional and loving forgiveness of each other.

A Drama of Misery and Mercy

John 8:1-11

Jesus went to the Mount of Olives. Early in the morning he came again to the temple. All the people came to him, and he sat down and began to teach them. The scribes and the Pharisees brought a woman who had been caught in adultery; and making her stand before all of them, they said to him, 'Teacher, this woman was caught in the very act of committing adultery. Now in the law Moses commanded us to stone such women. Now what do you say?' They said this to test him, so that they might have some charge to bring against him. Jesus bent down and wrote with his finger on the ground. When they kept on questioning him, he straightened up and said to them, 'Let anyone among you who is without sin be the first to throw a stone at her'. And once again he bent down and wrote on the ground. When they heard it, they went away, one by one, beginning with the elders; and Jesus was left alone with the woman standing before him. Jesus straightened up and said to her, 'Woman, where are they? Has no one condemned you?' She said, 'No one, sir'. And Jesus said, 'Neither do I condemn you. Go your way, and from now on do not sin again'. (John 8:1-11)

THIS INCIDENT of the adulterous woman as narrated by John exemplifies a brilliant triptych illustrating three distinctive but consecutive stages of response and of interpretation and a very specific theme underlying the narrative. In this case, we are immediately informed about this unifying theme by a formal and solemn announcement that *'this woman has been caught in the very act of committing adultery'* (John 8:4). Each panel sequentially represents not only the diversity of responses to the announcement expressed by the various characters at play, but more significantly, as the story unfolds, each panel challenges us as to where we stand when confronted with personal and/or communal sinfulness.

The Challenge in Three Movements

The story is set in the temple precinct, the place of worship, the place of the Law and of Mosaic tradition, the place of God, all combining to give the event a social cum legal flavour. In this setting, with the leaders of the people immediately stating the case and appealing to the Law, the reader is immediately alerted to the fact that here we are dealing with more than just a civil crime to be processed according to a strict rule of justice, but a situation carrying strong cultural, social and moral connotations and implications.

However, the opening strokes of the story immediately reveal a shift of focus away from the woman and on to Jesus himself. He is the one who is primarily on trial here, being challenged precisely on his stand on the fundamental cultural and religious principles on which the very existence as God's chosen people stood from time immemorial.

The whole of John's Gospel narrative represents a critical drama predicated and structured by a chronic ongoing antagonism between Jesus and those who refused and opposed his message and self-identification as the living divine presence in the reality of the human story. Consequently, by appealing to the Law of Moses, in their mind the leaders have already condemned the public sinner deserving of punishment by stoning and the execution can begin. However, as the questioning dialogue opening the narrative of makes it very clear. the setting becomes the perfect excuse to confront and condemn Jesus himself for his critical and challenging outlook precisely on Law and temple This Jesus – where does he stand – for or against the Law of Moses and the sacred milieu of traditions and temple? The trap is clear. Should Jesus declare himself against the execution, then he clearly sets himself at odds with the sacred prescriptions of the Law. On the other hand, should he take a stand for the Law, then he makes a mockery of his own teaching and preaching about forgiveness and love of one's enemies.

That is the challenge thrown at Jesus. However, the Word of God is never a mere narrative of some event distant in time and place but implies always a challenge addressed to us as much as to Jesus, spurring us to become the living actors confronting the drama of our own situation in our personal time and place and reaching far beyond the plot and into the very nature of God and of our relationship with God. Consequently, the story of the adulterous woman directs us to look at the whole issue of sinfulness; and the challenge is really addressed to us. Where does our God stand? Is our God a God of justice and judgment or a God of compassion and forgiveness?

Unfolding from a scene of judgment and fear and leading to forgiveness and hope energised by the awareness of God's healing presence, broken or helpless we may be, this dramatic Gospel story becomes is a critical commentary on our *attitudes* to sin and perceptions of forgiveness. Specifically, it challenges our awareness of sinfulness and the dynamics of reconciliation, with the triptych articulating across three separate but interconnected panels subtitled (1) *'Condemnation and Judgment'*, (2) *'Fear and Guilt'*, and (3) *'Affirmation and Forgiveness'*.

> No Gospel story speaks so simply or so profoundly of the love of God made available for us in the person of Jesus of Nazareth. But it also speaks of the seriousness of the need for repentance. We need to accept both if we are to become what God would want us to be.[13]

Condemnation and Judgment

'The Law' founded on God's original call of Abraham to become a wondering Aramean (Genesis 12:1-2), formally proclaimed as the

---

[13] Francis J. Moloney, *This is the Gospel of the Lord, Year C*, Homebush NSW: St Paul Publications, 1991, 81.

beacon of a fledging people in search of identity on Sinai (Exodus 19-24), and codified over centuries of historical development, was much more than a moral code of behaviours or retributive justice. Sacred and sacrosanct, specific, and unquestionable to its ultimate social, political, economic, and religious details, at all levels of reality, it embodied the very DNA of the Old Testament People of God. Consequently, any breaking of the Law was a crime against its very own identity as God's chosen people attracting the harshest punishment, particularly severe in matters of sexual ethics and morality as stated at the very start of John 10:1-2.

> *If a man commits adultery with another man's wife, both the adulterer and the adulteress must be put to death* (Leviticus 20:11).

The Law was clear and for '*this woman was caught in the very act of committing adultery*' and the penalty was incontrovertibly death by stoning, the ancient punishment for infidelity still active in some cultures. No, there is no appeal, or any need of some official process and no mercy is possible either with the gathered crowd nor with the leaders. Smug and secure behind the dictates of 'the Law' to justify their judge-and-executioner charade, the self-righteous accusers have already condemned the woman who has publicly disgraced herself, and all they can see is the sinner, 'a thing' without dignity, not worth addressing as a person. She is identified with her sin, and like a despicable 'thing', she is dragged away and made a public display amid cat calls of abuse, ridicule, and condemnation because a public wrongdoing must have a public punishment, and in this way the accusers want to take away her life as a solution to her sinful ways.

No longer considered a person, *they talk about* the woman as an extraneous intrusion without possibility of forgiveness, compassion or healing, because the sinner is a terminal cancerous presence in the community or clan and only worthy of disregard, rejection, punishment and death.

Ironically, while justice and mercy are epithets attributed to God's very nature of *'The Just One, forgiving iniquity and transgression and sin'* (Exodus 34:6-7) revealed by Jesus as 'Abba' (Mark 14:36), and *'Mercy is the Name of God'* as Pope Francis proclaimed,[14] the charade in the temple court degenerates into an attempt on God himself, a de-humanising gesture in the name of a de-humanising God. Even the gift of divine justice and forgiving presence is manipulated by Jesus' opponents under the pretext of law into becoming rejection of the person.

No mercy is possible when the human heart is set on self-righteousness and revenge against human frailty or mistakes, and even the God of healing and mercy asserted and exposed by Jesus by advocating forgiveness of enemies becomes irrelevant. 'Don't sin at all – they seem to say – and then we won't condemn you!' More than a matter of condemning a wrongful act, the woman of the story is only a pawn in the maverick attempt of the opponents of Jesus to discredit him and to trap him on his claim of a God full of mercy and compassion who enjoins on us to love the sinner.

Probably, as observers from the distance of centuries, the cruel treatment meted out to the woman moves us to pity, or even to a sense of revulsion. However, are we any different from that crowd for whom forgiveness is only a matter of legal observance apportioned according to the gravity of the offence? Confronted with sinfulness and brokenness, we often think that God is angry with us and that we have to pay him back and, to appease him, we feel duty-bound to do something proportionate to the wrong we have committed.

Like the angry crowd in the temple court, too often we think that reconciliation is a matter of judgment and/or punishment, and quickly forget that, rather than a confrontation with a fearsome judge, reconciliation is a moment of encounter with a loving father who is longing for our return home where we belong with

---

[14] Pope Francis, https://www.penguinrandomhouse.com/books/540211/

him. Like the angry crowd, when confronted with personal or communal sinfulness we may feel duty-bound to escape into a ritual proportionate to the wrong committed so as to avoid God's punishment. However, when atonement is the result of our efforts to avoid God's punishment and escaping punishment is the focus of our seeking forgiveness through a sacramental performance, then reconciliation becomes merely a magic ritual to appease an angry idol, never an encounter with a loving Father-God obsessed with sharing his love unconditionally, regardless of who I am or what I have done longing for our return home to share unconditional love as illustrated by the parable of the Prodigal Father (Luke 15).

Fear and Guilt

Crouched ungainly and dishevelled in the dust, the woman says nothing; helpless and hopeless, she says nothing. No need to say anything! She knows... They all know... Helpless and hopeless, paralysed by horror and terror, , she cannot even beg for mercy because she knows that there is no mercy for her. Shattered, bewildered, terrified and devoid of all dignity, she personifies absolute Misery. Her silent terror, overcome by a barrage of insults and condemnation, she waits for those blows to rain down, her mind and heart throbbing with terror, self-hatred, shame, and hopeless despair is allayed only by the sickening hope that it may be quick. For the Pharisees, the sinner was a person devoid of all dignity, and, consequently, the sinner could only consider oneself nothing more than a social and moral outcast, abandoned by God and condemned by humanity. Paralysed by horror and terror, guilt, anger and self-hatred are her only companions.

This scenario may well sound like an overly emotional flight of fantasy, but I suggest that in many cases it is not extraneous to the turmoil that may explode from deep within our psyche when confronted with true or imagined evil or wrongdoing. When we approach the sacrament of Reconciliation focusing exclusively on our sinfulness and on the punishment that we may deserve rather than on God's love, then there is no room for trust in God's mercy and forgiveness. None of us in our life journey are total strangers to fear and self-hatred that may grip us when we encounter negativity and brokenness in our relationship with God and each other. Then we feel diminished, and seek escapes into self-condemnation or some ritual, even for a brief moment, that may apparently appease the heart by blaming 'the world', 'the other' or 'the establishment' for our tangled situation.

However, when we lose sight of the presence and action of God in the midst of our brokenness, then the sacrament becomes a self-styled ritual of cleansing and a judgment seat of fear, guilt, and self-deprecation. If our heart remains locked within itself, enslaved and motivated by fear, guilt, and self-hatred. there is no magic wand or ritual escape that can heal the anxiety that may gnaw at us for a lifetime When we are not prepared to accept that only love can heal our negativity and we want to heal ourselves and, on our terms, we can only wallow in guilt, shame, fear, and hopelessness.

Unlike the woman in the temple dust, however, as believers in a 'life-giving God-presence' even beyond ultimate death, in our Christian tradition we know that we still hold a life-giving divine 'sacred-moment' that will redeem brokenness and fear beyond all human possibilities. That is the power of the Sacrament (hence *sacred moment*') of Healing, conditional to the outlook of our God-relationship we bring to this divine presence and encounter. Conversely, when we lose sight of our relationship with God in the midst of our brokenness and sinfulness, the sacred moment throws us back on our own shattered resources, becoming a ritual of self-cleansing among the accusers of the temple.

The practice of frequent and regular confession, a central element in spirituality for a long time, holds great power for transformation and healing, but it hides grave dangers as well. If the sacramental practice is justified by fear, then we deny the power of God to enter into our life and heal our brokenness. Fear generates distance, anxiety and mistrust. Fear seeks safeguards, sets boundaries, and puts us in control of the process. Fear reduces the sacrament of reconciliation to a rite of exorcism and magic. Fear makes judgments and demands judgment of God. If we approach the sacrament as a matter of routine, then the only joy of the encounter with God is a sense of self-satisfaction at having avoided once more the punishment of God. We have done all the right things, we performed the correct ritual at the proper time and place, and we can now go on unconcerned until the time comes around again for the next ritual purification; we have done it all, and God has nothing to do with it except reward us or at least spare us his punishment.

In this context, questions have to be asked: What leads us to the Sacrament: fear or trust? When confronted with my sinfulness, do I find excuses, by blaming myself and/or others, or do I acknowledge my fragility and trust in God? What motivates us in seeking reconciliation: fear and concern with crouching in the dust of our sinfulness, or the awareness of God standing with us, unconcerned with who we are or what we may have done? In seeking reconciliation, are we motivated by fear or by love of God? Are we more concerned with crouching in the dust or with the awareness of God standing by us and with us?

Affirmation and Forgiveness

While these are pertinent questions confronting all of us in the face of sinfulness and brokenness, even questioning can become yet another palliative for justification and of self-deceit depending on where the focus of our heart and the intent of mind are. In particular, are we people of doing or of being?

Suddenly, in the unfolding drama, Jesus enters, proclaiming and embracing 'Mercy' where punishment and death seemed inevitable. At the opening of the third panel of the triptych, the focus of the original narrative suddenly shifts away from the historical event to

Jesus called into action, while up to this point, he has been a silent and apparently bored spectator of the drama.

Jesus' presence is always very challenging to his opponents and, as they had already attempted in the case of the healing of the man born blind (John 9:1-13), this is a perfect opportunity in their intent to trap him into compromising his very credibility by seeking his opinion on a matter of moral law and civil order.

> *They said to him, 'Teacher, this woman was caught in the very act of committing adultery. Now in the law Moses commanded us to stone such women. Now what do you say?* (John 8:4-5).

Now he must declare his stance in relation to their presumed God-sanctioned 'Law' and 'Tradition' in the light of his pronouncements on a God of love and his declared mission to reveal the living presence of Abba in human experience. Any stand against the execution would have made Jesus guilty of rejecting the divine sanctioned 'Law' that identified them as a people and nation of God. On the other hand, had he approved of the execution, he would have self-condemned and betrayed himself by denying his ministry of God's presence through healing and forgiveness in Love that he had declared, lived and preached in their midst.

Jesus' reply to the dilemma is a counter challenge expressed though three significant gestures. *First, he shows his boredom throughout the whole issue and its process* by bending down and writing with his finger on the ground, making me sympathise with many disinterested and annoyed young students of mine over many years who would take out their frustration on the classroom desk. For us today, is it too irrelevant to surmise that God can be bored and disinterested with our long and detailed shopping-like catalogue of sins?

Secondly, after making the bystanders aware of their own sinfulness and brokenness, Jesus refuses to be drawn into the ruse and neither condones nor condemns the woman who happens to be a sinner, by *acknowledging the person as she is* where everybody else could only see the sin and the sinner to be excised as a 'cancerous thing', because God is Mercy and God's love is always available to the believer even in spite of ourselves.

> *'Let anyone among you who is without sin be the first to throw a stone at her'* (John 8:7).

Thirdly, not interested in justification or excuses for human mistakes, and bored with our quibbling and playing reward-punishment games, in antithesis to the crowd, Jesus looks into her eyes and while the accusers would talk only about her as a sinful object to be thrown away, *Jesus talks to her.*

> *Jesus straightened up and said to her, 'Woman, where are they? Has no one condemned you?' She said, 'No one, sir'. And Jesus said, 'Neither do I condemn you. Go your way, and from now on do not sin again'* (John 8:10-11).

That face-to-face encounter generates mutual trust whereby the woman facing her own sinfulness abandons herself to Jesus, and Jesus acknowledges her as a person, weak and broken though she may be, but nevertheless a precious God-created individual. While the attitude of the accusers is conditional as they seem to say to her 'Don't sin anymore and we won't condemn you', Jesus has no choice but to reach out to her in forgiveness, without conditions or guarantees that she will never fail again fall in the future, simply because 'God's name is Mercy'[15] and as such God cannot resist the sinner who trusts and abandons themself into God's loving presence.

When facing our own sinfulness and mistakes, we must stop wallowing in self-pity or fear for the future, simply accepting that we are weak and broken but precious in God's eyes, self-aware that the faithful and trusting God truly loves and forgives unconditionally without conditions or guarantees from our human frailty.

---

[15] Pope Francis, https://www.penguinrandomhouse.com/books/540211/

In our relationship with God, do we seek personal interest by many words or just listen in abandonment and trust to God speaking to our human insufficiency and brokenness? Are we prepared to let go of securities, fears and personal plans so as to allow God to touch our personal heart and set our future life course? There lies the greatest challenge of the *'sacred moment'*.

In the words of Ronald Rolheiser,

> As long as we remain sincere, we will soon enough admit our sin and we will know too that God still looks on us with love.[16]

Conclusion

Am I prepared to trust that this God stands by me, knows me as a precious person, no matter what my mistakes may be? Am I prepared to celebrate reconciliation or am I satisfied with performing a ritual of purification? God's forgiveness and mercy do not need words of judgment, or of fear and guilt, because they speak only of trust! God trusts me to the point of taking me as I am and letting me go without any guarantee that I will not fall again.

> Part of our flawed human condition is that we do sometimes fail. I have discovered that no matter how hard I try, I continue to fail every now and then. I still make mistakes, poor decisions, hasty judgments, and badly chosen comments. Sometimes these are intentional behaviours and sometimes I 'mess up' without even intending to do so. The blessing of failure is that it leads me to greater truth if I do not let myself drown in discouragement, regrets or self-disparagement... It is out of our human lives that God reaches us... God reaches us in the way that God has always reached human beings – through our ordinary, flawed lives. No matter what the reason for our failures, we need to eventually mover to the place where we

---

[16] Ronald Rolheiser, 'Yes we are sinners, but Jesus love us', in *Terra Spiritus*, 2006. http://www.wcr.ab.ca/columns/rolheiser/2006/rolheiser032006.shtml

forgive ourselves for how we have failed... Look at your flawed life today and let God come into it.¹⁷

As we approach the great festival of life – in spite of and beyond death – let us stop wallowing in self-pity or fear of our sinfulness. Instead, let us hear those words addressed to us, '*Has no one condemned you?*... '*Neither do I condemn you. Go your way, and from now on do not sin again!*'

---

¹⁷ Joyce Rupp, *The Cup of Our Life. A Guide For Spiritual Growth*, Notre Dame IN: Ave Maria Press, 77-78.

Sight and Blindness – A Faith Intersection

John 9:1-41

A Question of Identity

AS WE APPROACH the climax of Holy Week, the Word of God takes on a strong sense of urgency, demanding we take a stand on who Jesus is and on who we are as believers. Liturgically, this is a time of high drama. As we approach the climax of Holy Week and the all-transforming event of Resurrection, the Word of God takes on a strong sense of urgency and a compelling demand to take a stand on who Jesus is and on what it means for us to follow him now as believer and as disciples. The drama is heightened by the clever narrative structure of today's Gospel – a fast moving dialogue: questions, interjections, rebuffs, condemnation and trusting faith, all rolled into one, inviting a decision for or against Jesus. Both the story of the Samaritan woman, last week, and the restoration of sight to a man born blind today are intensely dramatic encounters expressed through fast-moving dialogue and challenging questioning. Both events raise the same fundamental issue of who Jesus is and both share the same rejoinder: *Jesus is the active living presence of God in our everyday lives, a presence that privileges the lives of those caught in a tragic entanglement of fear, suffering, and hopeless blindness engendered by the refusal or the absence of this God with us.*

Antithesis and Challenge

Today's Gospel awakens in my mind the image of two powerful streams of consciousness moving rapidly in opposite directions, intersecting at one definite point only to proceed on to an equally opposite and unexpected conclusion. In this drama between accepting or rejecting God's presence along the journey of faith in the reality of our daily experience, Jesus is that very point of intersection. Although he barely enters only later in the intense emotional dialogue that ensues between the man, his family, and especially the incensed leaders of the people that the miracle sets in motion, Jesus is the one who is on trial as the focus of the search that eventually leads to a personal decision of faith. For the bystanders of Jesus as much as for us and for all time, God's presence and action will always exact a response in terms of acceptance or rejection, in this instance expressed by the evangelist through the antitheses of sight or blindness, light or darkness, faith or unbelief. Ultimately, faith is not simply an academic or intellectual assent to a body of academic or ritualised propositions but a matter of decision for or against the life-giving presence of God in our actual world expressed through Jesus' human life and death. In the end, as much as for Jesus' contemporaries, all of us have to confront the inevitable duality that underlies the whole event, each of the two contrasting and opposite positions leading respectively from blindness to sight or vice versa from sight to total blindness.

I am reminded of an insertion in the obituary pages of a daily newspaper that caught my eye, a very brief tribute to an eye specialist who had passed away, and it read simply, 'You did not give me sight; you gave me life' – signed, 'Jocelyn'. Whoever Jocelyn may have been, she unconsciously but clearly paraphrased today's Gospel by enlarging the gift of sight into the gift of total life, just as in the encounter with the Samaritan woman last week, water became the sign of life and the energy of God's immersion into our ordinary lives. Characteristically, throughout his whole narrative, John persists with amplifying an image into an active instrument and expression of life and salvation. Consequently, rather than a wonder-worker who performs strange deeds like miracles or, worse still, an imposter operating under the aegis of none other than Beelzebub himself (Matthew 12:25-28), by restoring sight to a man born blind, Jesus is the sign of the saving presence of God in our human story.

The evangelist John is a master craftsman in the use of symbols, particularly of water (John 1:26-33; 2:6-9; 4:7-46; 5:37; 7:37-38) and light (John 1:4-9; 3:19-21; 5:35; 8:12; 9:5; 11:9-10; 12:35-36.46), constantly weaving them throughout a narrative as 'signs' (σημεῖα) that projects the reader into a totally 'other and deeper level of reality', specifically the level of divine presence and action in the constant flow of human affairs. Jesus' miracles are clear signs of the living, active and saving presence of God in our stories. However, for the sign to be saving and life-giving, we need to be able to see beyond and through the external sign itself, and there accept the living and active presence of God in our real everyday life, Conversely, the sign remains meaningless at best or downright death-dealing at worst (Matthew 12:25-28).

That is the double-sided key that will unlock the sign of God; blind acceptance in faith that God does not abandon humanity in the darkness of struggle and death, or the blindness of self-righteous rejection on the grounds of that self-styled pretentious security that says, 'I know the answer to life's mysteries, as well as the workings of God' (John 9:29-31). On this latter premise, there is neither need nor space for God to enter one's life and give life and light. In the regaining of his physical sight, the narrative of the blind man is a sign of the journey of faith that the believer must undertake by moving from the darkness of unbelief, misunderstanding, self-righteousness and sinfulness to the newness of light revealed by the person of Jesus.

As he sat for a lifetime, abandoned, uselessly, by the pool, an object of ridicule, scorn, rejected by most and culturally condemned even by God to total darkness from his very birth as a punishment for sins he knew nothing about and most likely not of his own making but of his parents, the blind man was certainly not seeking a conversion experience. So, typically, Jesus takes the initiative as he had done with the woman at the well of Sychar and approaches the man as a person who happens to be blind and has never seen the light, and not as the blind man who is paying for his sins and the sins of his parents by being denied the light from his very birth. In that initial gesture of recognition and human promotion, Jesus destroys not only blindness but also all the moral, psychological, social connotations and taboos that the conditions of physical blindness carried in that climate.

The Challenge of Faith

Between the original restoration of sight and the final coming to faith of the man born blind, the plot is at its most intense. As readers and listeners, we are drawn into heated and emotional discussions between the various characters and personalities of the drama: the blind man, his parents, and most of all the Pharisees and the leaders. These considered themselves the champions of the true faith in Yahweh and the guardians of the Law and Tradition on which their whole cultural, political and religious ethos rested. Faced with the undisputed sign of a man born blind restored to full sight, these people too are confronted with the same probing and uncomfortable question of who Jesus is and are invited to look beyond and see in him the active presence of God in their midst.

They certainly do admit that only God can do such things, as the blind man himself reminds his interlocutors (John 9:33) but, contrary to Jesus' saving action through direct divine intervention in affairs of human promotion for the marginalised and disparaged, their interpretation and acknowledgment of God does not align with their self-styled expectations of Messiah. They claim that they know the truth about God, while they cannot put their faith in this Jesus whom they do not really want to know, cleverly disguising their refusal by claiming ignorance of where he comes from (John 9:29).

> 'We know that God has spoken to Moses, but as for this man, we do not know where he comes from... We know that God does not listen to sinner, but he does listen to one who worships him and obeys and obeys his will' (John 9:29-31).

Paradoxically, precisely this claim to 'knowing' in the end prevents them from seeing the active presence of God in their own lives, and their opposition to Jesus is such that they not only fail *to see*, but they categorically refuse *to look at* the sign and beyond the sign. In an ironic twist of fate, locked in their preconceived ideas and expectations, and categorically refusing to believe, they are the blind ones. By eliminating any manifestation of God in their own lives and personal expectations, as the narrative ends, they are the ones who are left in the dark and can only decide for rejection and death of Jesus and of God himself, . In stark contrast, by trusting in this Jesus whom he does not know and has never seen through sensory experience (John 9:36-39), the blind person becomes the seer able to go beyond the sign and see the active presence of God with him and discover finds both sight and life in spite of darkness, sinfulness, and rejection in the concrete reality of his time and place.

Here are two journeys in opposite directions with Jesus at the point of intersection between faith and unbelief. This is the paradox of faith that Jesus himself reveals in his final reproach to his self-righteous contemporaries and addresses to self-styled believers of all time.

> Jesus said, 'I came into this world for judgment so that those who do not see may see, and those who do see may become blind'. Some of the Pharisees near him heard this and said to him, 'Surely we are not blind, are we?' Jesus said to them, 'If you were blind, you would not have sin. But now that you say, "We see", your sin remains' (John 9:35-41).

As a sign, Jesus' healing is much deeper than physical transformation, touching an equally deeper level of the soul and of the human psyche, and setting off a whole process of probing questions, doubts, and of ' maybes' in the man's mind that eventually will bring him to fullness of life and faith expressed in that almost explosive 'Lord, I believe'. A blind person becomes the seer, because he is able to go beyond the sign and accompanying struggle and doubts into a deeper perception of reality and see the active presence in his own life of God who touched his. His answer now can only be one of acceptance of this Jesus who touched his eyes and commit himself to that presence because he has accepted that in spite of his blindness and abandonment, he knows that in this Jesus God is now standing with him and by him.

> *Jesus heard that they had driven him out, and when he found him, he said, 'Do you believe in the Son of Man?' He answered, 'And who is he, sir? Tell me, so that I may believe in him.' Jesus said to him, 'You have seen him, and the one speaking with you is he'* (John 9:35-37).

In the end, the only one who sees is the blind man. He sees because he accepts Jesus' injunction to move out of his apathy and static self-pity and abandon his expectations and presuppositions. He sees because he trusts in this Jesus as the only one who can truly heal him. Is our faith a blind trust in a God hidden from our physical senses and apparently unknown, but always there, touching us in our blindness and inviting us to journey along with him, not knowing where he is likely to take us? With the best of intentions or fired by some emotional pseudo-spiritual fervour, we seek frantically for a meaning or a solution to our struggles in rituals, religious placebos, or personally satisfying practices, only to entrench ourselves even further in darkness, defeat, meaninglessness and despair. In the end, only the acceptance that God stands by us in our darkness can restore sight to our blindness, strength to our weakness, and wisdom to our sense of loss and confusion. In the end we can only trust and find fullness of life in God, or despair and curse the darkness.

At the end, in striking similarity to the encounter with the woman at the well (John 4:26), Jesus leaves no doubt as to his identity to the lost, rejected and blind man, by making a direct reference to the revelation of God's active presence to Moses in the encounter with the burning bush by self-proclaiming with the very name of God: *God said to Moses, 'I am who I am'* (Exodus 3:14). In Jesus, our God seems fascinated with the down and out, and plunges unconditionally into the very fibre of their life. There lies our challenge too. As we face the many and varied crossroads of our lives, where do we really stand in relation to our God? No doubt, we claim faith; but this faith is perhaps of our own making, according to our expectations and agendas, suiting every whim and turn of our lives. Or is our faith a blind dependence in God physically hidden and alien to our tangible sensitivity, but always there, stirring us in our blindness and bidding us to accept his living and active presence in our darkness, loneliness, misunderstandings, and even sinfulness?

That second self-revelation of Jesus, *'You have seen him, and the one speaking with you is he'* (John 9:37), against all possibilities and expectations, became the existential turning point for the blind man well beyond any restoration of sight and must become the beacon enlightening us the disciples, provoking wisdom to see this eternal presence and energy throughout the rocky journey of our own life. Enlightened by these words, let us engage the trust to jump blindly into the darkness which life and faith often confront us. Strengthened by this unseen presence, may we have the courage to let go of our self-styled securities for the one security of God's presence, come what may in the uncertainty of an unknown future, along with our God touching us where we are most vulnerable, insecure and fearful because our God will always be the 'Presence of "I AM"'.

Signs of Death – Instrument of Life

John 3:14-21

'Give Up Giving Up'

SEAMUS WAS A MOST PECULIAR MAN, a philosopher by his own reckoning, who would occasionally knock at the presbytery door, either holding a little brown bottle wrapped untidily in a brown paper bag or begging for a 'bob for a cuppa', which to the initiated meant the little brown bottle in the small brown paper bag. We soon came to a compromise. 'I'll give you the real cuppa', I proposed, 'and I'll share one with you'. He did not seem to mind. And that was the beginning of a repeated ritual that invariably led to a long and often multi-lingual philosophical dissertation on his part – multilingual, because he would readily jump from English into Gaelic and maybe revert back to English again – a confused and unintelligible blabbing making no sense to me and being of no concern to him.

It was Ash Wednesday and I had just walked out of the church after the rite of distribution of the ashes. On noticing the mark on my forehead, he immediately launched into one of his now unavoidable and to me unintelligible monologues. I sat nodding aimlessly ignorant of whether in agreement or disagreement, just sipping a cuppa, compliant with the first Lenten penance that had just befallen me. More by instinct than by any comprehension at all, somehow, I picked up the gist of his relentless discourse. Seamus was holding forth with conviction on the theology of Lent, and I knew that, if I were patient enough, eventually that broad brogue would revert into intelligible English.

And my patience was rewarded. Well into the incomprehensible monologue, while nodding my head alternatively in affirmation or negation for some time, clueless as to whether I should nod either way at all, I suddenly became aware of an unexpected turn of consciousness: Seamus obliged by drifting from Gaelic into English. Now at least I could understand the words, if not the sense of his convoluted address and I will be forever grateful that I picked up that final punch line. Whether aware of the depth of his insight, and whatever nuances he ever put to his words, Seamus sentenced with authority, 'Lent! What's all this business of giving up and giving in! At my age! – (he appeared much older and more haggard than his chronological years!) – What is the point? *I think that this year for Lent I give up giving up!*' And with that, he got up from the bench, returned the cup and, as the well-known identity that he was, continued his daily meanderings through the neighbourhood.

That was the last I saw or heard of Seamus, but whatever Seamus meant by those ambiguous words, I hear them resonate in my memory with deep and challenging wisdom every Lenten season. I wonder if my Irish friend ever realised or even remembered the power of his ambiguity, but his ambivalent statement unwittingly gave expression to the authentic life-centred Lenten journey, not in terms of deprivation or personal acts of penance, or of repetitive actions, rituals, and traditions but as a commitment to a radical and all-embracing conversion of mind and heart – a heart and mind set on a centred journey of self-fulfilment with our God, in the face of struggles and negativity, without ever giving up hope and courage whatever obstacle or adversity we may encounter.

An Ambiguity: Life Through Death

Seamus' ambiguous *'give up giving up'* resounded strongly the ambiguity expressed in the encounter of Jesus with Nicodemus

(John 3:1-21) where, in Jesus' own words, the sign of ignominy and death has become the instrument of life and love, sounds a warning against being too quick in finding ready-made answers in our response to God, and instant solutions to our questions and struggles.

When we bring God into our story, we will often be tempted to manipulate God according to our whims, or to blame God for the unplanned, the unexpected, and the unwanted crushing into our lives. This 'heart-less' attitude will uphold conventional presupposition of a legalist and vindictive idol-god, instantly and unconditionally punishing human frailty and weakness and creating a God according to our likes and dislike in response to a quick-solution-and-immediate-response syndrome. In this case, it makes sense to reach out for the placebos that will appease God and even the Christian tradition of Lenten fast and prayer can become a personal performance by which we exorcise our misguided expectations while leaving us totally unmoved and unconverted in heart and mind.

By contrast, Seamus' ambiguous statement is a challenge to look at Lent as a call to grow in hope not as a conquest through *doing* something that presumably will please and appease God, but by *being* a person of hope and trust in God, regardless of the weakness and negativity we may experience in our journey and even of death. Consequently, the ambiguity of the signs of death – like ashes or a cross marked on our forehead are a stimulus to courage and hope that draw energy from a patient God even against all evidence to the contrary, God does not give up on us nor does he give in to hopelessness and desire for punishment in the face of human brokenness and frailty, and therefore we need not so much perform acts for immediate satisfaction, as incarnate instead that same hopefulness and patience in our journey of life and conversion.

We often think of conversion as an instantaneous lightning bolt changing not only our lifestyle but also our very personality, a total transformation brought on by submitting ourselves to some ritual, enduring beyond human bearing some masochistic pain-filled action, or by canonising some artificial God-imposed demand. Conversion is not a once-and-forever moment of instant transformation, but a work in progress lasting a whole lifetime, a life-long journey of seeking God through and in spite of human weakness, sinfulness, and barrenness, without ever-losing heart or allowing guilt, blame or self-hatred to dominate and weaken our resolve. For the believing disciple, conversion is never instantaneous, but a transformation of mind and heart that will only reach its fulfilment when this mind and heart are set on God journeying patiently with us each step of our way, without violence or judgment.

As sensory beings, we need some form of outward sensory experience of the journey of faith and conversion like the triad of Lenten practices of prayer, penance and work of charity, not as ends in themselves as if by themselves they create change and conversion. They must be outward visible signs of that deeply personal change of perspective and disposition of mind and heart that will make room for God and foster growth towards God in us, as Seamus' strange and unreflective insight points us precisely to this inner and challenging transformation.

Death as Harbinger of Life

In his conversation with Nicodemus, Jesus proclaims this ambiguity of hope and healing precisely through the signs of death by referring to an ancient incident that occurred during the great journey of liberation from Egypt to the Promised Land. In their long wandering through the desert, the Israelites encountered a plague of venomous snakes, and Moses was instructed to raise a dead snake on a stake, with the reassurance that anyone looking at it would be cured of their deadly bites (Numbers 21:4-9).

> *The Lord said to Moses, 'Make a poisonous serpent, and set it on a pole; and everyone who is bitten shall look at it and live'.*

> *So Moses made a serpent of bronze and put it upon a pole; and whenever a serpent bit someone, that person would look at the serpent of bronze and live* (Numbers 21:8-9).

Healing and salvation through a dead body hanging on a stake is an unlikely contradiction at the best of times; however, that is precisely the ambivalence Jesus appropriates to himself as the climax of the mission entrusted to him by the Father. Life through death is the ultimate ambivalence of Lent, which should lead the believer to 'give up giving up' and journey through the desert and carry the cross with strength and hope.

> *'And just as Moses lifted up the serpent in the wilderness, so must the Son of Man be lifted up, that whoever believes in him may have eternal life.'* (John 3:14-15)

As Christians, we have no greater ambiguity, and the sign of death raised up to the heavens is the ultimate and unchanging source of hope and life. Of itself, the cross has no meaning beyond an ultimate instrument of suffering and death. However, when this instrument is seen as the place where we encounter God, then we truly have every reason to rejoice in hope and never lose heart, even if the call is to journey through suffering, confusion and contradictions. In a supreme act of contradiction, the cross becomes the ultimate sign of God's presence in our lives and of divine identification with the human story to the extreme of ignominy, pain, suffering and death. Christianity is not a masochistic philosophy that canonises the cross as a good to be pursued for the sake of a pie in the sky when we die. Death is horrid and the cross is its most despicable instrument. However, what Jesus is saying is that God's self-giving to broken and weak humanity is so whole-embracing and overwhelming that even the most cruel and abominable death is not too great a price to pay for God in his yearning to identify with our brokenness and to draw us into himself.

> *For God so loved the world that he gave his only Son, so that everyone who believes in him may not perish but may have eternal life* (John 3:16).

If we are to understand Jesus' life and mission, we must look at the mystery of life out of and through the lens of death and annihilation. Throughout the Gospel of John, this pronouncement underscores the whole narrative and 'the hour' of the cross is the beacon guiding his whole life (John 4:21-23; 5:28; 12:23 16:32). As for discipleship, Jesus repeatedly reminds us that we become ourselves to the extent that we let go of ourselves, until that final letting go of life in order to find Life.

> *Unless a grain of wheat falls into the earth and dies, it remains just a single grain; but if it dies, it bears much fruit* (John 12:24)

Later on, just before his arrest and execution, Jesus will proclaim to the assembled crowds in the temple and to his opponents alike, '*and I, when I am lifted up from the earth, will draw all people to myself*' (John 12:32), and in that embrace we can all once again rejoice, hope, and have life forever. No more reasons to give up on any account, because now we are embraced by God himself, even if from the ultimate symbol and an instrument of death like the cross.

Nicodemus, like the sincere and observant Pharisee that he is, is searching for the truth and is waiting for his Messiah, the truth of a Messiah that will restore the covenant and the unique relationship of God and its people, recreate the greatness of Israel by destroying its enemies, and re-install the sanctity of Torah and Temple. Nicodemus' God is a political God controlling humanity through judgment, justice and punishment, and in turn, being controlled by the meticulous performance of rituals and the correct observance of legal tenets governing every skerrick of human activity. Nicodemus '*came to Jesus by night*' (John 3:2), is symbolic of a deep darkness of mind and heart; and, as he searches in the darkness of doubt, there is little love of his God, and even less acceptance of a God opening his arms in embrace from a cross. Though sincere in his search, Jesus' kind of God does not make sense. It is too contradictory, too close to human reality, too redeeming of human depravity and sinfulness. In the Pharisaic mentality, this kind of God is an impossibility as absurd as *'entering a second time into the mother's womb and being born again when one is old'* (John 3:4-5) and makes you 'give up' into judgment and fear your understanding, your hope, and your faith.

That is the deadness and heart-darkness that Jesus challenges in Nicodemus, and in each and all of us when we say we love God, and yet our hearts remain trapped by fear and hopelessness. To the searching Nicodemus, Jesus spoke plainly and bluntly.

> *'Very truly, I tell you, no one can see the kingdom of God without being born from above...' Nicodemus said to him, 'How can anyone be born after having grown old? Can one enter a second time into the mother's womb and be born?' Jesus answered, 'Very truly, I tell you, no one can enter the kingdom of God without being born of water and Spirit. Do not be astonished that I said to you, "You must be born from above"'* (John 3:3, 5, 7)

Contrary to the ruthless judge syndrome of condemnation and punishment, the identification of God with humanity is total even to the extreme of death and the ultimate contradiction of the cross where God reveals himself as love. As radical and unpalatable this philosophy may sound to the apparent God-seeker, Jesus made no apology for his claim but lived and died by it. He did not seek death for its own sake, or as a payback to an angry God, as a certain disturbed and distorted spirituality would have us think. Jesus died to proclaim the human possibility of faithfulness to God in the face of injustice, violence and evil in this world.

To the Nicodemus in each of us, searching in the confusion of the dark of night, Jesus is making one of his most powerful and affirming proclamations.

> *'Indeed, God did not send the Son into the world to condemn the world, but in order that the world might be saved through*

him. *Those who believe in him are not condemned; but those who do not believe are condemned already, because they have not believed in the name of the only Son of God. And this is the judgment, that the light has come into the world, and people loved darkness rather than light because their deeds were evil. For all who do evil hate the light and do not come to the light, so that their deeds may not be exposed. But those who do what is true come to the light, so that it may be clearly seen that their deeds have been done in God.'* (John 3:16-21)

There lies the foundational call of the Lenten journey: we have to confront a transformation as radical as ashes becoming the energy of new life and as whole-embracing as returning to our mother's womb and being born again, as Nicodemus himself probes.

Let Go into God

To human logic, the way of salvation and of discipleship is nothing less than a total and crucial reversal of values; the cross becomes a throne, nakedness a royal mantle, destitution the absolute richness, and death is the only certainty for life. Most of all, Jesus came to reveal a God of love and compassion who embraced people without distinction or conditions in their multi-faceted brokenness. Such stance, however, was too challenging for those who were not prepared to accept God on such terms, and Jesus' faithfulness to the program assigned to him by the Father put him on an inevitable collision course with his opponents. He died for it, without flinching or compromising on his belief that the love of the Father conquered and nullified even death, and that, because of that love, life would emerge even from death.

Jesus let go of his life in complete and unconditional trust and faithfulness to the God whom he came to reveal as the very antithesis of fear, oppression and hatred, To achieve that kind of liberation for humanity, he had to become the victim of those very powers of evil and go through death epitomised by the dead but healing serpent in the desert so as to gift us with hope and life even in Seamus' ambiguity in our life. The seed had to be destroyed and obliterated, but humanity is now empowered into a new life, with new possibilities for peace, justice and freedom. Jesus could easily have embraced the status quo, kept his belief and his ideas to himself, performed the required rituals and observed the religious laws of a devout Israelite of his time, and thus saved his life. In that case, however, the seed would have remained a single fruitless and lost seed, and the world would still be enslaved to both God and humanity, and dominated by fear, injustice and unredeemable sin.

With Nicodemus, 'giving-up' then takes on a new and life-giving perspective. We all 'have to be born again' into a new vision and a new understanding. We have to look at the cross and accept the fullness of life that emanates from it, flooding us into a new hope and a new awareness. We have to believe in ultimate love exploding out of ultimate death. It means never giving up, whatever the barrenness or apparent fruitlessness of our efforts. It means to accept the presence of God in absence, loneliness and struggle. It means to accept the life-giving action of a patient and understanding God even in the midst of human tragedy. It means to work tirelessly at nurturing our relationships with God and with each other, when to all appearances we are wasting time, energy and water on an apparently dead stump of the tree of life.

It means to accept that in the economy of faith and conversion, what matters most in not the instant result, but the determination to journey on in hope with our God sustaining us in our tiredness and our weakness. It means to convert from fear of punishment by a vindictive idol-God, to the confidence in an Abba-God, rich in patience and bent on nurture and love. It means to focus less on our sinfulness and more on the lavish and loving embrace of a forgiving God. It means to move from hopelessness brought on by the memory of past mistakes to a joyful hope in a future with God. It means to journey on, looking at the cross on Golgotha and seeing life exploding from an empty tomb.

God never gives up on his eternal plan of intimacy and love, and with Seamus, we must '*give up giving up*', accepting this love and living by the consequences of this acceptance. God will never give up on us, either individually or communally, and our most authentic Lenten practice must be to refuse 'giving up' on ourselves, on each other and on God, no matter what life puts before us and what shape our journey will take. Yes, Seamus was right: no more fear, no more hopelessness, no more judgment or condemnation; just total trust in a God of love, embracing each and every one while nailed to a cross. and with Seamus, we must '*give up giving up*', accepting this love and living by the consequences of this acceptance.

Life through Death

John 11:1-45

A Drama of Identification

BEFORE EVERY SUCCESSFUL DRAMA there stands a meticulous and well-performed full dress rehearsal. It is during such a rehearsal that every detail is carefully analysed and executed, in order to ensure that the eventual performance delivers not only technical and artistic perfection, but more importantly that it transmits the message behind the artistry and technicalities, touching deeply into the psyche of the audience.

The dramatic narrative of the death and raising of Lazarus (John 11:1-44) put to us on the Fifth Sunday of Lent (Year A) is very much the full dress rehearsal of what we will celebrate over the next two weeks, culminating with the central event of our Christian identity: Death and Resurrection. Here we have high drama, and the event is crucial to our understanding of what is about to happen to Jesus on the one hand, and on the other of what constitutes the human destiny, if we but accept that God is with us in life and in death at all times. Although death seems to be all around us in its multifarious manifestations, in anticipation of Easter Sunday, the episode of Lazarus reminds us that our God is a God of life and not of death. At the same time, this same Word confronts us with a strange paradox: life is couched in the spoils of death, and the apparent destruction wrought by suffering and death ushers in a totally and unfathomable new life.

Lazarus is dead; a brother is dead, a friend is dead, and we cannot ignore the pain and utter sense of tragedy that death engenders. It is wrong to deny such pain and pretend that death is nice by sweeping it under the carpet or hiding it under the guise of some dangerously twisted spirituality that glorifies death for the sake of a pie-in-the-sky type of reward. There is no pietistic sentimentality as Jesus comes to the full realisation that his friend is dead and demands to see his face one more time. Jesus weeps at the sight of the tomb for ever sealing his friend in silence and darkness, and, in those tears, he gives full expression to the sense of utter defeat and distress that are the inevitable companions of death.

On Palm Sunday 2023, Pope Francis addressed the crowds in St Peter's square by reminding the world that in in confronting Lazarus' death as a forbearer of his own death, Jesus experienced *'the distance of God so he could be completely and definitively one with humanity'*, and in in those tears, God weeps with every person standing before the multi-faceted deaths that threaten human existence. On that same occasion Pope Francis highlighted the many 'abandoned Christs' that exist in society:

> The poor who live on our streets and that we don't have the courage to look at, migrants who are no longer faces but numbers, the discarded with white gloves: unborn children, the elderly left alone, who could be your mum or dad, as well as the sick whom no one visits, the disabled who are ignored, and the young burdened by great interior emptiness with no one prepared to listen to their cry of pain and who don't find another path but suicide.[18]

There lies the only acceptable meaning of death: identification of the divine with broken humanity. Now God knows the pain and the agony of loss and destruction, and we are no longer alone in the agonies and the torments of humanity and in our own death.

---

[18] https://cathnews.com/2023/04/03/pope-released-from-hospital-presides-at-palm-sunday-

The Touch of Life

It is precisely in the midst of that world of loss, sorrow and pain that Jesus does the unthinkable for the grieving Martha and May and the bystanders. He demands that the tomb be opened. On previous occasions, clearly challenging the strict rule of defilement and risking severe condemnation, Jesus had actually touched dead bodies already on the way to burial, (Luke 7:11-17) or a young girl lying in death (Luke 8:49-56) restoring both to life. On this occasion, in spite of the misunderstanding and protests by Lazarus' own household (John 11:39), Jesus actually demands to confront death face to face, and breaks open the tomb, that absolute and ultimate grasp denying any trace of life forever.

This scene may hold a spectacular appeal to our Hollywood-saturated imagination, but it was shocking beyond acceptance within the culture of the time, where the very concept of death spoke of moral desecration and corruption, and any physical contact with a dead body meant becoming morally corrupted and defiled. From the very beginning, Jesus refuses to share these sentiments spawned by fears and taboos, but in that gesture of desecration, he not only demands to confront death face to face, but he emmeshes himself fully in the human story to the ultimate extent of personal identification with pain, loss and death itself. Yes, whatever our phobia, fears and death, God is now with us in life and in death, because in Jesus he has come so that we may have life, and life in its fullness (John 10:1), as John has him declaring just before being notified that his friend Lazarus was ill.

Because Jesus is there, death is no longer the final word, and he demands that we too be opened and set free from our fears and the taboos of death. Because he is there, life explodes for Lazarus, even in a dead body trapped forever in a tomb and bound inescapably by all sorts of restraints. There lies the crux of the Lazarus event. As he tries desperately to reveal to grieving family and friends, he touches death; and to bewildered disciples and bystanders, Jesus' very presence in this world is life-giving, even in the place of physical death.

'I am the resurrection and the life.* Those who believe in me, even though they die, will live, and everyone who lives and believes in me will never die' (John 11:25)

Challenging the astonished and grieving Martha and bystanders beyond human possibilities, Jesus then adds the pivotal question of life and faith for all time: *'Do you believe this?'* (John 11:26). Faith is the crux of the event, and of the challenging questioning thrown at us by the narrative. Jesus is not the magician of the sideshows, but he is there as the revelation of the living and life-giving God in the midst of full humanity, sharing fully our death and suffering. Through Jesus, God only wants life, in spite and beyond death and suffering. God brings life and destroys death and all forms of human death beyond all possibilities, but only to the extent that we look beyond our expectations, fears and taboos, and accept this eternal presence in the daily rollercoaster of our human story and forever.

'Unbind Him!'

The worst thing we can do to the Word of God is to reduce it to a dead body wrapped in garments of death and abandoned to the darkness and coldness of a centuries-old tomb. The Word of God is never a narrative but an injunction that demands a response, and this Word is always *for us and about us now*, otherwise that Word will remain forever entombed and dead.

Suddenly, in the midst of the shocked bystanders, a name rings out *'Lazarus, come out!'*, and a ghostly figure wrapped in the ritual garments of death stood silent against the darkness of an open cavernous tomb.

'Lazarus, come out!' Nothing could resist that call personally and individually by his name, not even the bonds of death that entangle a lifeless body buried for four days in a sealed tomb and still wrapped in burial garments. Horror must have gripped those bystanders at Jesus' next imperious command addressed to them resonates:

> *The dead man came out, his hands and feet bound with strips of cloth, and his face wrapped in a cloth. Jesus said to them, 'Unbind him, and let him go'.* (John 11:43-44)

Yes, the Word is alive and unequivocal and personally challenging, and so in the midst of death and suffering, we are called by name out of the death into life. However, while Jesus gives and restores life as a sign of God's life-giving presence in our humanity and God always calls us by name, this presence will be realised only through human intervention. *'Unbind him and let him go.'* Jesus needs the mediation of other people to free Lazarus from the bonds of death, and we are the ones who must make it happen by experiencing and touching death and by unbinding the shackles of death and annihilation all around us, embodied in our apathy and unbelief, our fears and our presuppositions, our darkness and sinfulness. For those bystanders, shackled in their taboos and terrors as much as for us, probably callous at the experience of too many deaths, the message is the same and inevitable. Holy Week and Easter call us as real people addressed by our personal name into fullness of life forever and demand that we face death, not as the experience of total loss and destruction, but as the place we share with God in our midst of who we are as we are.

We Are Lazarus

For all its dramatic energy, this Gospel narrative is much more than a dress rehearsal for what lies ahead for Jesus but a challenging blueprint for us in our claim to faith and in our future destiny. While we can be silent, critical, or distant spectators during a dress rehearsal, the power of the real drama lies in its capacity to draw the spectator into the depth of his or her soul, awaken powerful emotions, and throw out a personal challenge. In every good drama, we transcend the spectator role. Instead, we are plunged into the actor persona. While we can feel emotionally awakened by the story of Lazarus, Resurrection must sink deep roots into our psyche, making us the living actors caught inevitably in the drama of life.

If the temporary raising of Lazarus gives us a hint of what God can do in his effort to gift us with life, Holy Week and Easter proclaim what God actually does definitively for each of us. Caught up in the humanity of Jesus, our destiny is an explosion of life without end in spite of and out of death.

In the raising of Lazarus, we are given the sign of God's life-giving presence in our midst. In Jesus' Resurrection, we have the final and unchanging expression of what we are in the mind of God – a God whom not even death could keep away from us. ' Lazarus' calls us to faith in spite of death, Easter reveals the ultimate result of this faith. If the story of Lazarus invites us to confront the inhumanity of suffering, the horror of looking at death in the face, and the darkness of walking through death, for the believer it also points inevitably to fullness of life. Easter reassures us that we are not alone in our journey to life through death. God has done it all before, and God will do it all over again with every human being who accepts his life-giving presence in life and death. And through it all, the crucial question that Jesus addressed to Mary resonates powerfully and persistently for us too, 'Do *you* believe this?'.

Conclusion

Much of the time, honestly, it does not feel like death has been defeated. Like Mary and Martha, we cry out in pain and ask our agonising questions — about job loss, wayward children, financial crises, chronic illness, loss of loved ones, war and terrorism — whatever casts death's shadow across our lives. Even as we cry out of the depths, however, we live and wait in hope. Like Martha and Mary, we learn that God does not act exactly when, where, or how we think God should act. But God will act in God's good time, and death will not have the final word. The day of resurrection will come.[19]

---

[19] Pope Francis, Do You want to fast this Lent? (2018), www.bangorparish.com/wp-content/uploads/Columban-Sr-Ash-Wednesday-Thoughts-for-Lent.pdf

Triumph and Execution (Holy Week)

Luke 22:39-71; 23:1-56

A Drama of Contradictions

ENCOUNTER, NOT PERFORMANCE is the catchy title of a book published posthumously under the authorship of Fr Frank Wallace SJ. While the book deals specifically with prayer, I have often found myself broadening the vision and its insights, prompting me to question what motivates me to celebrate specific events and to re-live the cycle of liturgical seasons. Do I celebrate in order to do something or in order to encounter God on God's terms?

I believe that the question is particularly relevant to this week of our liturgical year – a week full of high drama, of deep pathos, of raw emotions, but most of all of unavoidable challenges. The liturgy of this week is not about a sentimental recall of the past, but an injunction to evaluate where we stand in our personal journey of faith right now. Within a few days of each other, the same people of Jerusalem proclaimed 'Hosanna' and 'Crucify'. That becomes our challenge as we face the roller coaster of daily life, particularly when struggles and misunderstandings seem to crush both faith and hope into an illusion, and God may appear to be so far away from our painful reality. For the believer, Holy Week is decision-making time.

'Blessings on the King who comes!... Crucify him! Crucify him!' Such is the fickleness of the human heart, and the result is death. This is also the contradictory and challenging message of any celebration during what we call 'Holy Week', a celebration that

begins with a royal welcome and ends with an execution reserved only for the most rebellious of slaves. As a celebration, however, we need to remember that the Word of God is not just a recall of something that happened to Jesus two thousand years ago, but a word addressed to us and about us today. As we enter the great liturgical week, Palm Sunday announces a double warning to the believer. First, it alerts us that faith is not a matter of routine performance or a mnemonic recall but a request to make a personal decision for or against God within the fickleness and challenges of life. Secondly, this week, the Word of God sounds a stern warning that faith is a dangerous commitment because it demands an uncompromising and non-negotiable acceptance of God in our personal and collective stories, including the pain of contradiction and betrayal. As we celebrate from the perspective of two thousand years, where do we stand in that crowd calling out 'Blessing' and 'Crucify'?

Strident opposites of light and darkness, table fellowship and betrayal, promises and denial, a criminal and a Messiah, welcome and execution, life and death – opposites pitted against each other on a roller coaster of emotions ushered in by a festive *'Hosanna'*, and soon supplanted by a death-dealing *'Crucify'* screamed out in the one breath, and by the same people, on the blood-stained darkness of a Friday afternoon. The liturgy of the Easter Vigil paints the drama of Holy Week as a 'glorious duel between life and death', with light and life triumphant over suffering, execution and death.

The passion narratives are bookended by two significant cries. On the one end, Jesus is facing arrest, abuse and execution, abandoned by all, ripped by fear to the extreme of doubting the Father's love. On the other, after pleading with the Father to *'take away this chalice from me, but not as I wish but your will'* (Matthew 26:39) we hear his dying scream on Golgotha *'into your hands I commend my spirit'* (Luke 26:43). For Jesus, there is no contradiction or compromise as he remains steadfast on the course to his death, asserting trust and abandonment to the Father in the face of human doubt, injustice and betrayal. In the end, for Jesus and for all of us who claim to be his disciples, the duel between life and death is the duel between fidelity to God and fickleness of the human heart.

High drama indeed, but that is not the end of the story. Finally, the ultimate contradiction and the dramatic climax pulsating with deep emotions. A death-shattering cry of 'He is alive!' proclaims that a dead body buried for three days in a tomb has walked out, free, alive, and glorious, never to die again. This is the drama the liturgy puts before us over the next seven days.

The Drama is Now

A seriously good drama is much more than a re-enactment of some historical event or a performance recalling something long-lost in the past. The real power of a dramatic representation lies in its capacity to capture the audience so intensely and personally that they relive their own individual and collective life-stories by identifying with the persona being portrayed on screen and stage. In this way, more than tugging at the emotional chords of the heart, a truly dramatic performance must lead to an encounter with our own selves and our world.

And we are caught up in it all. We are not just spectators to an ancient story beginning with the waving of palms reserved for a royal welcome and ending with an execution reserved only for the most rebellious of slaves. Holy Week is not a monolith cast in stone commemorating some unexplainable event in a lost and forgotten land, tugging at the chords of our hearts, but not touching the reality of our daily lives. We are caught in every nuance of the drama, or the drama has no meaning and even less impact. This week's liturgy invests the totality of our experience and gives vent to the full gamut of emotions evoked by extraordinary events; human and divine, lived experience and undreamt-of possibilities, life and death and life again. Good Friday and Easter are *now*, and they are for those who accept God in their lives. The journey of Jesus through death and into the fullness of life is our journey and our final destiny as well. In Jesus and like Jesus, we are meant to live God's gift of life, fully, in spite of death and beyond death, but that final outcome necessitates confronting contradictions as painful and as violently senseless as he did on his journey to Calvary.

In this perspective, as significant and world-transforming as the original event of Jesus of Nazareth may have been two thousand years ago, the events and stories re-enacted and retold over the next few days, speak to us and about us. The richness and depth of ritual and storytelling of Holy Week can never remain a performance, but must become a life-giving and transforming encounter with our God, through the re-telling and re-enacting of the life and death of Jesus of Nazareth.

When the story of Jesus' passion and death remains at the level of memory or performance (like Mel Gibson's 'The Passion of the Christ'), it is easy to fall into some shallow sentimentalism at the vivid representation of the most excruciating of deaths and feel warm and fuzzy at the thought that 'Jesus did this for me'. As another author puts it, 'this may leave us very grateful for Jesus, but less keen on our heavenly Father!'[20] The Passion story that we read throughout this week is not about payback or retribution, because God is not the bloodthirsty idol that can only be appeased by the most horrific death of his Son. Such a perspective is blasphemous in the Christian understanding of what we celebrate these days. It makes God a cruel tyrant rather than the Father proclaimed by Jesus, waiting to embrace us in our mistakes, and the only good news one can draw from such dramatic sentimentality is called box office intake. The very thought of Jesus' death as a payback for our misdemeanour shrieks against human justice as much as destroying the very idea of a God of love.

---

20 Gerard W. Hughes, *Oh God, Why?*, Oxford: The Bible Reading Fellowship, 1993, 138.

The story of Jesus' unwavering faith in the Father in spite of the tragedy of Good Friday, is a call to commit ourselves to accepting that, whatever our personal hells, in Jesus, God has plumbed their darkest depths. Yes, Jesus descended into the hell of our fears, our physical and emotional torments, our sense of alienation and abandonment, our pain and misunderstandings, our sudden and tragic experience of death in its multi-faceted manifestations in trust of and abandonment to the Father. And because of that trust-filled descent into all that is evil, life blossomed anew like a flower out of the cruellest winter. May we be people who have the courage to shout 'Hosanna' even when everything in us and around us screams crucifixion, and never condemn God for the struggles of our lives! Because our God has lived the hells of humanity in full, we are now able to sing 'Alleluia' even beyond and in spite of death! This is not meant to be a canonisation of suffering and death. Suffering is evil, and death is abhorrent, the consequence of evil, and the denial of God. To claim that suffering is good, even if couched in terms of a reward in an afterlife, is blasphemous, as it reduces God to an angry, cruel, and sadistic puppeteer who enjoys the sight of us floundering, hopeless and helpless, in the mire, and rewarding humanity in proportion to the degree of suffering one has endured throughout the earthly journey. Declaring himself as the giver of life in its fullness (John 10.10), human fragility and suffering are the catalysts that ignite Jesus to compassion. Jesus did not choose the cross because it was good, nor did he choose suffering as a reward to be sought after. Jesus accepted suffering and death as part of that human and divine journey leading to fulfilment and salvation only as an expression and an instrument of that radical Yes to the Father that he lived and witnessed throughout his earthly life.

In a play of contradictions, this week we look at the cross and are invited to see life, to enter the darkness and have the courage to hope. The saving power of Jesus' passion and death does not lie in excruciating pain or emotional pep-pills for their own sake. We are saved through the cross and by the cross, because in that icon of death and destruction, ironically, we encounter God, and God encounters the whole of humanity, precisely when our humanity is at its most vulnerable, disfigured, and seemingly hopeless.

Suffering is redemptive not because it pleases a God who demands of us superhuman endurance of masochistic proportions. Suffering and death are redemptive because now we can say with certainty that God, in Jesus, identifies totally with our human story, complete to its most shocking and most excruciating expressions. In the Christian understanding of reality, fidelity to God-with-us is the key to the mystery of the cross and the ultimate and crucial dilemma of faith. When confronted and lived with trust and in abandonment to God, the experience of rejection, execution and death becomes a sacramental sign of encounter with God in our lives.

Fidelity to God is the key to the mystery of the cross and the ultimate crucial dilemma of faith. Jesus did not choose the cross as an end or a good in itself, and to claim that – whatever its shape – suffering is good is to make God a cruel tyrant rather than the 'Abba' of Jesus. The triumph of Easter is only subsequent to the execution on Friday, and embracing the death-dealing cross as a symbol of hope is a dangerous stance. However, when confronted and lived with trust and abandonment to God, our human experience of rejection, execution and death becomes salvific and life-giving.

The Drama is Us

Jesus' Passion is not about his sufferings, but about his passion for love. He is so passionate about the Father's love and about the mission entrusted to him by the Father that not even suffering and death are too high a price to pay. The Passion narrative is bookended on both sides by a cry of despair and a letting go into the hands of the Father, in total abandonment, fidelity and trust. In the garden, gripped by fear and enveloped by the terror of the night, doubting the very presence of the Father's love in his own life, he remains uncompromising and ready to face even death, if that is the price of fidelity to God.

'My Father, if it is possible, let this cup pass from me; yet not what I want but what you want!' (Matthew 26:39)

These are Jesus' final words before letting himself be arrested, taken away, abused and eventually executed like an abominable criminal. And on Golgotha, Jesus screamed his despair at the prospect that the Father may have abandoned him to a most cruel death. Yet, in the end he still calls out to the Father,

'Father, into your hands I commend my spirit'. Having said this, he breathed his last (Luke 23:46).

For the Christian, fidelity is the key to the mystery of human suffering and of a God hanging in death on a cross. But fidelity can be painful and even death-dealing, as we know from our daily experience reflected in this week's liturgy. The triumph of Easter is always subsequent to the execution of Friday, just as the tragedy of Good Friday can only make sense through the lens of Easter Sunday. Embracing the cross as a symbol of hope and liberation can be dangerous and fickle. It can readily become a psychological palliative for our troubled hearts, or a dangerous escape from the painful reality at hand.

The real power of the cross lies in its symbolic power of encounter. Yes, the cross is the place of encounter between us and God, the bond linking inescapably our story today with the story of Jesus then. He not only paid with his own life for the fickleness of the human heart, but he walked to his death choosing to trust in an abandonment to the Father, while facing personal doubts, and human contradictions. In Jesus, we have a total immersion of the divine into the human, and so we humans can now walk through death into the divine. When confronted with trust in and abandonment to God, the signs of rejection, execution and death become a sacramental sign of encounter and life with God, and the cross is the place where God meets us.

In this way, the cross, which dominates stark and foreboding this week, becomes the place where we encounter God, and we share life and death with God. Golgotha has nothing to do with self-inflicted masochism but, as we gaze on that cross, now we can truly claim that having taken upon himself the totality of human suffering in Jesus, God knows human suffering to its ultimate destructive power in death. God now knows what I go through, when physical pain wracks my body, when loneliness and abandonment crush my spirit, when my future looms so hopeless that I even doubt that there may be a future at all, when I am the victim of injustice, or when I am called to forgive the hurt inflicted on me by others. God knows rejection and insult, physical and mental abuse, betrayal and falsehood. because he has been there in the flesh.

Pope Francis said that in his Passion, Jesus experienced the distance of God so he could be 'completely and definitively one' with humanity.

God knows death to the point that my death becomes the only human way to enter into God's reality, just as death was the ultimate way of God entering the totality of our human reality. And because God knows it all and knows it with a knowing of the heart as well of the mind and body, I am no longer alone and abandoned in my struggles, in my sufferings and even in my death.

He has been there! He is there! He will be there forever, in our life journeys and beyond. Now we can truly hope and rejoice, because in the end not even death, the ultimate evil, is foreign to God or could keep God away from us. Yes, we are saved from fear and death, and we can sing Alleluia even though our bodies may have to go through crucifixion. He has done it all before, and he is with us for the fullness of life. Good Friday and Easter Sunday remind us that life is only possible when we are prepared to let God into our pain and abandon all our expectations and securities into

God's hands. Then truly pain becomes redemptive, an instrument of God working his way in our lives and journeying alongside us on our way, even throughout our most hellish experiences.

May our celebration of Holy Week be truly life-giving and re-invigorate our minds and hearts, not through the memory of a blood sacrifice, but by the acceptance of the total immersion of the divine into the human story! May we learn that the most human facets of our existence are impregnated with divine presence! May we recall that God lived through it all and did not shun the earthy and the broken, totally embracing earthiness and brokenness in their extreme manifestations and deadly conclusions! God truly became man through suffering, so that human suffering may become an instrument and stimulus towards our divine destiny of oneness with our God. Only in this sense can suffering be redemptive. Only in this perspective can we celebrate Holy Week as the triumph of Easter Sunday through the execution of Good Friday.

The story of Jesus' unwavering faith in the Father in spite of the tragedy of Good Friday, is a commitment to accept that, whatever our personal hells, in Jesus, God has plumbed the darkest depths, descending into the hell of our fears, physical and emotional torments, alienation and loneliness, pain and misunderstandings, our tragic experience of our many deaths in trust of and abandonment to the Father-God. And because of that trust-filled descent into all that is evil, life blossomed anew like a flower out of the cruelest winter. In our contradictions, may we have the courage to shout 'Hosanna' and never condemn God for our struggles because in Jesus, God lived the hells of humanity in full, no matter the shape of our life-story and walked into the fullness of life.

Oneness in Love and Service

Matthew 26:26-29 / John 13:1-17

Metaphors of Life and Love

ACROSS THE FOUR GOSPEL NARRATIVES, few incidents carry more significance and energy than the events of the Last Supper. On that last evening of his earthly life, Jesus gathered those who were his own, and in the intimacy of a family meal, he opened his heart and poured out his soul to his disciples in an explosion of unconditional love and deep trust, as one does with intimate and trusted friends.

Following the synoptic accounts and Paul (1 Corinthians 11:23-26), for centuries the liturgy has highlighted the Eucharist as the focus of Holy Thursday and the centre point the Christian Tradition.

> *While they were eating, Jesus took a loaf of bread, and after blessing it he broke it, gave it to the disciples, and said, 'Take, eat; this is my body'. Then he took a cup, and after giving thanks he gave it to them, saying, 'Drink from it, all of you; for this is my blood of the covenant, which is poured out for many for the forgiveness of sins'.* (Matthew 26:26-29)

However, while the three Synoptics focus almost exclusively on Jesus' Eucharistic institution as the ultimate self-giving to his disciples for all time (Matthew 26:26-30; Mark 14:22-25; Luke 22:14-20), strikingly, the Fourth evangelist does not mention the Eucharist at all in this particular context of the Last Supper. Rather, for John, that good-bye meal is an experience of deep emotions and a powerful revelation embracing both life and death at the same time. In an attempt at conveying his message in a long conversation, Jesus seems to struggle for words, resorting to speak in images and metaphors. Mingling together past memories, present emotions, and reassurances for the future, he hands over to his disciples his last will and testament, summing it up in that one word *'love'* by which he expresses both his feelings of deep love for his *friends* and reveals who God is and who we are for God.

In particular, two metaphors carry a unique and powerful significance as expressions of that *love* which he left us as his parting gift: the metaphor of the vine and branches (John 15:12-16), and the parable in action of the washing of the disciples' feet (John 13:1-17). The double parable in word and action are not only central to the event of the Last Supper but, in their intimate connectivity, they are both revelatory and constitutive of the new order inaugurated by Jesus' life, death and resurrection, The two elements are paradigms of the new reality, while at the same time underscoring the very nature of Christian faith and of discipleship.

Sandra Schneiders suggests that if we are to understand both what Jesus was about and what our faith response should be, we need to look at the experience of the Last Supper where the symbiosis between the image of the vine and the parable in action of the washing of the feet represent the very foundation of our relationship with God and with each other.

Vine and Branches

This relationship between God and each one of us is so intense and so life-giving that it finds full expression in the life-giving sap that, life-blood-like, floods every fibre of the vine: roots, trunks, canes, and branches, seeping deep into the leaves and the tiniest shoots and tendrils, to bring life and abundant fruitfulness to every part of the plant according to its specific and delicate structure and needs.

Such intensity of love and life with God is difficult to fathom and may almost sound irrational and too much to accept. But that is the intimate life and love connection revealed to us by Jesus on the night of his good-byes. We share the same vital energy and life of God, and the love that bonded Jesus to the Father is the love-bond that God yearns to establish with each of us individually and all of us collectively. The same one vital sap flows through God, each of us individually and all of us collectively, all sharing the same Spirit-DNA. By contrast, no life is possible, and the dead branches no longer connected to the vine are thrown away into meaningless nothingness. To be a disciple, then, is to live the very life Jesus lived, expressed in the dynamism of a metaphor that speaks at once of vigorous vitality, for the sake of rich and abundant fruitfulness. We are the object of an incredible God-empowered love, and our task is simply to accept this uniquely personal relationship with our God, obsessively possessive of me and you. We are God's work of his labours, his memories, and his joys. We are God's possession from all eternity and for all eternity, and the very life-sap of energy flows through us, the branches, as it flows through Jesus: the sap of life put there and nurtured by the Father.

'I am the vine, and you are the branches, and my Father is the vine dresser.' (John 15:1)

Our God is driven by an obsessively possessiveness, *'so that we may have life, and have it in abundance'*. (John 10:10)

A mind-shattering revelation indeed, but also a challenging demand for us to live the same relationship of oneness of life and love with each other. Totality of love imbibed by the image of the vine demands totality of faith expressed through service, equality and real friendship; precisely that kind of service, equality and deep friendship which Jesus expressed through the symbolic action of washing his disciples' feet. On the contrary, when we try to structure a discipleship in terms of a personal spirituality divorced from the social dimension and relatedness to others, our efforts are naive, futile and ultimately self-destructive (John 15:4-6).

There is absolutely no escaping the two imperatives of *abiding in God's love* and of *loving one another*. Just as Jesus was the living witness of the active and loving presence of God in our history, likewise the disciples are to witness the same active and loving presence through and to each other. We will be true disciples witnessing to Jesus only if we are prepared to let the love-sap flow fully into our daily life and relationships, in a deeply human and concrete way. Only by living fully the life of love we claim to share, in a deeply human and real way, we will witness to Jesus and become credible signs and effective instruments of God's loving presence. Only by incarnating with each other this mutuality of human-divine energy in our daily humdrum and relationships, people will take notice (John 14:31; 17:20-24) and they too will know the God of love who longs to be with them and embrace them in his love (John 14:31; 17:20-24).

Foot Washing

The personal life-relationship between God and each of us individually imaged through the vine and branches can only be incarnated and become a credible witness through the relationship of service to each other exemplified by Jesus washing his disciples' feet (John 13:1-17), a gesture which, for John, takes the place of the Eucharistic institution, giving us the same message of total self-giving that he would incarnate the very next day on the cross. In the symbolic gesture of breaking of bread at table, Jesus revealed what he was going to do next day, giving us the exemplar of our relationship with each other. Just as the broken body and the blood spilled on the cross will always be the ultimate manifestations of Jesus' total and unconditional self-giving love for his disciples, the Johannine community has always identified the washing of the feet as the expression of the same self-giving and carrying the same injunction of unity and love that must exist among all those who belong to the Kingdom.

Both the Synoptics' narrative of the Eucharistic institution and John's parable of the washing of the feet carry the same strong directive by which the disciples were to *remember him by actively doing* to each other what he did for the world. At the institution, Jesus tells them *to do this in memory* of him (Luke 22:19). However, the injunction has nothing to do with repeating a ritual, but it points directly to the mutual re-incarnation by the disciples of the total self-giving that Jesus would suffer the very next day, even at the cost of a broken body and spilt blood. Likewise, after washing his disciples' feet, Jesus bids them the same *doing* to each other as he did to them.

'I have set you an example, that you also should do as I have done to you.' (John 13:15)

Jesus' gesture and instructions are catechesis in action. They reveal both that faith/love attitude that must inform all interpersonal rapports, and the mode of living concretely authentic human relationships towards all. Rather than being an abject sign of self-abasement (κένωσις), by washing of the disciples' feet, Jesus proclaims that the giving of one's life for one's friends (John 15:13), sisters and brothers, is the ultimate sign of love and the only adequate response to the Father's love for us (John 17:5.22.24). By vesting as a servant and taking on the role of the slave towards the master and of a disciple towards the teacher (John 13:4-5), Jesus reverses the reputed roles of authority and turns upside down the order of power. Jesus makes no secret of the fact that service is the fundamental expression of God's love for us and of mutual relationship in discipleship.

Discipleship demands that we be totally and unconditionally available to others, because it is only through this unconditional availability that full life will sprout from the vine and community will be redeemed from the level of a utopian idea at best, or of cohabitation at worst. For the believer, either everything is on a level of deep friendship, or it is nothing at all, and any form of pecking order makes community impossible. Service can only be understood and exercised from a position of equality and within a relationship of friendship and love.

The need to acknowledge each and every one as neighbour irrespective of culture, status, beliefs or personality is an indisputable responsibility of our claim to faith, and we can do no greater violence to the Word than to avoid reaching out to the needy and broken who walk the road with us. This call to openness and mutual friendship of relationships is a recurring theme running through most of the parables of Jesus, and this gesture of washing the disciples' feet is but a visual expression of what Jesus repeatedly proclaimed through parables such as the 'Pharisee and the Publican' (Luke 18:9-14) and of 'The Good Samaritan' (Luke 10:25-37).

If we dare to claim belief in Jesus, we have to look at how we perceive and understand others, and then confront the challenge of identifying our own stance in life from the perspective of our faith claim. Conversely, any form of discrimination, distancing and separateness on grounds of 'us-and-them' makes a lie of our claim to faith and becomes an open denial of the active presence of a loving God in our life and in the life of those we discriminate against or distance ourselves from because they speak another language, express a different culture, worship in a church, a synagogue, a mosque, a temple, or shun and condemn worship altogether.

Peter's reaction to Jesus' washing his feet and the ensuing dialogue is typical of the struggle of coming to terms with Jesus' demands against the natural tendency to control, select, compare, or set boundaries within the social context of the Kingdom. In his typically fiery way, Peter objects to having his feet washed precisely because Jesus seems to be doing the wrong thing to the wrong person and for the wrong reason. What Peter is really rejecting is the challenge to authority structures based on power relationships. He demands that things be neat and tidy and efficient, so that he knows where he stands in terms of rights and duties. But most of all

Peter is refusing a model of salvation through service and through death to self.

Service is bilateral, requiring as much giving as receiving, and my readiness to accept service from another person is as much a sign of human maturity as it is an element of growth for the whole community. The complete sharing of the foot washing may require that I remain open and available to others sharing with me their charisms as well as their pain, and, in that case, my role to service consists in being served rather than serving others. That is undoubtedly the hardest demand of discipleship, because then I have truly no control and no power; it leaves me destitute and totally dependent and available to my brothers and sisters. Availability to being served is a true call to growth into deeper intimacy and total openness to love. It is a call to allow the love of the foot washing to be given to us in community.

In a world that proclaims that self-assertion is the norm of success, that individualism is absolute, that economic usefulness is the sole criterion for social acceptability, that material advancement is the ultimate goal in life, that labelling and stereotyping is the accepted mode of determining social relationships – in such a world, our commitment to washing each other's feet becomes a disturbing but vital counter-witness. This kind of trustful and open availability proclaims to the whole world not only the possibility of true and authentically human love energised by God's very life and shared by every individual person, but it also proclaims our readiness to make ourselves available to bringing about a world governed by justice, equality and love. We must be those trusting, wise and courageous ones who will have to make it happen or it will never happen at all. God relies on our weakness to bring about his dream of oneness in love, and we must make it happen through our openness, trust, readiness, and that one universal energy called *mutual love* which alone breaks down barriers, eliminates distinctions and individuality and makes us all one.

Together at the Breaking of Bread (Holy Thursday)

Matthew 26:26-30 / Luke 24:29-32 / John 6:53-57

Revealed at the Table

IT MAY SOUND LIKE A TRIVIA QUESTION, but have you ever noticed how often the Gospel narrative seems to link significant events of recognition of and/or revelation by Jesus within the context of a meal?[21] Two meal-centred bookends encompass the Gospel narrative of the Paschal Mystery: the Last Supper and Jesus' self-revelation at the end of the Emmaus journey, with two disciples who, in a futile attempt at obliterating forever the memory of their tragic lot, leave Jerusalem behind and trudge their way back to Emmaus, full of disappointment and self-pity, only to recognise Jesus when he accepts their invitation to break bread with them (Luke 24:13-35).

Jesus said his earthly good-byes during that intensely emotional experience around the table, at the Last Supper. On this central event of the Christian Story, each narrative differs from the others, and yet, all of them convey a powerful sense of *intimacy* and *revelation* – intimacy between Jesus and his disciples, and revelation of who the disciples are for God and who God wants to be for the

---

[21] Matthew 9:9-12; 14:13-21; 15:32-39; 26:6-13.17-29; Mark 1:29-31; 2:15-17; 6:30-44; 8:1-10; 14:12-21; 16:14-16; Luke 4:38-39; 5:29-32; 9:10-17; 10:38-42; 19:1-10; 22:14-23; 24:13-35, 38-43; John 2:1-11; 6:1-14, 22-70; 12:1-8; chapters 13 – 17; 21:9-14

disciples (John chapters 13-17). The technical injunction to *break bread* is both the ultimate moment of recognition of Jesus in the life of the disciples, and the primary source of energy that must propel the disciple to embraced totally and unconditionally the presence and action of Jesus in the roller coaster of life experience.

Some friends of mine tell the story of their grandfather who, having survived the atrocities and the starvation of the Second World War, like thousands of others, migrated from Europe to this country to start a new life and to try to forget the horrors of the past. As he got older, however, and with the onset of dementia, he developed some very quirky mannerism, one having to do with memory and food. The destitution of food which he had to survive through the atrocities of war and prison camps in Europe crystallised in his fading mind becoming the rationale of his unusual behaviour and the energy of a message that he left to his children and grandchildren. Occasionally, he would get up in the middle of the night and startle the whole household by knocking loudly on bedroom doors and calling out at the top of his voice, 'Eat! Eat!' As people would exit their rooms to quieten him down, to their surprise each member of the household would find outside their bedroom door a bread roll laid out ready for eating.

The painful memories of starvation and misery of his youth had become an obsession, but so also was his concern for those who lived with him. He did not want to re-live those bad memories ever again, nor did he want any of his family to suffer depravation anymore, and so his way of showing concern was not just to tell them but to provide for them real food and encourage them to eat. Somehow the *memory* of the past became a stimulus for present action, by inviting the members of his household not only *to eat*, but by *providing the food* that would heal his own memories and sustain those who heard his story.

An amusing incident carrying clear Eucharist connotations in terms of *memory and food* and resonating strongly of those core Eucharistic words of Jesus:

> '*Take and eat* (because) *unless you eat the flesh of the Son of Man, and drink his blood, you have no life in you.*' (John 6:51-53)
> As the old man would call out,
> 'If you do not eat, you will die; and I not only tell you this much, but I give you to eat to ensure that you will not die!'

Memory, recognition, food and drink shared, bread broken and wine consumed in fellowship. This is Jesus' goodbye and last will and testament. This is Eucharist.

At the Last Supper, Jesus self-gave himself to his disciples by enjoining on them to *eat and drink* and to do it '*in memory*' of himself. However, the memory of what Jesus said and did at the Last Supper with his disciples goes far beyond a mnemonic recall or the repetition of an ancient ritual. Rather, it projects us into a threefold dynamic action of God: (a) inviting us to *eat and drink* God-enriched food, (b) providing us with that unique food that flows from *God's own self giving* to humanity, and (c) energising us into making that memory a living and life-giving gift by becoming *food and nourishers for each other* in the reality of each day. The Eucharistic implications of Holy Thursday and of every Eucharistic celebration are not just a matter of observing a repetitious ritual, but of incarnating and living by the injunction of eating flesh and drinking blood so as to live. In the words of Pascual Chavez,

> (Christians) live eucharistically, not so much because they often celebrate the Eucharist, but because they live Eucharist and spend their life for others.[22]

Food: The Fundamental Need

Food plays a fundamental role in our lives, both individually and as a community. Not only does it nourish and sustain our daily life,

---
[22] Pascual Chavez, 'Making the Eucharist in Order to Make Oneself Eucharist', ACG 398, http://www.sdb.org/en/rector-major/1215-archive-rm-agc-acs/2241-archive-rm-en

providing energy for growth and work, but, most of all, food shapes our lifestyle and our social interactions. Indeed, food has the power to create and/or destroy whole social groups and cultures. Every day, we are exposed to the shocking revelation of the destruction and havoc wrought by lack of food in two thirds of the whole world. Nor are our own suburban sprawls immune to this tragedy which is so vast and so deep that we cannot comprehend or want to admit. We feel so helpless in confronting it, and indeed in spite of the media saturation or even because of it we have been lulled into an almost inert sense of hopeless complacency.

Poverty is not a virtue, and the lack of food is a tragedy that screams indictment and condemnation to any politically correct conscience. Pope Francis has made 'the cry of the poor' the point of discrimination and ultimate authenticity of the Christian believer. Life deprived of food becomes cheap and meaningless. A hungry person will leave home and country, as the plight of thousands of refugees on our doorsteps has demonstrated so graphically and so tragically to us in the last few years. If need be, a hungry person will kill a fellow human being in order to obtain food as the basic necessity of life; and historians and sociologists tell us that both the search for and the super-abundance of food are primarily responsible for the thousands of wars and social upheavals that have shaped world geography and written the history of humankind over the last forty centuries.

Have you ever stopped to think of what happens to food? The very moment we ingest food, a whole biological/physical process is set in motion that will transform those elements of food or drink into something totally different and powerfully life-giving. Whatever our likes and dislikes, the food we eat quickly becomes flesh and blood and bone, energy for growth, for work, for enjoyment, and for healing. The food we eat becomes what we are, not only physically, but socially, emotionally and spiritually as well. Indeed, our lifestyle, our mutual relationships, our pattern of work and growth are shaped and conditioned to their deepest level, by what we eat and by our eating habits.

Food and drink carry a powerful and critical social and spiritual import. Even in our age of fast foods and grabbing from the shelves, we still yearn to spend time with family and friends around the table, where we can be ourselves while giving and receiving the gift of mutual presence and shared generosity by interacting with each other. In this context, even a cup of coffee shared and consumed with a friend over a five minute chat takes on a new vitality and meaning, becoming the symbol and instrument of a much deeper and much more life-giving reality. We are together as we are and share our mutual life as it is. The gathering around the table is the diamond tip of deep friendship, of shared experiences, and sentiments and of rich growth through being and becoming a living presence to one another.

In this perspective I propose that the many meal-centred incidents throughout the Gospel narrative become the human expression of God's life-giving energy in action when we accept this self-giving God in human affairs. At the Last Supper, Jesus engaged in a long conversation with his disciples (John 13-17), revealing the mutual relationship between us and 'the Father-God', a relationship energised by his life-giving presence within the limits of our human story. When accepted and imbibed into our daily experiences, God himself becomes the energy of a totally new life exploding within the fragility of our human frame and a new way of living our banal daily events and encounters. This new divinely-energised life is so intensely personal and intimate that we can only approximate it to the sense of unity, love and personal sharing expressed through table fellowship. In his self-giving as food and drink as his will and testament before his death and resurrection, Jesus invites himself into our life saying: 'Yes, it is me, and I want to be present in love to you and to one another to such an extent that not even death will keep us apart anymore'.

'Take and Eat... This is My Body'

These experiential considerations are important, as they open up vital insights into the mystery of the Eucharist for each of us individually and for all of us as a community of believing disciples. Through Eucharist, God enters our lives and shares our experiences at the deepest imaginable level, and in every conceivable dimension of our stories. Only a God madly in love with humanity could have envisaged such a dramatic scenario as to make himself food, so as to create that total, even physical and personal intimacy with each and every human being who is prepared to enter into the human-divine relationship. As Matthew tells us,

> *While they were eating, Jesus took a loaf of bread, and after blessing it he broke it, gave it to the disciples, and said, 'Take, eat; this is my body'. Then he took a cup, and after giving thanks he gave it to them, saying, 'Drink from it, all of you; for this is my blood of the covenant, which is poured out for many for the forgiveness of sins. I tell you, I will never again drink of this fruit of the vine until that day when I drink it new with you in my Father's kingdom'.* (Matthew 26:26-30)[23]

Throughout history and in every religious tradition, the meal together was and still is a sacred sign, a sacred moment (= *sacrament*) expressing friendship, intimacy and personal sharing and, true to his cultural ethos, Jesus was never a stranger to such sacred moments; but the Word pushes our understanding of Eucharist far beyond the ingestion and the bodily processing of food. What the Word is saying is that Jesus was not a faith healer, a rabblerousers, a ghost, or the object of some mass hysteria but a living sign of God's presence and relationship with and within humanity.

In a very different Eucharistic context, the words of Jesus are quite shocking and almost crude, and nowhere more so than in John's Eucharistic discourse (John 6:22-66). The Fourth evangelist

---

[23] See also. Mark. 14:22-26; Luke 22:14-20; 1 Corinthians 11:23-25)

makes no mention of any Eucharistic meal during Jesus' Last Supper with his disciples, developing instead a very powerful Eucharistic teaching in chapter six, within the context of another meal feeding thousands: the multiplication of the loaves and fishes, where once again, the evangelist places a crucial event in the ongoing narrative of the self-revelation of Jesus in terms of food and drink. What is more significant, however, is that immediately after the spectacular miracle, Jesus introduces an 'I' discourse, thus not only identifying himself with food, but accentuating the self-revelatory nature of the story and confronting his hearers with such shocking realism that many of his followers could not accept the 'intolerable language" and turned their backs on him. They did not recognise him because this was certainly not the Jesus-Messiah they were expecting or looking for.

> *Jesus said to them, 'Very truly, I tell you, unless you eat the flesh of the Son of Man and drink his blood, you have no life in you. Those who eat my flesh and drink my blood have eternal life, and I will raise them up on the last day; for my flesh is true food and my blood is true drink. Those who eat my flesh and drink my blood abide in me, and I in them. Just as the living Father sent me, and I live because of the Father, so whoever eats me will live because of me'.* (John 6:53-57)

Jesus pulls no punches, nor does he mince words. With that absolute authority and total integrity that marked all his life and ministry, he tells us to *eat* his *flesh* and *drink* his *blood*. If we feel uneasy and a little shocked at the realism of these words, we should not be dismayed. We simply join the majority of his listeners who after an abundant feed in a desert place, at no expense at all, could not accept the reality of God's intimate presence in their life. They turned their backs on him and *'no longer walked with him'* because they could not accept a God so intimately immersed in our flesh and blood as to become our flesh and blood through the instruments of food and drink. There is a tremendous sadness and a deep loneliness in those final words of Jesus to his disciples at the end of that story. '*So Jesus asked the twelve, "Do you also wish to go away?"*' (John 6:67).

The God the Jews had come to know and fear over the centuries was the God on high (Psalms 93:4; 113:5; Hebrew 1:3), the Protector of Israel against its enemies (Psalm 82:3; Isaiah 31:5; Zechariah 12:8), the Law Giver (Isaiah 33:22), and the Just Judge (Psalms 75:7; 96:10; Isaiah 11:4). The people of Israel prayed to him in their need and paid strict ritual homage, so as to ensure his favours and continued protection. In many ways, some of us will readily identify with this kind of faith and with this image of God. When that happens, however, we fail to see that the God Jesus came to reveal is the totally 'Other God', the '*Abba*', who longs for intimacy with his children, to the extreme of complete identification with my life and your life. And this longing for intimacy has no more powerful expression that through the sign of food and drink.

> We all know of this desire to give ourselves at the table. We say: 'Eat and drink; I made this for you. Take more; it is there for you to enjoy, to be strengthened, yes, to feel how much I love you'. What we desire is not simply to give food, but to give ourselves. 'Be my guest', we say. And as we encourage our friends to eat from our table, we want to say, 'Be my friend, be my companion, be my love – be part of my life – I want to give myself to you.'[24]

Through that persistent injunction to eat and drink, Jesus is saying that in the Eucharist meal God becomes part of our very self, our flesh and blood and bone and tissues, part of our struggles, joys sorrows and hopes. God in His total self-giving becomes the energy by which we live and grow and die. Yes, God is my *energy*, no matter what I am or what I may think I am. No matter what may ever happen to me, God becomes my *strength* and my *hope* because, by sharing at the Eucharistic meal, I absorb him into my

---

[24] Henri Nouwen, *Jesus. A Gospel*, ed. Michael O'Loughlin, Maryknoll NY: Orbis Books, 2001, 88.

very body, into my emotions, my achievements and even into my mistakes. Ours is no longer a God of fear, 'El Shaddai' then, or the 'Distant One' as for those shocked first followers of Jesus. Ours is a God who shares my experience fully and deeply to the point of becoming flesh of my flesh and bone of my bone, as well as energy for our becoming. The question is: What kind of recognition do we carry to our Eucharistic celebrations?

Total self-giving for total identification!

> *'Take, eat; this is my body... Drink from it, all of you, for this is my blood of the covenant.'* (Matthew 26:26-28)

> When we consume the consecrated bread and wine, the elements are transformed into our bodies through the natural process of digestion... (and) we are engulfed in an infinite embrace... creating ripples that radiate to every level of our being, body, soul and spirit, and flooding with the inexhaustible energy of divine light, life and love'.[25]

Truly my body is his body, his life, and his total self. St Paul calls it incorporation, oneness of intent and experience (Romans 6:10-11), and St Augustine, instructing his newly baptised, captures this same realism when he proclaims,

> Let us rejoice and give thanks that we have become not only Christians, but Christ. My brothers and sisters, do you understand the grace of God our head? Stand in admiration, rejoice; we have become not only Christians, but Christ.[26]

And Henri Nouwen echoes:

> Jesus is God-for-us, God-with-us, God-within-us. Jesus is God giving himself completely, pouring himself out for us without reserve. Jesus doesn't hold back or cling to his own possessions. He gives all there is to give: 'Eat, drink, this is my body, this is my blood... this is me for you!'... God

---

[25] Thomas Keating, *Manifesting God*, New York NY: Lantern Books, 2005, 34-36.
[26] https://www.catholicculture.org/culture/library/catechism/index.cfm?recnum=3008

not only became flesh for us years ago in a country far away. God becomes food and drink for us now at this moment of Eucharistic celebration, right where we are together around the table. God does not hold back; God gives all.[27]

No wonder the early Church called its ritual meal *Eucharistia*, a word precisely meaning *Thanksgiving*. We have reasons to give thanks indeed, and to rejoice and to hope!

'Do This in Memory of Me'

The fact that the four accounts of the Lord's Supper and in Paul (1 Corinthians 11:23-27), Matthew (26:26-30), Mark (14:12-21) and Luke (22:14-23) differ more or less markedly in expression and small details reflects the diverse traditions out of which they grew. But while this may be interesting for biblical scholarship, they all share the injunction of the Lord to *do this in memory* of him as the one linking factor. This has far more serious and personal implications than mere theological speculation. Each community *saw the injunction to do* as addressed to them, *in their real and very specific* cultural and religious *situation*, in their actual needs and struggles, in their rejoicing and hoping, in every individual and communal attempts at coming to terms with the Lord who was no longer physically present to them after promising them that he would not leave them alone (John 14:18). In Eucharist, God becomes who we are, where we are, as we are in our specific cultural, ethnic, religious or social life situations. No barriers, no holding back, no distinctions of worthiness or unworthiness, first or last, saints or sinners, all are made one in the energy and synergy born of the presence of God in their lives and in their community. Matthew actually adds the words 'all of you...'.

'*Drink all of you from this...*' (Matthew 26:26-27)

---

[27] Henri Nouwen, *Jesus – A Gospel*, 87-88.

The *doing in memory* of the Lord's Death and Resurrection, *all* together, implies a *community dimension* as the vital and foundational element of Eucharist, such that we cannot afford to overlook without destroying the very nature of the mystery.

We have all had the experience of eating together, an experience which is often linked with some very special, personal and communal event. A family gathering, a successful business or academic achievement, a visit from a relation or an intimate friend after a long absence, an anniversary, a wedding, or a birthday, even after the sadness of a good-bye or a funeral. These are but a few occasions when we feel the need to be together, occasions when, like the 'prodigal father' did on the return of the wayward son (Luke 15:11-32), we invite our friends and relations to share a meal or, as someone would say, 'to chuck a party' or just 'to have a drink'.

What matters least of all on these occasions are precisely the food and drink as elements in themselves. It is the feeling of celebration, sharing and intimacy, of togetherness and affirmation, of joy and compassion and hope that really bring us together. It is a need to *be with others* in mutual presence, and allowing others to be with us that gathers and binds a group of individuals into a celebrating community. The food and drink shared and consumed on such occasions by *all* of us *together*, certainly have their role to play and an important role at that. They become the instruments and symbols that give meaning to our gathering, both signifying and creating that common-union of ideals and intent that brought us together in the first place. However, just as we cannot envisage a celebration without the symbols of food and drink, so we cannot pretend to invite someone to share our meal unless the basic attitudes of togetherness, friendship and mutual acceptance are already there.

Eating bread and drinking wine together does not automatically create community, as we see all too well in our age of fast foods and grabbing from the fridge. However, we need the symbols of eating and drinking around the table to express the oneness that binds us together in the reality of our lives. Neither the symbols of bread and wine in themselves, nor the mechanical, quasi-magical, and monotonous repetition of what the Lord said or did, will ever constitute or create Eucharist. Eucharist is the sharing here and now of those attitudes of mind and heart symbolised by the breaking of bread and pouring of wine, *all together, in memory* of the Lord. It was precisely in a peak moment of powerful togetherness, of deep intimacy, of good-byes and of bewilderment, of memory and dreams, of death and of life that the Lord Jesus *'took bread... said the blessing... gave it to his disciples'* and told them to do the same over and over again.

In writing about early Christian communities, Luke reminds us

> *They devoted themselves to the apostles' teaching and fellowship, to the breaking of bread and the prayers... All who believed were together and had all things in common; they would sell their possessions and goods and distribute the proceeds to all, as any had need. Day by day, as they spent much time together in the temple, they broke bread at home and ate their food with glad and generous hearts, praising God and having the goodwill of all the people. And day by day the Lord added to their number those who were being saved.* (Acts 2:42, 44-47)

Clearly, for the early Christian communities, the coming together to break bread and to do what the Lord did was not only subsequent to but a necessary consequence of the *fellowship* (κοινωνία) and of the total sharing of a whole life. Only then did Eucharist make sense to those early believers as total *communion* with the Lord and with each other. The Eucharist can never and must never be reduced to a private 'me-and-God-and-no-one-else' kind of devotion, because then we would neither celebrate memory nor do what the Lord did on that one night of his earthly life.

When participation in the Eucharist is understood more as a precept to be fulfilled than a Grace to be accepted; when we go to Mass for the gifts which God has waiting for us rather than for the Gift which is God himself, we are driven to the conclusion that even though the external forms seem Christian, the reality is far from being so.[28]

The early Church never thought or spoke of Eucharist except in terms of *oneness* and *community*, because *that* is what the Lord intended it to be. On the contrary, Paul had some strong words of condemnation for the Corinthians who had lost sight of the deep significance of what they were doing, to the point of total disregard of each other's needs.

> *For when the time comes to eat, each of you goes ahead with your own supper, and one goes hungry, and another becomes drunk* (1 Corinthians 11:24. See 11:17-34).

I wonder what the Apostle and those early Christians would say if they were to witness some of our celebrations today.

Eucharist: 'To Become' Bread and 'To Do' Eucharist

Viewed in this way, the Eucharist becomes both a challenge to think and to live in a certain way, and a commitment to build up the Body of Christ together with our brothers and sisters. '*Do this in memory of me*' has truly been called a *dangerous memory*, because, when taken at their face value, those words are far more than an exhortation to repeat a ritual.[29] Jesus is not asking us simply to replicate a ritualistic performance, but to do what he did and what he was about to do in a few hours for his disciples and for the whole world: total and absolute giving of himself to the world and for the world.

It is important to note that, while the Fourth evangelist dedicates a large section of his Gospel to the Last Supper without

---

[28] Juan E. Vecchi, 'This Is My Body Which Is Given For You', *ACTS of the General Council of the Salesian Society of St John Bosco*, 371, 2000, 18.

[29] Johann Baptist Metz, in https://en.wikipedia.org/wiki/Johann_Baptist_Metz

ever making any mention of a specific Eucharistic theme, as in the traditional language and understanding of the Synoptics, nevertheless, the Johannine narrative of the Last Supper carries a strong similarity of intent of the Institution through the parable in action that was the 'Washing of the Feet' (John 13:1-13). Not only is Jesus' washing of disciples' feet the parable in action of the total self-giving of God to us, but at the end of the gesture of absolute self-giving, Jesus enjoins on his disciples,

> *'I have given you an examples that you may copy what I have done to you.'* (John 13:15)

Thus, both the narrative of the institution in the Synoptics and the washing of the feet in John express exactly the same attitudes and finality: the total self-giving of Jesus in view of what was to happen within a few hours, culminating in his total abandonment to death, and the same message to his disciples:

> *'Do this what I have done to you, and do it to each other together and with one another.'* (John 13:15)

In the Johannine narrative of the Last Supper, Jesus' washing of the disciples feet substitutes the Eucharistic theme of institution (John 13:1-15), and, at the end of parable in action, Jesus tells his disciples to '*copy*' what he has done to them. Interestingly enough, the Liturgy carries the same import. At the Celebration of the Lord's Supper on Holy Thursday, while focusing on the events of the Upper Room, the Gospel retells the parable in action of the washing of the feet, instead of the Synoptics' narrative of the 'institution', with the same injunction '*to do*' to each other as he has done for us.

> *'For I have set you an example, that you also should do as I have done to you.'* (John 13:15)

Celebrating Eucharist then means to take seriously Jesus' powerful and unequivocal injunction to incarnate in real terms the attitudes that fired him as he broke bread with his disciples on that last evening of his earthly life. We have *to do Eucharist* and *be Eucharist*. We have to wash one another' feet (John 13:1-20) and break bread for each other and, like Jesus' self-giving, *we must become bread for each other*. People will only recognise Jesus as the self-giving God in every facet of real life through our own personal self-giving to each other. For the old man in our original story, the memory of his life's struggles prompted him to celebrate a ritual of reaching out to others. Celebrating his present blessings and healing his memories through that ritual made him do something practical and hands-on for others. He who had experienced famine and suffering felt the need *to do something* for others, so that the memory became a healing gesture for himself and a commitment to make abundance available and nourishing to his household.

To break bread together means *availability* to each other without distinctions or personal judgments. It means to go out to those we live with in *spontaneous* and *joyful self-giving*, even at the expense of our own likes and dislikes and personal plans. It means *readiness* 'to bear one another's burdens', even when we feel that our crosses and burdens are more than enough to carry. It means *fostering harmony* through sensitivity to another's needs and mutual encouragement. It means taking up one's *responsibility* for the welfare and happiness of each and every member of the community regardless of position, tasks or personalities. It means readiness to *forget and forgive* when we are hurt and hurt deeply as well as readiness to *accept forgiveness* from brother or sister – (and accepting forgiveness is far more difficult that to offer forgiveness to another person!). It means *fostering* each other's God-enriched *gifts* and talents of human qualities by affirming, encouraging and rejoicing.

From this perspective, the Eucharist can never be reduced to a personal devotion or a routine chore. I am led to the Eucharist because of my encounter with God who sends me to meet my brother and sister and to be in fellowship with them.

The practical implications, of course, may be staggering! What about when I refuse to meet my brother and/or sister? It is no use then to protest faithful observance of the law on the rhythm of an alarm clock. It is hypocritical to entrench oneself behind private devotions, pretending that my many personal prayers at thanksgiving time will become the magic wand that will settle differences, if I am not prepared to take the first step towards a settlement and reconciliation (Matthew 5:23-24). It is idolatrous to think that God will change both minds and attitude of that brother or sister if I remain entrenched in my own views and my personal agenda.

The daily Eucharist builds the community, as we have heard mantra-like so many times. But the very celebration of Eucharist presupposes human conditions of time and place and people who are prepared to accept into their own lives that very unity of intent and relationship that the daily Eucharist signifies. Because we share at the table of the Lord, we must let ourselves be challenged. Failing to accept the challenge is to make a mockery of the Eucharist. Already Augustine had warned us,

> The faithful know the Body of Christ, if they do not neglect to become the Body of Christ'.[30]

> The Eucharist is truly understood and perceived not only when certain things are done *to IT* (when it is celebrated, adored, received with the proper dispositions, etc.), or when certain things are done *because of IT* (we love others, struggle for justice, etc.), but also and above all when it becomes the *form*, the spring and the working model which imprints itself on the communitarian and personal life of the believers... Therefore, the Eucharistic celebration is fulfilled when it acts in some way to cause the believers to give their 'body and blood to their brothers and sisters, as Christ did.[31]

---

[30] St Augustine, *On the Gospel of John: 3:3.*
[31] Carlo M. Martini: 'La Dimensione Contemplativa', in Carlo Colli (1982), *The Spirit of Mornese*, New Rochelle NY: Don Bosco Publications, 1982, 186-187.

All this makes heavy demands of time and energy. It frustrates and tires us out, leaving us shattered. That is why the Fathers of the Church spoke of *becoming bread*, bread for the hungry, bread that is broken, cut, torn, chewed up and transformed... All this hurts, and it hurts very deeply and intensely!

> Sometimes I will be rejected and misunderstood; I may not see results in my ministry, and I will need to give when nothing seems to be returned. To follow is to serve when the body and the spirit are weary and to never know what lies ahead... Sometimes we feel like there is a part of us that's been *eaten out* and *chewed on*... We will expect some emptying to go on in our lives, some eating up to take place. But it will not destroy us because... we (are) sustained and strengthened by our love of God and our faith in his ever-abiding presence. We can have problems, frustrations, difficult situations and not allow them to embitter, disillusion or destroy us.[32]

Our contribution may appear small – probably insignificant – to world wisdom, but it absolutely essential. John links his most powerful teaching on Eucharist to the miracle of the multiplication of the loaves and fishes, where the almost insignificant contribution of a small boy who was prepared to share the poverty of his means – five loaves and two fish – became the instrument by which thousands of people were fed (Matthew 14:13-21; Mark 6:30-44; Luke 9:10-17; John 6:1-14). There is a clear link between sharing Eucharist and becoming Eucharist by making ourselves available to God who then works his way through our available destitution. Commenting precisely on this specific Gospel event, Basil Pennington writes:

> What happens in our lives is not measured by our talents, nor even by our dreams, but by our willingness to say yes to the Lord each day and use our gifts as he inspires and directs... How many loaves do you have, really, the number

---

[32] Joyce Rupp, *Fresh Bread and Other Gifts of Spiritual Nourishment*, Notre Dame, IN: Ave Maria Press, 1987, 118-119.

is not important. He can do as much with one as with seven. We all have the gift of life, the power to love, to be there with him for others. Given that, there is nothing we cannot do with him, in him, through him.[33]

That is the only way to realise concretely and to set free the energy of God's loving presence, promised by Jesus at the Last Supper, revealed at the Resurrection, released by the Spirit at Pentecost, and imbibed by each of us individually and all of us together at Eucharist. Then the world will know that our God is madly in love with each and every one of us indistinctly, uniquely and personally and that our destiny is to be one with him, in κοινωνία (fellowship) with the whole world. Then the world will know the gift of peace and love that it yearns for so insatiably, that very peace that Jesus gave repeatedly to his fearful and confused disciples in the Upper Room: at his goodbye meal (John 14:27) and again as the ultimate sign of his Resurrection (John 20:21).

---

[33] M. Basil Pennington, *Who do you say I Am? Meditations on Jesus' Questions in the Gospels*, Hyde Park, NY: New City Press 2005, 87-88

The Cross – The Place of Encounter with God (Good Friday)

John 18:1 to 19:42

Good Friday: A Celebration of Death!

THIS IS UNDOUBTEDLY the most dramatic day of the whole liturgical year, bringing into play memory, emotions and ritual. However, it is easy to reduce this one day to a spectacular celebration of life in spite of anything and everything to the level of a yearly mnemonic recall of some past event, an annual re-enactment of something that happened long ago and far away. The annual celebration of Holy Week may momentarily tug at the emotional chords of our hearts, but, unlike a good drama, in the end this annual ritual may leave us emotionally moved, but quickly forgotten for another year. This is not an annual celebration of the past, but a jolt in awareness of our own self and *our story today* and throughout the whole of history.

Holy Week Liturgy plays on emotions, but it goes beyond emotions; it feeds on memory, but it is more than just a recall of the past; it is ritualised through words, symbols and gestures, but it is more than a re-enactment. If we leave these days out there in the past, isolated from our life today, then Good Friday and Easter Sunday have no meaning. As the little boy asked me sincerely, 'Why do we call it "Good Friday" when we remember that Jesus died on a cross'?

Like a good drama, Holy Week must touch the depths of the human heart, awaken a new awareness of self, and encourage us to strip away the persona that we embrace and hide behind our true identity. Holy Week is very much a present and personal drama for anyone who claims to believe; a drama *now, here, about us, every day, as we are*. To celebrate Holy Week means to move away from being spectators to becoming actors in the drama. While we can be silent, critical or distant spectators during a dress rehearsal, the power of the real drama lies in its capacity to draw the spectator into the depth of one's soul, awaken powerful emotions, and throw out a personal challenge. Like in every good drama, we must allow ourselves to transcend the spectator role and to be plunged into the actor persona. Celebrating Holy Week is about making choices and deciding on where we stand with our God and with each other, or, as someone said, a time when as Christians we are called 'to look up and take heart, to look at the cross and dare to hope'.[34]

Our Experience of the Cross

The media is not good news! It is rare these days to pick up the printed media or listen to the evening news without being confronted immediately with stories of terrorism and violence on a local or world scale, with natural disasters and incurable diseases, with family violence, abuse and multi-dimensional crime, with the plight of refugees and homelessness. Not only do natural or catastrophic disasters leave us bewildered, but our personal, immediate and inner worlds may seem to collapse for whatever reasons: marriage breakdowns, job loss, onset of serious life-threatening illness, estrangement between parents and children. To all this, we must add the personal struggles that we face each day in so many diverse ways, and the result is a cosmic sense of negativity,

---

[34] Pope Francis, https://www.catholicnewsagency.com/news/254024/pope-francis-advice-for-holy-week . .

depression and mistrust in our world, in our story, in ourselves. All these situations so overwhelm us with a deep sense of helplessness and hopelessness that we feel as if our life has lost all its meaning and purpose.

Suffering inevitably leaves us bewildered and disturbed, because, in most cases, there is no rationale for such events or for the immensely tragic consequences they bring with them. As we watch from the comfort of our living room, hopefully questions arise, persistent and unresolved. *Why?... Why these things? ... Why these people? ... Why (not) me?* Such events are more than social issues but touch us at the very depth of our being and as such, they are spiritual and religious questions that cut deep into our consciousness and inevitably, even if unexpressed, they bring into play the ever-present question of God. We may not always express it in as many words, but we cannot avoid the question lurking deep and gnawing in our hearts. '*Why do such things happen – Why does God allow these things to happen?* – innocent children to die of starvation, thousands of people wiped off the face of the earth without a trace in an instant of explosive madness, hardworking people being denied dignity and work, socio-political-economic selfish power-hungry – *Where is the God of love who is meant to care for us? Where is God at all?*

If we are to accept the insights of developmental psychology, there are only two possible outcomes of such bewilderment: either an irrational bitterness, or a call to faith. As Erik Erikson puts it, *despair* or *hope*. When one's earthly hopes are shattered, when our lives collapse and lose their meaning, when we feel flattened and bowed down, when everything seems totally hopeless, one can either fall into bitterness and despair, or one can develop a stronger hope and courage that never seemed possible. Christianity opts unquestionably for the latter, and, in the face of all possible or unimaginable negativity and apparent hopelessness, the Christian Story suggests a one-word response: Easter! However, Easter is inevitably conditioned by Good Friday. Life must go through death, and then we can say, 'Look up and take heart; look at a cross and dare to hope!'

That is the message that today's celebration puts before us; death and life, despair and hope all rolled into one. Jesus chose life (John 10:10), even if that life could only sprout forth through death. It is up to us to choose and decide.

Life through Death

Unlike any other religious tradition, Christian faith stands on the ultimate paradox proclaiming that the only way to life is through death. The cross dominates large and incessant throughout the Gospel narrative, and Jesus not only embraces this cross as the faithful fulfilment of the mission to him entrusted by the Father and his life-giving instrument for the whole world, but he makes it an absolute demand for anyone who claims to follow him in discipleship. The vehicle of the most abominable death becomes for us the ultimate and unavoidable instrument of life. In the words of Paul to the Christians of Corinth,

> *The language of the cross may be illogical to those who are not on the way to salvation, but to those of us who are on the way see it as God's power to save. Here we are preaching a crucified Christ; to the Jews an obstacle that they cannot get over, to the pagans madness, but to those who have been called... the power and the wisdom of God. For God's weakness is stronger than human strength.* (1 Corinthians 1:18-23)

For centuries, Christianity stands accused of making an apology of the cross, pretending to canonise suffering, as good, and absconding the reality of suffering into 'another world', or in an after-life. What this week screams to the whole world is that, in the Christian economy and understanding of reality, nothing could be further from the truth. Death is evil and suffering can never be good news. Gerard Hughes claims that the passive and indiscriminate acceptance of suffering as a presumed instrument towards a deeper relationship with Christ is blasphemous and a denial of Christ himself.

> The deformed notion of the passion divinises suffering which, in itself, is an evil and to be avoided. Suffering does not save: its effect is normally to destroy. Passively and indiscriminately to accept all suffering, as though in so doing we were imitating Christ, can be a denial of Christ. If we are victims of injustice and oppression and deceit, whether from secular or religious authorities, then to accept it passively and encourage others to do the same 'for the love of Christ' is to collude with evil, not to resist it.[35]

To claim any inherent goodness and value in pain and suffering as if willed by God makes a mockery of the God whom we address as Father. To claim that God wills suffering and death for us makes God into an angry, cruel and sadistic puppet, who after throwing us into 'this valley of tears', smugly leaves us floundering, hopeless and helpless, just to see if we can make it to the shore. Such a bloodthirsty God may well make millions on a Hollywood portrayal of 'The Passion of the Christ' but, as Gerard W. Hughes concludes, 'this can leave us very grateful to Jesus, but less keen on his heavenly Father',[36] whom Jesus addressed as Abba.

What the Christian claims, however, and what the Church celebrates in Holy Week and Easter is the conviction that there exists a positive and life-giving oneness between human suffering and God, expressed through the mutual and unbreakable sharing of death and life, suffering and hope. If there were no suffering, if all our longings were merely in the here-and-now, not only there would be any need for hope, but there would be no possibility of hope, and life would be the ultimate inescapable tragedy.

---

[35] Gerard W. Hughes, *God of Surprises*, London: DLT, 1998), 128.
[36] Gerard W. Hughes, *Oh God, Why? A Journey through Lent for Bruised Pilgrims*, Oxford: The Bible Reading Fellowship, 1993, 138.

If suffering were good and life-giving, 'the most effective service of God would consist in our imposing the maximum suffering on ourselves and on others.'[37]

As the one sent by the Father *'to bring life to the full'* (John 10:10), Jesus did not choose the cross, nor did he embrace it because it was good. If pain and suffering in themselves were harbingers of salvation and redemptive, why did Jesus spend most of his earthly life healing and relieving pain and death, and then send his disciples to do the same? Why spend a lifetime dedicated to human promotion and redemption when suffering is a precious currency for eternal bliss?

> Suffering, in itself, is an evil and to be avoided. While it is true that some people are ennobled by suffering, the majority are diminished or destroyed by it... Suffering does not save: its effect is normally to destroy. . . (and) to accept it passively is to collude with evil.[38]

God's will for us is life, and not destruction and death, as Jesus' first self-disclosure in the synagogue of Nazareth proclaimed and all his subsequent actions revealed (Luke 4:16-19). To a widow grieving for the death of her only son, Jesus gives him back to her, bursting with life (Luke 7:11-17). Lepers cry out in despair and anger at a world that rejects them and labels them unclean, only to be restored to health and dignity by his compassionate presence (Luke 17:11-19). At the risk of defilement and condemnation, Jesus holds the hand of a young girl lying in death, restoring her to fullness of life and joy (Mark 5:41-42). A woman afflicted by a physical ailment and by an even more painful moral stigma is allowed to touch him, and healing and affirmation are the result (Mark 5:25-34).

Jesus was not about suffering and pain for the sake of pharisaic ritual purity or moral judgment. On the contrary, human fragility

---

[37] Ibid.
[38] Gerard W. Hughes, God of Surprises, 138.

and pain are the catalysts that ignite compassion in Jesus of Nazareth. He physically touched pain, suffering and death, and by touching and embracing that human fragility, Jesus not only condemned and healed the darkness of pain, fears and self-condemnation, but he also declared the moral imperative to remove pain, fear, suffering and death that in a myriad of ways obscure and denigrate the preciousness of each person.

If we hold on to some distorted belief by which suffering is a sign of God's favour and that God can only be appeased by human struggle and pain, then why deceive ourselves blind by engaging in activities of human promotion and redemption, be these in terms of justice, wellbeing, health, or just plain companionship or compassion? Jesus did not choose suffering as a good to be sought after and even less to be imposed on others. In the garden, he prayed to the Father pleading for deliverance, '*Father, if it is possible, let this cup pass me by*' (Matthew 26:39; Luke 22:42); and on the Golgotha, Jesus screamed his despair to the point of doubting the Father's presence and love, '*My God, my God, why have you abandoned me?*' (Matthew 27:46).

> Life has a way of testing what we really believe. Life tested Jesus. What do you believe about God when powerful people murder your cousin? What motivates you to keep on hoping for change in people when you experience isolation and rejection? What do you believe about God when you are nailed to a cross, and all your dreams seem to have crumbled into nothing? Jesus preached the importance of living in a trusting relationship with God, free from notions of a God ready to hand out physical misfortune, loss, or death as a punishment.[39]

More than a tragic climax of his life and mission, *for Jesus the cross is the inevitable condition of his filial relationship and submissive obedience to Abba, as his complete immersion into the human story,*

---

[39] Michael Morwood, *Praying a New Story*, Melbourne: Spectrum Publications, 2003, 99-100.

and as the one necessary path for fullness of life for those who claimed to follow him. The cross will be salvific only to the extent that it is an expression and an instrument of that radical 'Yes' to the Father that Jesus lived and witnessed throughout his earthly life. What saves us and leads to fulfilment is fidelity to God and to God's ways, and such fidelity is often painful and distressing, as it demands that we let go of our well-laid plans and comfort zones and accept God on God's terms.

The Cross: The Place We Share with God

Unwanted and less-than-human though the cross may have been for Jesus and for the whole of humanity of all time, Jesus accepted it as part of that human and divine journey that would lead to fulfilment and salvation. Jesus did place the cross as the categorical condition of discipleship, as the rationale of Christian faith, and as the only way to fullness of life (Luke 9:23; Matthew 3:38). However, such claims have nothing to do with masochistic predispositions or self-inflicted stoicism. Jesus did not embrace the cross and enjoined on us to take up ours because suffering was good in itself.

His proclamation at Nazareth holds the key to Jesus' claim and invitation (Luke 4:18). In that self-proclamation, Jesus sets out a program of redemption from all that is evil and unjust and soul-destroying in our world, but such a task of redemption on behalf of others often demands a level of self-giving and of courage that is painful, self-sacrificing and even death-dealing.

> It was because Jesus lived out this prophecy that he suffered, for he threatened those whose power, prosperity and security depended on keeping the poor in their poverty and the downtrodden in oppression. If we let Christ be Christ in us, oppose injustice and speak the truth in love, we shall also suffer at the hands of those whose power we threaten. This is to share in the Passion of Christ.[40]

---

[40] Gerard W. Hughes, *God of Surprises*, 139.

The cross then becomes the place where we encounter God in Christ, a necessary means of discovering the real God in us and walking with us, as the disciples of Emmaus eventually discovered. Jesus invited those two disciples to look on their own suffering as a key to self-discovery and a stimulus to hope (Luke 24:13-35).

This is also the message of Good Friday, where we see a Jesus subjected to and struggling with the most painful experience imaginable, to the point of experiencing the ultimate level of physical, emotional and spiritual agony, to the point of screaming out in anguish the ultimate human despair, '*My God, my God why have you abandoned me?*' (Matthew 27:46). This means that now we can truly claim that having taken upon himself the totality of human suffering, having been there himself through Jesus Christ, God knows human suffering to its ultimate destructive power in death.

God knows what I go through, when physical pain wrecks my body, when loneliness and abandonment crush me to death, when my future looms so hopeless that I even doubt that there may be a future at all, when I am the victim of injustice, or I am called to forgive the hurt received. God knows rejection and insult, physical and mental abuse, betrayal, and falsehood. God knows death to the point that death becomes the only human way to enter into God's reality, just as death was the ultimate way of God entering the totality of our human reality. As the story of Lazarus tells us, in Jesus, God confronts death face to face, and calls life out of death, and, as Thomas Keating puts it, 'in the crucifixion of Jesus, the impossible happens. God dies'.

> God is not just an onlooker of human history and of our individual melodrama, applauding our efforts and lamenting our failures from a safe distance. He *joins* us in our sufferings. In the crucifixion of Jesus, the impossible happens. God dies.[41]

---

[41] Thomas Keating, *Manifesting God*, New York, NY: Lantern Books, 2005, 59.

Because God knows it all with a knowing of the heart as well of mind and body, now we are no longer alone or abandoned in our struggles, in our sufferings, and in our death. Along the road to Emmaus, Jesus not only claimed that it was necessary that the Messiah should suffer and die, but he made himself their compassionate travelling companion. By falling in step with two people who trudged their way in darkness and pain seeking for an escape more than for an explanation, God not only dies an abominable death, but our God is also the one who walks, mostly unknown along the road of our pain, loneliness and misunderstandings.

> Jesus knew what it was like to be in darkness, to feel isolated, to need to pray about things and make sense of what was happening in his life. In times of loss, pain, and tragedy, we can turn to him because he knows what is like to be in our shoes. He has been there. We can turn to him for the healing that comes from compassion, from being understood... God is not an overseer directing circumstances from elsewhere. God is intimately IN the pain with us; we are living IN God'.[42]

The necessity of the cross that Jesus enjoins on his disciples is the necessity of letting God into our pain and abandoning into God's hands our false images as much as our false expectations and securities. When we have the courage and strength to do that, then truly pain becomes redemptive and truly life-giving, because it becomes the instrument of God working his way in our life and journeying alongside us on our way. With nothing to hold on to of our own making, then only God can make us into what God has always wanted us to be. It is as if God invites us into himself through our vulnerability and dependency, even to the point of our most hellish experience. In our creedal statement we proclaim that Jesus '*died, rose and descended into hell*'. Every time we

---

[42] Ronald Rolheiser, *Moral Intelligence* in http://ww.rolheiser.com/ (Accessed 2007-02-18).

proclaim those words at liturgy, we commit ourselves to accepting the fact that in Jesus, God has plumbed their darkest depths of our humanity, whatever our personal hells, our paranoias, our fears, our physical and emotional torments, our sense of alienation, and abandonment.[43]

Because God has descended into all that is evil, for the believing disciple life blossomed anew like a flower out of the cruellest winter. Incarnation reached its ultimate fulfilment on the cross on Calvary not as a blood sacrifice, but as total immersion of the divine into the human story. From that moment onwards, every human facet becomes caught up into that divine presence that did not shun the earthy and the broken but made earthiness and brokenness constituent elements of the divine reality. Only in this sense can suffering be redemptive. Only in this perspective can we speak of abundant fruitfulness through suffering and death.

It is in our pain that we encounter our God present and life-giving. When we are wrecked with pain, lost in a dark tunnel of confusion and mental anguish, trapped by fear at a doctor's worst diagnosis, burning with anger, exploited by lust and avarice, imprisoned in loneliness and longing for compassion and companionship God knows it. Ignored and rejected because of one's skin or language, victim of injustice and ridicule, plumbing the depths of despair, God knows it all. God is an active player in our humanity and in the multi-faceted deaths we encounter every day in ourselves and all around us. On the cross, humanity dies with God and on human crosses God dies with humanity. We are no longer alone, because imprisoned though one's life may seem or feel, God is there falling in step with us, and, Lazarus-like, calling each by name into life.

Life may be couched in the spoils of death, and the apparent destruction wrought by suffering and death ushers in a totally and

---

[43] Ronald Rolheiser, *Forgotten Among the Lilies. Learning to Love Beyond Our Fears*, (New York, NY: Doubleday, 2005, 158-159.

unfathomable new life. The Lazarus story gives us the clearest witness of a God who weeps in the face of death and suffering, and yet confronts this death face to face and out of that confrontation brings us life, where none was supposed to be (John 11:1-37). In the midst of death and suffering, God calls us by name out of the death of chronic and endemic apathy, hopelessness and unbelief. As for Lazarus, God invites us to confront the inhumanity of suffering, the horror of looking at death in the face, and the darkness of walking through death, in order to be called to fullness of life. Easter proclaims what happened to Jesus when he had the courage and fidelity to abandon himself into the hands of the Father. The Lazarus narrative proclaims what happens to us when we have the same courage to accept God in our life even at the cost of death.

Easter reassures us we are not alone in our journey to life through death, because God has done it all before and will do it all with every human being that accepts God's life-giving presence in life and death. The key is that question Jesus addresses to Martha: 'Do you believe that?'

The Cross – Harbinger of Hope

In the end, life is quite simple really. We either accept that God is totally caught up with us, yes even in extreme pain and isolation and in the most excruciating death, or we lack that acceptance and hope, and then nothing at all makes sense anymore. By accepting the weeds among the wheat and being reassured that God has placed the good seed there, life's hardships are not so overwhelming and no longer death dealing (Matthew 13:24-30). Indeed, in spite of and through those hardships, we can still achieve a full and fulfilled life, we can still rejoice and love and be grateful, because we know that he is there and therefore 'all is well, and all is well, and all manner of things will be well'.[44]

---

[44] Julian of Norwich, https://en.wikipedia.org/wiki/Julian of Norwich

On the contrary, if we do not accept God's presence in our daily cross, then that life becomes more and more unbearable every day, crushed by loneliness, anger and despair.

The paradox of our existence, of an infinite longing trapped within a finite being, and the tragedies of our life will only make sense through Jesus' words

> *'Very truly, I tell you, unless a grain of wheat falls into the earth and dies, it remains just a single grain; but if it dies, it bears much fruit.'* (John 12:24)

For a person without faith, suffering and dying are a senseless tragedy and an unmitigated evil, but for those who hope, even suffering and dying are blessings. Our little deaths challenge us to let go of what is less authentic and not life-giving in our life for the sake of fullness of life. After all that is what Jesus came for:

> *'I came that they may have life and have it to the full.'* (John 10:10)

As we get older, we encounter more and more a sharp split in our own life experience. Some have an almost palpable inner peace about them. They are grateful for life and what it has given them, and in this way, they become life-givers all around them. At the same time, as we grow into a more mature age, some of us become progressively more angry, bitter and grasping at the bare straws of life, blaming everyone else for their paucity of wheat and fruitful peace.

There, the dividing line is hope. Hope throws a new perspective on everything, while without hope, we see ourselves as a victim and the world as the universal enemy. Trapped by our limits, crushed by the tragedies of life, bewildered by the unexpected and unexplainable, we will never achieve full satisfaction, and the cross will appear unbearable and offensive. But we know that Good Friday is only the prelude to Easter Sunday, and Easter Sunday is only possible because of Good Friday. If the two were not linked and if we were not caught up in this dynamism of death and resurrection that forms the basis of our hope and faith, then life would be a cruel hoax and our God would be a sadist puppeteer, pulling the string for the sheer pleasure of seeing us suffer.

Hope is not just medicine for the end of one's days. It should colour one's attitude all through life. When we start to live with hope, every day becomes an occasion of joy, even in the midst of suffering. Hope is not a matter of eagerly awaiting the arrival of the Grim Reaper to usher us into our heavenly hope where we can be finally happy. Much more realistically, it shows itself by our living with joy and detachment today. If we are bound for eternity, we will live in this world with one foot planted in heaven. We will have already stopped running the frantic, never-ending steeplechase after material satisfaction and have set our eyes firmly on the many signs of God's presence to be found in our daily lives. Then we will live in trust, like a child in her mother's arm with the cross urging us:

Make me an instrument of your peace... where there is despair let me bring hope!

Expectant Stillness (Holy Saturday)

Genesis 1:1-5

LITURGY IS NOT CHOREOGRAPHY, nor a nostalgic and empty memory nor a repetitive re-enactment of some past event. Liturgy is living presence, re-expressing in the now of real time the fulcrum of God's saving relationship with humanity, articulated through word and symbol. For Christianity, this fulcrum finds its ultimate expression in the Paschal Mystery represented by the Death and Resurrection of Jesus, and, therefore, Holy Week is both the climax of the liturgical celebration and the source of meaning-maker for the believer across the full span of the whole liturgical year.

In the understanding of the Church, Easter is never a single event, but a continuous season of growth in self-awareness and of deepening maturity of the believer's relationship with God. This ongoing transformation takes on a unique intensity of expression, particularly on the final day of the Lenten season, the day Christians call Holy Saturday. Augustine of Hippo refers to this day as the visible representation of the whole Paschal Mystery bestowing significance and energy to the life of the disciple. The compelling sequence of symbols and implications that the day offers carries a universal and cosmic dimension, and expresses powerfully the import of the Death and Resurrection of Christ in relation to the whole universe, for the life of the world, and for each individual in the reality of their life.

Liturgically, silence dominates the last hours of Good Friday and well into the nightfall of Holy Saturday. It is the silence of loss, of mourning, and of death. All life has vanished, and the

Expectant Stillness (Holy Saturday)

Lord of creation, the very Source of life, lies dead and buried in the silence of a tomb. The tomb is the ultimate sign of non-life, and its unredeemed darkness leaves us with a plethora of questions but ultimately silences all answers or rational expressions.

As if the whole world stood still, today's liturgy underscores the dynamic silence and the stillness stirring deep within. Apart from the sombre tones of Morning Lauds appropriately called 'Tenebrae' (Darkness), chanted in monasteries or by some rare, cathedral choirs, churches are empty, divested of all decors, deprived of light and sound, and most of all destitute of any liturgical expression. This is the one day of the whole liturgical year when the Eucharist is not celebrated until the solemn Vigil after nightfall or the early hours of Easter Sunday morning. It is the silence that thrusts us into the primordial state of *'formless void and darkness that covered the face of the deep'* (Genesis 1:2) of the opening lines of Genesis 1 which opens the sequence of Old Testament readings during the great Vigil.

While death seems to be the central theme of Holy Saturday, from the perspective of the liturgical and biblical contexts, these references give rise to challenging questions about life and not about death. It is crucial then that we fathom the deep significance of this day, otherwise the power and life-giving energy of the evening celebration is nullified and lost into another repetitious ritual leading to a meaningless celebration.

Two quite inadequate views seem to dominate both the meaning and the praxis of Holy Saturday: a highly emotional response or a pragmatic expression. Across the centuries and the plethora of cultural expressions, Holy Saturday has often taken on gloomy and negative connotations, a mournful mood where any form of celebration would seem to be most inappropriate on a day when we commemorate the funeral of Jesus. Focusing precisely on a funereal ambiance and highlighting death, this is only a day of emotions and deep sadness as we mourn the loss of the Lord of life, and any expression of hope and peace are to be banished.

On the other hand, from a more mundane perspective, a shallow understanding of Holy Saturday may have led us to see a day of great activity, a day of preparation for the solemn liturgy of the Vigil and of the following day. While this is the less appealing but often a necessary aspect of Holy Saturday, this functional concept has unfortunately fed into the perception of our consumer society which readily embraced a pragmatic and commercial view of the foundational pillars of the Christian liturgical cycle (Christmas and Easter), and once again hijacked the powerful energy of Holy Saturday into an orgy of tingling cash registers.

I suggest that neither of the above attitudes has anything to do with the real meaning of Holy Saturday. Indeed, any form of mournful sentimentality as much as hyperactive performance are equally destructive of the power inherent in this one day of the year. Holy Saturday is not about the silence out there, but about the stillness deeply in here, in the depth of the heart that yearns for life and invites us to look at the fullness of life from the perspective of death and at death from the standpoint of life.

There is a strong sense of deja vu in Holy Saturday, as the day begins with the ultimate silence of death, only to erupt a few hours later into an explosion of light and a cosmic symphony of new life that re-enacts the opening image of the primal story of creation and the opening stanzas of the Vigil celebration in the evening.

This is the day of silence and stillness, not the inert silence of the absence of all reality, of emptiness and nothingness, but a silence pregnant with life and harbinger of fullness of life. This is the silence of the primordial reality at the very beginning of time.

> *In the beginning when God created the heavens and the earth, the earth was a formless void and darkness covered the face of the deep, while a wind from God swept over the face of the waters. Then God said, 'Let there be light'; and there was light. And God saw that the light was good; and God separated the light from the darkness. God called the light Day, and the darkness*

he called Night. And there was evening and there was morning, the first day. (Genesis 1:1-5)

Silence can be death-dealing and overwhelming, particularly when predicated of the darkness of the tomb. But silence can also be life-giving and revelatory of our true self and generative of those questions that stir deep in our heart and challenge the core of our psyche. In a world pounding obsessively with a dissonance of perennial words and sounds, we become totally insensitive to any messages the cacophony may convey. However, the instant the whirring and pounding halts, suddenly an unwelcome uneasiness takes hold. Paradoxically then, silence becomes the harbinger of personal meanings and we become aware of a new level of truth bubbling from inside of self and not screaming incoherently from outside. This is the silence engendered by the emptiness of Holy Saturday, a silence that invites listening with the heart and looking at the depth of self.

Today we are invited to confront the silence of our lives and to listen with the ears of the heart, as Saint Benedict, the father of western monasticism, would invite us to do, allowing stillness to uncover the full reality of who we are at the most profound and most real level of our self, on the one hand, and, on the other, reveal who God is in the concrete reality of that personal self. In the memory of the Lord dead and buried in a tomb, we are finally confronted face to face with the inevitability of death in us and all around us and of the absolute finality to what we call life. However, we can never separate death from life, and it is precisely this absolute finality that must thrust us into confronting the meaning and essence of life. For the primal story of Genesis 1, the *formless void and the darkness covering the face of the deep*, is the place where *the wind of God sweeps over the water*, a harbinger of the explosion of creation, culminating into fullness of life.

At various junctures of our personal story, we all come face to face with death in its most diverse manifestations and experiences, and all of us have to grapple with the sense of loss and emptiness that the multifarious deaths engender. The loss of a dear one, the sudden terminal diagnosis, natural disasters and children escaping violence only to lie as lifeless bodies washed up on an unknown foreign strip of sand. All these, and a myriad other situations, bring us face to face with the reality of death, and we cannot escape their challenge to life by engaging in some form of denial, pretence, rationalisation or alibi. These are our Holy Saturdays, but these are also the fundamental silent challenges stirring unavoidably our spiritual DNA and disturbing radically the depth of our soul. If everything ends in death, then nothing on earth makes sense and life appears as an empty wasteland. Death is the inescapable ultimate reality of life and, unless we allow death to prod and question us and push our vision beyond the narrow horizon of the physical and the within of what is quantifiable, then life becomes a meaningless obsession and death is but a horrid embrace of nothingness. Yes, today we celebrate a Jesus in the tomb, but that sepulchral silence speaks of life in its ultimate fullness because *a wind from God swept over the primordial face* of the created world and of the human story.

In the Christian economy of salvation, Holy Saturday enjoins on us to look beyond and within measurable reality, pointing to the decisive paradox that death is not a closure of the human story, but a beginning of an eternal journey shared totally by God with humanity. Jesus proclaimed that he has come that they may have life and have it in full; but this fullness is conditional to a total loss of life for the sake of life.

> '*I came that they may have life and have it abundantly. I am thee good shepherd. The good shepherd lays down his life for the sheep.*' (John 10:10-11)

Likewise, in his conversation with Nicodemus, Jesus pointed out that the ultimate symbol of death raised on a stake in the desert was the definitive emblem of eternal life (John 3:14). Today we celebrate the One who died that we may have life, and this One is the living and life-giving presence of God totally enmeshed in our humanity. God's immersion into the human story is absolute and total to the extreme of death, and therefore we are no longer alone in facing death, nor is God extraneous to the multifaceted human deaths. The prayer of the Church on this day reminds us that, at his death, Jesus descended into hell. In the context, rather than a physical place or a state of mind, hell represents everything that is non-life and anti-life in our living experience and in our story. In Jesus, God spared himself nothing that belongs to the human experience, but embraced the most unsavoury elements of our story, including the abandonment of death. Yet, God in Jesus drew life precisely out of that non-life trapped in the nothingness of an empty tomb.

Holy Saturday is not a day of mourning and bereavement, but a day of rejoicing and hope urging us to celebrate our human-divine identity and our destiny. God knows our death and our sense of deep emptiness and loss, having experienced and embraced these realities in Jesus. There lies the rationale for our rejoicing and our hope. God knows, and God is there to offer us fullness of life now in spite of the apparent defeat and disintegration of the tomb. As Joan Chittister puts it,

> Holy Saturday faith is not about counting our blessings; it is about dealing with darkness and growing in hope.[45]

Hope is not a passive waiting for the pie-in-the-sky-when-we-die, but a dynamic engagement in the life of each day as the place of God's revelation and of God's life-giving presence. Hope is confronting both present and future with courage and determination, aware that life is a gift shared unconditionally by God, in spite of and beyond death, because not even death could keep Jesus away from his disciples. Hope is unconditional immersion in the reality here and now, a reality not only tainted

---

[45] Joan Chittister, *The Liturgical Year. The Spiralling Adventure of the Spiritual Life*, Thomas Nelson 2009, 154.

but at times distorted and disfigured by pain, sin and death, and yet energised by the living presence of God. Hope is commitment to create conditions that foster and enhance life and joy in the very midst of loss and struggle. Hope is embracing the little deaths of each day and letting go of what is less authentic and less life-giving for the sake of that fullness of life for which Jesus lived and died and came back to life. Hope is being at ease with uneasiness and ambiguity, never satisfied with ready-made answers but always seeking a God who seeks us in life and death.

Hope is a positive realism that looks at life with an affirming eye and acknowledges the goodness around us and within us, rather than through the lenses of brokenness that sometime overwhelms us. Hope is embracing life with only one security: Jesus shared our experience to the extreme of death and came back to life; and that is our story and our destiny.

These are the sentiments that underscore the great Vigil celebrated at nightfall and bringing to its explosive climax not only a day that had begun immersed into stillness of mind, and powerful eloquent silence of the heart, but climaxing the whole season of Lent as a journey into spiritual maturity and wholeness of life. Behind the structures and symbols of the celebration, we can read the paradigm of Easter for the Christian believer. Light, word, water and food are the basic realities of human sustenance, but they are also the realities by which the solemn Vigil breaks the silence of Holy Saturday, reproposing the cosmic nature of Easter and symbolising the living gifts offered to us at Easter.

Once again, the language and rich symbolism of the Vigil throws us back into the beginning of the Judeo-Christian story, when

> *God said, 'Let there be light'; and there was light. And God saw that the light was good; and God separated the light from the darkness. God called the light Day, and the darkness he called Night. And there was evening and there was morning, the first day.* (Genesis 1:1-5)

Expectant Stillness (Holy Saturday)

Each breaking of the new day of the creation story is a reminder of the fundamental truth of Christian belief. In the biblical tradition, the primordial chaos was spectacularly redeemed by God calling forth fullness of light and life out of chaos and dark emptiness. At the dawn of the new economy, Christ broke through the darkness of the tomb, exploding into a new day of fullness of light and life, shattering forever the enslaving clutches of death on humanity.

This is the day of paradoxes when the stillness and silence of the previous twenty-four hours culminate in the celebration of the solemn Vigil at nightfall, an unrestrained festival of symbols and Word reminiscent of the primordial chaos and darkness exploding into life. The opening words of the Easter hymn speak of an intense duel between life and death and proclaim that death has no longer any hold on us because life has conquered death forever. Everything is now possible even out of the coldness of the darkest tomb, in spite of the hordes of deaths that may threaten and afflict us. Liturgically, in word and symbol, the Vigil breaks the expectant silence to proclaim that, because of that empty tomb and that greeting of peace by Jesus to his disciples, hereafter the deepest darkness of our life is shattered by a flickering flame gradually but inexorably exploding into a reverie of light and song.

Within the structure and symbols of the liturgy of the great Vigil, we can read the paradigms of the new reality inaugurated by Easter in the life of the disciple. Light, word, water and food are the life-giving and sustaining elements in the new economy inaugurated by Jesus breaking through the bonds of death forever, re-expressing the very sparks of the dawn of the new reality redeemed from all sepulchral darkness and emptiness, and symbolising the enduring gifts proffered to the believer on Easter morning and for all time. The coldness and inertia of our hearts can now glow and overflow with a new fire, giving warmth, hope and joy where there is sadness and despondency. Our life is no longer an arid wasteland, and our fragility is no longer a waterless and death-dealing desert, because the flood of God's presence and love has now taken hold of our story and has saturated the parched lands and the wilderness of sinfulness that we inevitably have to cross on our life journey.

Redeemed from the darkness of sin, the Christian believer is now called to be a bearer of light, to persevere in listening with the stillness of the heart to the promptings of the Spirit, and to journey through life as a witness of hope and peace in spite of death all around, because in Jesus God conquered death, and not even death can keep God away from us.

The Impossible is Real

The impossible becomes possible, then probable, and finally inexorable.

THE HUMAN HEART is prisoner of a life-long paradox. Enslaved by an insatiable yearning for love, peace and joy, but most of all for life in its fullness and forever, such deep and intense craving shatters against the inevitability and finality of death, which not only puts an end to our hearts' yearnings, but it obliterates the very possibility of life itself. From a purely human perspective, death is horrid, non-negotiable and all-destructive. Unless, of course, we are prepared to believe in an empty tomb that only a few hours before held a dead and mangled body, an emptiness screaming the humanly unthinkable that the one who lay there before is alive beyond and in spite of death.

That is the challenge of Easter: to believe that the ultimate and impossible longing of the human heart is no longer a mirage, but a reality. Life explodes in and through death. The stories that the liturgy puts before us at this time of year speak of horror and death, but at the same time, they proclaim the impossible: life has blossomed in its fullness in spite of the horror of death.

That Sabbath Day in the Upper Room

Let us imagine the atmosphere in the Upper Room on the evening of Passover, the great annual festival commemorating an apparent human impossibility that had exploded into reality for those who lived through it many centuries before. Passover celebrated divine-driven freedom from slavery by a powerless and anonymous band of slaves, against the might of Egypt. It was a yearly celebration and a memory projecting the heart into a yearning for a future full of hope for all generations to come.

However, just a couple of days later, Jesus' disciples re-gathered in that room – not in the mood for celebration, their longing hearts harbouring only disappointment, sadness, fear and resentment. Indeed, you could cut the air with a knife, air of death, full of emptiness, of anger, of fear, of disillusionment and of mistrust. Although to the end, they had failed to understand who Jesus really was and what he was on about, and their motives for following him were often more dubious than praiseworthy (Matthew 20:20-23), those disciples had staked their lives for Jesus, who augured so abundantly for their personal future and to their misguided expectations of political liberation and freedom from their oppressive political, social, and religious foreign power and culture.

Whether it was two leaky fishing boats or a profitable tax collector's table, they had gambled both present and future, leaving behind all their personal securities and families to follow the preacher from Nazareth, who promised so much and spoke joy and peace to the outcasts. They had gambled it all because they believed in him for their own sake.

For whatever reason, and not necessarily the most praiseworthy one, that band of ignorant and simple people had left behind in trust the security of their home and trade to follow this young preacher from Galilee, who seemed to ensure so much. '*We had hoped that he was the one to redeem Israel*' (Luke 24:21), they would late complain. Of course, it is easy and attractive to follow and to trust the Lord when he speaks to us words of affirmation and healing (Luke 15); when, in our own imagination, his message sounds like a radical call to arms against the hated Romans (Luke 12:49-53); when he works spectacular deeds like feeding five thousand people on two fish and five barley loaves (Luke 9:10-17). It is easy to claim discipleship when we let our imagination run wild and we create our own style of discipleship, twisting and misplacing the words of the Lord to suit our own expectations (Matthew 20:20-23; Luke 22:24-30). It is all so easy, then. But now all those self-styled expectations had vanished; all those dreams of first and second place in the Kingdom had turned into a nightmare of deception and fear. All that 'following the Lord' now seemed completely futile and cruel.

Now the young man from Galilee who worked wonders and spoke such words of promise was dead, the most ignominious death of a rebellious slave, and their own world had crumbled into despair and deceit. All they had to hold on to now was the memory of a dead teacher, of a wonder worker executed like a fraudulent criminal. Yes, they felt cheated, let down, and totally hopeless. Their longing hearts now could harbour only disappointment, sadness, fear and resentment. Their dreams and plans shattered, all that was left was to go back to what they knew before, fishing, farming, and tax collecting, trying to put out of their minds that whole tragic chapter, in the hope that time, if ever, would heal the wounds of their misguided adventure.

An Empty Tomb

In this scenario, the light of hope is trapped by darkness, and the energy of life has been swallowed up by the all-embracing gloom of death. It is dark outside that Upper Room, the place of promise and intimate friendship just a few hours before, a darkness that seemed to exude from the all-embracing blackness gripping the hearts and souls of those who had witnessed and lived through the unbelievable tragedy of what we call Good Friday.

Just before daylight has the strength to break out, the only sign of life is shadows, as three black clad figures shuffle hurriedly and stealthily through the narrow alleyways leading out of the village. In the whole-enveloping inner and outer darkness, they are looking for the darkness of a tomb. Only a mother grieving the cruel and untimely execution of her son can comprehend the pain of loss and death. It is all-pervading, and overwhelming. One more visit to 'the place they laid him' (Mark 16:6), for one more tear, one more memory, one more embrace of that cold unmovable stone that seals away forever life and any loving embrace.

But the tomb is open and empty. The ultimate sword piercing the heart of a mother! Tombs are meant to hold dead bodies, delivering a strange message of marriage between finality and eternal presence at the same time. But an empty tomb is a sad and cruel reminder of absolute nothingness, without presence and without memories. The cruel game of tragedy and pain has now reached its ultimate climax in an empty tomb, freezing the human psyche into absolute fear and horror. Even the last fickle reminders of life now have been obliterated.

Unless, of course, the unthinkable, the unbelievable, and the impossible happen, by which the empty tomb becomes the ultimate sign of life through death and beyond death. This is the message of a 'young man, dressed in a white robe' (Mark 16:5) who, in Mark's account, stands at the place of death, but with a message that in its apparent absurdity does nothing to allay the fears of those who persist on looking for a dead body in an empty tomb.

> *'Do not be alarmed; you are looking for Jesus of Nazareth, who was crucified. He has been raised; he is not here.'* (Mark 16:6)

But precisely in the midst of such overwhelming gloom, death, and heart-wrenching memories, the disciples experience the unthinkable and the humanly impossible. Jesus stands there, in their midst in that same room, once again reassuring and affirming them, eating with them, inviting them to touch him, and speaking words of peace. Bewilderment and hopelessness explode into a sense of wonder and joy that defies human words, and projects those who lived through it into a totally new level of reality and self-understanding. Both by the empty tomb and in that Upper Room, the disciples experience a radical event that defies human rationality but proclaims the impossible become real. Jesus is not dead, but alive. No logical process or explanation holds any value here because resurrection delves into the deepest level of the human heart, awakening precisely that ultimate and eternal longing for life in its fullness and forever.

In that Upper Room and before an empty tomb, the disciples discover that the impossible is now not only a possibility but a reality for them, before their very eyes and in their hands. If we but accept it, that experience of reality is for us too. When the one we love walks the streets and greets us again after being dead and buried for three days, then everything is possible and there are no longer limits to our yearning, hoping and dreaming. The Lord has truly risen, as he said he would, and *in that impossible encounter, the disciples experience in the flesh that not even death could keep God away from them.*

In that Upper Room, where the freedom and hope of the first Passover had died with the memory of the crucified one, now they experience ultimate freedom from the slavery of fear and death, and absolute hope reassuring the yearning heart that, whatever the journey ahead, life and not death is the final destiny. In the face of such impossibility become real in their hands and before their eyes, the bottom line for the disciples was that only a direct intervention of God in human history could have brought about a transformation of such magnitude as to bring life out of the very depths of the tomb and push the limits of our yearning beyond the barriers of death. Only God could have done this, and this God is standing right there in their midst beyond all human possibilities or power of understanding.

Transformation versus Information

In a bizarre parody of Easter, someone suggested that Jesus did well most things, but failed miserably on the most important one. Had he chosen to walk this earth in our times, full of ubiquitous technological wizardly, a minute bug inside the tomb would have revealed to the whole world in real time what happened in that place of death and confront us instantly with undisputable evidence for our faith and belief. Apart from the bizarre presupposition underlying such a suggestion, the best one can say is that probably our electronic wizardly would have returned nothing but the silent emptiness of the darkness of death.

It is an acknowledged fact that, historically and chronologically, the various Resurrection narratives make little sense, and it is a futile exercise to pretend to set out some logical and coordinated sequence of time and place. As an experience of Jesus dead and risen again, the disciples and the narrators are totally at a loss in their attempt to portray something wholly other, without any measurable resonance; indeed, totally counter to what is normal human experience. Hence, when it comes to details of place, time, situations and protagonists, the telling is confusing, and in some cases contradictory.

When we look at the various Easter narratives, we find a total lack of sequence and logical rationality. In total confusion and without any literary connection to each other, the four evangelists range across a whole gamut of details, times and places, painting the diverse reactions of those who lived through the event. Time seems to be suspended and geographical references have no boundaries. Jesus seems to appear simultaneously in different places, one person or a multiplicity of characters seem to be the recipients of the same appearance according to different narratives. Taken on their whole, the Easter stories make no sense. And rightly so because the *Gospels are not about information but about transformation.* Information seeks the whys and hows of some vacuous and mysterious resuscitation of a body, where living energy is held in suspense to be revitalised by human intervention. Jesus' Resurrection, on the other hand, is a total and radical transformation, challenging and supplanting all that is non-life, and exploding into fullness of life where absolute and total death reigned supreme.

Easter is about life, tapping into life experience and demanding a personal life response from each individual in their diverse situations and in their understanding of life, where they are and as they are in the world. Resurrection is an experience transcending human categories of measurement and analysis, yet powerful enough to energise a radical and eternal transformation totally investing one's personal life and the lives of all those who claim discipleship. Resurrection belongs to the realm of faith, or it has no meaning. The one thing we know for sure about the Resurrection of Jesus is that we are not dealing with some miraculous unexplainable resuscitation of a dead body, but with a powerful encounter with self and one's God.

In this multiplicity of responses, a common thread runs through all the Resurrection stories, linking the diversity of personal experiences into the proclamation of the Easter 'Alleluia' as the individual and collective event of salvation. In every Easter narrative, there comes a moment where a shift, takes place and that is the saving moment of the whole event. This is the shift from unbelief to recognition of Jesus, from concern with self to concern with Jesus as the revelation of God's love, and from obsession with death to rejoicing at life. When the first witnesses cease to search for a dead body, and their obsession with death and grief turns into recognition of Jesus as the living and undying presence of God in their personal and collective lives, then Resurrection becomes real and saving for those who lived through the events.

The Resurrection narrative that brings together and at the same time contrasts Peter and John, following the bewildering message of the women who find the empty tomb (John 20:3-10), is a classic example of this duality of vision and shift of perspective. Frightened and confused, both disciples rush to the burial place. John, much younger, outruns his companion but, in deference to the older man, he stops and allows Peter to enter the tomb first. Here the Gospel writer makes a very significant observation. Peter looks into the tomb first and he sees the burial cloths, but no sign of the body of

Jesus. John, in turn, looks into the tomb and we are told that *'he saw and believed'* (John 20:8). Both men look at the same event under the same circumstances. Peter is searching for a dead body, just as the women were, or as Mary of Magdala was doing when she asked the gardener to tell her where they had hidden the body of Jesus (John 20:11-18). On the other hand, like John, the true disciple is searching for Jesus as the revelation of God, and in that search, their eyes are opened, and they experience Resurrection.

Likewise, on their escape from Jerusalem, the two disciples of Emmaus trudge along, their thoughts dark and their hearts so utterly closed within themselves that they become completely unaware of reality, except for their own problems and their seeking for self-pity (Luke 24:13-35). Trapped within their own selves, they do not notice the stranger who comes up and falls in step with them. All that matters, really, are their personal problems, their own sense of having been let down and betrayed, and this stranger must know that they are the victims of injustice and deceit. They just missed the point of it all, the living presence of God journeying with them. Focusing exclusively on themselves rather than the Unknown Stranger who walks with them, they are at pains to wallow in self-pity, and they tell him their sad and mournful story. By contrast, the stranger invites them to move away from their navel-gazing self-pity by tapping into the depth of their heart and engaging their personal and collective memory of God with his people.

Looking back on what God has done and inviting intimacy in the present, the breaking of bread becomes the spark that opens their eyes into the sudden explosion and recognition. Yes, *'the Lord, has risen indeed'* (Luke 24:34). Emmaus is not just an escape or a pretence, but a challenge to let go of our expectations and to make choices on how we see things and events, an invitation to look at the world with the eyes of God. Then we will discover life anew. Then we will be able to celebrate Resurrection.

Faith is seeing and believing, but to achieve faith, the disciples must be prepared to move on from seeing what one wants to see, into allowing oneself to see in spite of what one actually sees. Easter calls for a reversal of action and of perspectives. Fullness of life may demand that we stand peering inside an empty tomb, like Mary and the other disciples, often so overwhelmed as to focus entirely our search for a dead body, with little understanding, nothing to show for our efforts, and nothing to hold on to. Like for Mary (John 20:11-18) and the Emmaus disciples (Luke 24:13-35), we must stop focusing on the signs of death and accept that God, in Jesus, is standing there beside us, alive, calling us by our name, urging us to embrace the apparently human impossible as the place where God is waiting to abolish our death and give us life.

Easter is Here and Now

For God, there is only present, and the Christian story is never information about a past, challenging human rationality or relegated to dusty history books. The word of God is always about us, *here, now*. The experience of the disciples is not just an event of two thousand years ago, and our celebration is not merely a yearly ritual, no matter how heart-warming or emotionally charged it may be. It is not a matter of retelling that Jesus is alive and once again with his disciples, a palliative message we proclaim to ourselves to quieten the burning yearnings and restlessness of our hearts. For believers, the Word of God is always addressed to us and is about us, and the '*He has been raised; he is not here*' proclaiming life in spite of death is, at the same time, both our story and our commitment to be lived today and for all time where we are and as we are. Easter is a living and lived experience as real and as personal as sharing a meal of fish together, or encountering a stranger on the road, or strolling along the beach, as some of the Easter narratives tell us.

Our Easter rejoicing is not just a memory of Jesus who conquered death in Palestine two thousand years ago, but a proclamation to the whole of history that that conquest marks out our own destiny for all time. Having immersed himself totally into humanity to the very depths of ultimate death and despair, then our humanity becomes the place where God is and wants to be, even in death. Conversely, outside of this human-divine perspective, resurrection has no meaning and even death would have kept Jesus trapped in its clutches. The same is true *for us in our full humanity and nothing, absolutely nothing can separate us from the love and life of God made visible in Jesus Christ*, as St Paul reminds us (Romans 8:39).

However, so long as our God remains a dead body in an empty tomb, and we are not prepared to accept the reality that he is alive beyond the death and pain that often invade daily life and our flesh and blood, then all our festivities are empty make-beliefs, leaving us like the disciples in a place of darkness and fear. We are the ones called to confront seeming impossibilities of long ago and far away and respond to it with our lives here and now. That is the crux of the Christian story incarnated in the Resurrection of Jesus. Like the disciples seeking some sense in the darkness of daily life, we are the actors in and respondents to the Easter experience, embracing the paradox of a rich source of hope and soothing peace and of deep love, when and where everything in us and around us points to darkness and hopelessness. Mary despairs, Peter is struck silent, not knowing what to make of those abandoned burial cloths, John sees the same thing as the fisherman of Capernaum, but John sees through the appearances and believes. That is our Easter story too: seeing and accepting life through and *in spite of death within and all around us*.

Like for the first disciples, life for each of us can so easily turn into a scenario of loss of immeasurable consequence, of emptiness, and of hopelessness without rhyme or reason, testing faith to its very limits. Life will have harsh moments, our world will confront us with incomprehensible tragedies, our souls and bodies will grapple with darkness and scream pain, and our hearts will yearn for freedom and intimacy. But because the wounded Jesus left behind an empty tomb and walked back into the lives of those who were totally broken and desperate, then we can hope against all hope. Death and suffering are not the end of the story, and we can rejoice in the midst of sadness, and the darkness of our struggles will inevitably have a life-giving and love-enriched conclusion.

To celebrate Easter means to live on the edge of impossibility and call it the highway to complete reality and fulfilment. No matter what our individual and collective stories may be, to celebrate Easter means to have the courage to make our daily deaths turning points of encounter with our God, places where God is at work in spite of all appearances to the contrary, or what our disillusioned hearts may try to tell us. From now on, the only way for us to look at death and see life beyond death, is to gaze into an empty tomb, yearning not for a dead body, but embracing life in its fullness through that absent dead body. Faith in the resurrection is seeing through death, hearing through the silence deep in our hearts, rejoicing when the world weighs heavily on our shoulders. Faith in the Resurrection is acknowledging God's presence when loneliness seems to enshroud us on all sides and embracing and being embraced by our God precisely when physical, spiritual, emotional, and psychological death is all around us and dominates every dimension of our lives.

Having experienced Resurrection, now the disciple is called to let go of everything that is death dealing: fear, anxiety, hopelessness and guilt. On the contrary, joy, hope, trust and peace are the hallmarks of this season of transformation and new beginnings. Are we such people of transformation, of new beginnings, of renewed energy, and of fresh awareness? Or are we just celebrating another empty ritual reminding us only of the passing of time and the inexorable cycle of seasons? Are we perhaps gazing at an event of the past with no significance and even less bearing on our daily lives? Easter is not a time or a ritual. Easter is a commitment to accept God and to reveal God's presence whatever our human story may put before us.

Not only a harbinger of peace, joy and hope, Easter must become a stimulus that kindles the burning yearnings of our hearts for life and love, through the energy of our living and loving God – the God who in Jesus not even death could keep away from us.

A Verb of Transformation

Underlying all the Resurrection narratives is the assertion that, because of Easter, fear turns into courage, grief into joy, absence into presence, loss into hope, darkness into light, and distance becomes intimacy. As the original pre-Easter story tells us, life can easily turn into a scenario of loss of immeasurable consequence, of emptiness, and of hopelessness without rhyme or reason, testing faith to its very limits.

For all its power of transformation, the resurrection of Jesus is wrapped in silence, and we do not encounter any spectacular Old Testament theophany. Yet, as if by an irresistible compulsion and urgency to spread the news, the disciples, fired by excitement and wonder, proclaimed the message to each other through an impromptu communication network of word of mouth. The women frightened and bewildered, tell the disciples (Matthew 28:8; Luke 24:10), and Mary of Magdala does likewise after her incomprehensible meeting in the garden (John 20:18). Having recognised the Risen Lord at the breaking of bread, the Emmaus disciples immediately 'returned to Jerusalem' to make the unlikely proclamation, only to be told that their news was already second hand (Luke 24:33-35). Just as the original disciples could not hold to themselves the experience of their encounter with the Risen Lord, but had to scream it to the world, so our belief in the Resurrection commits us unconditionally to become ambassadors of the Good News in our world, or our faith is a futile looking into a hollow, dark and empty tomb.

In a world where death has become a tragic multi-dimensional daily occurrence of war, racism, terrorism, street violence, exploitation, abuse, abandonment and destitution, words like hope, peace and affirmation may sound hollow and almost offensive to victims. And yet, Easter screams to the world that in this very world, hope, peace and good will are possible in spite of everything else. Together with the message that he has gone ahead of them into Galilee where they will see him (Mark 16:7; Matthew 28:10), Jesus' first greeting to his distraught and broken disciples was, *'Peace be with you!'* (Luke 24:36), In Scripture, Galilee is 'the Galilee of the nations', a potpourri of cultures and traditions. But, because of this, Galilee is also the place of simplicity and ordinariness, where everyday life unfolds with all its unchallenged commonality and sometimes the tragic realism of struggle and suffering. That is the Galilee of our lives, and there is where we are called to live and accept the Easter proclamation and, in turn, become witnesses and proclaimers of the living and active presence of God beyond death.

Privacy is not of God or of faith, and Easter's call to transformation and new beginnings, of energy, and of renewed sense of presence has a double dimension. Easter is not a passive attitude but an active verb. Immersed in the joy and peace that comes from the realisation that not even death can keep God away from us, then the world must know the truth in us and through us. Confronting a tragedy and loss of life at sea on one Easter Sunday morning where five nuns on their way to the Americas lost their lives, Gerard Manly Hopkins reminded us, that Easter is *a verb of cosmic transformation into a totally new reality of hope, peace, and faith-filled joy, in spite of all appearances to the contrary.*

> Let him easter in us, be a dayspring to the dimness of us, be a crimson-cresseted east.[46]

Having been touched and called to review and renew our perceptions, our attitudes and our behaviour, transformation can only be authentic when these elements exude naturally from the

---

[46] Gerard Manley Hopkins, *The Wreck of the Deutschland.*

realm of self to become energy for new perceptions, attitudes and behaviour in others. We must be the instruments of Easter revelation because the Word of God makes us both recipients and actors in the story and commits us to be ambassadors of the presence of God and bearers of joy and peace in the real world of every day.

Every time evil and hurt are conquered by forgiveness and love, every time a simple gesture of friendship raises a smile in a brother or sister, every time we open our hands and reach out to that person in need of companionship and compassion, Easter becomes an active verb. Every time we have the courage to face life without losing heart and nurture a single moment of peace and serenity in someone else, death is supplanted by life. In all these times, Easter becomes real, we re-live it in ourselves and bring it about in our world.

Conclusion

Easter celebrates the *active presence of God* in our life; a presence revealed through healing, courage, hope, love, compassion, forgiveness but often forgotten, tucked away in the recesses of our *memory*, overgrown with concerns with our own agenda or with the pain that they may engender. These are the *glimpses of God*, the good wheat strewn along the path of life even when trapped by noxious weeds (Matthew 13:24-43). To believe in Resurrection demands that we bring these glimpses of memory to consciousness so as to become spurs and stimuli to *future hope* in spite of the pain of loss and dryness of a rocky desert. We need to change perspective and look at the good wheat sown there. For the person of faith *God is forever* the 'God of surprises' as Gerard W. Hughes would say,[47] *walking unknown with us in our struggles* and even denials and escapes, and eventually revealing himself unexpectedly when and where we least expect to find him.

---

[47] Gerard W. Hughes, *God of Surprises*, Darton, Longman and Todd, 1996.

We need to change perspective and look at our story from the point of view of life and not of death because death has been conquered and subdued by life in Jesus' Paschal Mystery of death and resurrection. Having revealed himself as the Living One in spite of death on all sides, Jesus calls his doubtful disciples and this confused and fragmented world into the ultimate awareness of life, screaming to the universe and for all time that not even death could keep him away from his disciples. Therefore we can face our future into eternity with courage and hope and have no fear of brokenness and personal darkness, because *not even death can ever keep God away from us. That is our destiny and an infallible source of peace and joy, come what may.* That is Easter for all and for eternity.

Resurrection: A Journey into Self-Discovery (Emmaus)

Luke 24:13-35

Emmaus: The Paradigm of a Journey

JOURNEYS ARE EXPERIENCES that touch us deeply, much more intensely and radically than we realise. Journeys bring us in touch with people or take us away from each other; they create intimacy or distance; motivated by life or by death, they are a source of joy or sorrow. We undertake a journey fired by enthusiasm born of a dream of what the new destination may hold, or we may carry with us a nightmarish burden of anxiety, fear, pain and suffering. Sometimes we journey alone, seeking companionship and sometime the journey thrusts us into sharing the time and energy of compassion with a stranger. We journey in hope and joy, and we journey in loneliness and insecurity. Most of all, we journey in faith, faith that our expectations will be realised, our pain healed; faith that our strivings will bear fruit and that our brokenness will not overwhelm us. Journeys embody the full gamut of emotions and experiences that shape life, and it is only in that fullness of life with all its diverse attributes that our journey will lead us to God.

Journeying is one of the primordial images of the relationship between God and humanity. From the call of Abraham to the restoration after the Babylonian exile, the Old Testament could well be described as the saga of a God who journeys with a chosen people; indeed, in spite of the betrayal by this people and through the darkest hours of their millennial story. As for the Christian tradition, journey is the hallmark of Luke's Gospel. Beginning with Mary and Joseph trudging their way from Nazareth to Bethlehem, the story reaches its climax with two unnamed disciples trudging their steps away from Jerusalem and onto Emmaus. In between these two bookends, we have Jesus, his eyes set on Jerusalem (Luke 9:53), always on the move towards the place of fulfilment, and calling people to journey with him.v

However, the Word of God is not about retelling some distant incidents of relative significance to the present. On the contrary, the Word of God is addressed to us and about us, and the millennial image as well as Jesus' own life journey in Luke is a mirror into which the disciple is called to reflect themselves and there find their paradigm of discipleship. The Christian journey implies faith in a God journeying with us, and the post-Resurrection story of the two disciples returning to Emmaus encapsulates the most powerful statement of transformation and discovery that takes hold of us when we are prepared to accept the active and living presence of God along the journey of life. Thus Emmaus becomes the paradigm of the disciple's journey of faith.

In a remarkable piece of writing titled *Tuesdays with Morrie*, Mitch Albon tells the story of a radical and challenging journey: the last few months of the life journey of Morrie Schwartz, the psychology professor, now struck down with ALS, the brutal and unforgiving Lou Gehrig's neurological disease for which there is no known cure. Mitch Albon, the successful journalist from the *Chicago Tribune*, has long since lost contact with his old Harvard psychology professor having dropped out of his class many years before. A chance recognition while scanning through television programs, not only brought back old memories, but it become the catalyst of a remarkable story of complete transformation for Mitch himself.

On discovering that Morrie was now a television ambassador in an information campaign on the disease, Mitch decides to call on Morrie. Deeply fascinated by the unbelievable attitude to life of the dying professor, that first call becomes a weekly journey from Chicago to Boston, precisely every Tuesday, to spend time with Morrie, but mostly to be energised by the conversations with this dying friend. In a series of challenging discussions, Morrie confronts the fundamental issues of life in such a way that Mitch himself cannot escape facing his own life questions and his own search for meaning.[48] In a moment of deep personal reflection during his return flight, Mitch comments:

> Now the truth is that I was losing Morrie, we were all losing Morrie – his family, his friends, his ex-students, his pals from the political discussion groups that he loved so much, his former dance partners, all of us... But it was also becoming clear to me – through his courage, his humour, his patience, and his openness – that Morrie was looking at life from some very different place than anyone else I knew. A healthier place. A more sensible place. *And he was about to die.*[49]

There lies the key. It is all a matter of perspective, a 'looking at life from a very different place': from the perspective of life or from the perspective of death. Mitch can only see the impending death, and all he can experience is the sense of utter loss, while Morrie, the dying one, challenges him to look at reality from the stance of life, in spite of impending death. With remarkable similarities to the Christian understanding of life and death, a little later in the conversation, Morrie will say with conviction,

> If you love a person, then that person will never be dead to you ... Love is how you stay alive.[50]

---

[48] Mitch Albom, *Tuesdays with Morrie*, Hodder Books, 1997.
[49] Ibid. 63 – (*Italics* are mine).
[50] Ibid. 133-134.

Resurrection: A Journey into Self-Discovery (Emmaus)

As I read Morrie's story almost with compulsion, I felt irresistibly driven into another story of long ago, the powerful Resurrection story that Luke locates along the road between Jerusalem and Emmaus (Luke 24:13-35), a story of a life journey through death and beyond death.

Jerusalem is the place of fulfilment of the ancient promises, the place where God is, and to which Jesus was driven (Matthew 20:18; Luke 9:53), where his whole life and mission unfolded, and where salvation was to explode in all its revolutionary power. However, this place which Francis J. Moloney calls 'the fulcrum of God's saving history' is also the place of the unexpected, of betrayal, of deceit, and of death.[51] Jerusalem is the place of the two absolute dualities where the disciple is forever caught in the dilemma between these two perspectives: life or death. In turn, the dilemma gives rise to two poles: self-styled expectations and securities on the one hand, or abandonment to the unexpected and the unwanted of God, on the other.

Escape and Pretence

It is difficult to imagine the atmosphere in the Upper Room on that very special Sabbath Day, the annual celebration of freedom and hope, recalling the divine intervention of God centuries earlier in setting Israel free from slavery at the hands of all powerful Egypt. But the mood on that holiest of days is anything but celebratory. For whatever reason, and not necessarily for the most praiseworthy one, that band of ignorant and simple people had left behind the security of their home and trade to follow this young preacher from Galilee who seemed to promise so much. Ironically, with all their expectations and personal agenda, in the end they failed to recognise

---

[51] Francis J. Moloney, *The Living Voice of the Gospel*, Mulgrave Vic: John Garratt Publishing, 2006), 192.

who Jesus was, even when he was standing right beside them. '*We had hoped that he was the one to redeem Israel*' (Luke 24:21).

But now, the stark reality hit home. They had seen him condemned, mistreated, crucified, dead and hastily buried in a borrowed grave. The deceit was now complete, and the danger to one's personal safety was raw. The fact that some women, no doubt victims of mass hysteria brought on by traumatic emotional stress, should announce that they '*had seen a vision of angels who said that he was alive*' (Luke 24:23) only added to the mockery and the pain of the open wound. Suddenly, those people gathered in that Upper Room had had enough of Jerusalem, of its unfulfilled promises, and of all the events that had taken place there, culminating in death by crucifixion.

The only escape from this mind-shattering nightmare was precisely that: escape – escape from the scene, escape from the people, and escape from the very memory of it all. If the whole of Jesus' life journey was towards Jerusalem as the place of fulfilment, two of his disciples now decide that the only sane and rational thing to do was to move away from Jerusalem and pretend that nothing of this ever happened to them by finding refuge in the tried and true of their previous life. In the words of Francis J. Moloney, leaving fearful and anxious, their hearts burning with anger, anguish, and disbelief

> They are leaving the place of God's presence in their midst and moving away from the pivot of God's salvation history.[52]

and with Michael Winstanley, we must agree that 'perhaps this terrain is not unfamiliar to us in our own life's journey.

> We can readily sense the tragedy, the poignancy of their situation, the pained expectant waiting... We detect the tone of anguish, bitterness and near despair, and glimpse that

---

[52] Francis J. Moloney, *This is the Gospel of the Lord – Year A*, Homebush, NSW: St Paul Publications, 1992, 115.

empty void which is their future. Perhaps this terrain is not unfamiliar to us in our own life's journey.[53]

This is the anguish, meaninglessness and uncertainty that gets hold of us when we are confronted with pain, unavoidable but not of our own making or choice. This is the anger and pointlessness that comes rushing into our hearts and minds when our best-laid plans come to nothing, and our commitment to discipleship appears at a dead end. This is the hopelessness that often results from a self-styled discipleship, where the focus of our life is entirely on our own private salvation, rather than on God calling us into a personal relationship.

They trudge along, their thoughts dark and their hearts so utterly closed within themselves that they become completely unaware of reality, except for their own problems and their pining for self-pity. Trapped within their own selves, they do not notice the stranger who comes up and falls in step with them. Where did he come from? Who is he? Who cares, anyway? All that matters are their personal problems, their own sense of having been let down and betrayed, and this stranger must be made aware that they are the victims of injustice and deceit. Like Martha in another incident in Luke's Gospel (Luke 10:38-42), they so focused on themselves that they missed the point of it all, the living presence of God journeying with them. Focusing exclusively on themselves rather than the Unknown Stranger who walks with them, they are at pains to wallow in self-pity, and they tell him their sad and mournful story.

> They have their own ideas... They have made up their own mind about who Jesus is and what he should have done for the nation.[54]

---

[53] Michael T. Winstanley, *Come and See*, London, Darton, Longman and Todd, 1985, 112.
[54] Francis J. Moloney, This is the Gospel of the Lord – Year A, 114.

One of the most common and most frightening human experiences is the experience of loss: loss of friends, loss of opportunities, loss of livelihood, loss of time, loss of health, loss of purpose. However, each loss, painful and frightening though it be, also holds the key to a future direction. If we are to grow into wholeness, we must let go of certain elements that have been an important part of our life and make choices in favour of something else. In turn, each choice ushers in further losses and painful letting go of a reality that, until then we held absolutely vital to our well-being. To reach our destination at the end of the road, we have to leave behind much more than physical distance, and we must experience separation from items and situations that are crucial and significant to us. We must be aware and remain open to otherness and trust in others, or we will never make any process along the road of becoming who we are meant to be in life.

Faith is seeing and believing, but to achieve faith, the disciples must be prepared to move on from seeing what we want to see, into allowing ourselves to see, in spite of what we actually see. Emmaus is not an escape or a pretence, but a challenges to let go of our expectations and to make choices about how we see things and events by looking at the world with the eyes of God. Then, we will discover life anew. Then we will be able to celebrate Resurrection.

A Matter of Perspective

In our original story of 'Tuesdays with Morrie', during one of his musings, Morrie remarks to Mitch,

> The culture doesn't encourage you to think about such things – (life and death) – until you are about to die. We are so wrapped up with egotistical things... we are involved in trillions of little acts just to keep going. So we don't get into the habit of standing back and looking at our lives and saying, Is this all? Is this all I want? Is something missing? ... You

need someone to probe you into that direction. It won't just happen automatically.[55]

This is precisely the strategy of the Stranger on the road to Emmaus. By inviting the two disciples to confront themselves with their own expectations and presuppositions, they are summoned into a shift of perspective *from a concern with self and self-pity to focusing on the living Jesus, the saving Word of God walking our roads and sharing our table fellowship.* Questions then rush into our minds, many and persistent, and we cannot ignore them; those same questions that Jesus addressed to the curious disciples at the very beginning of John's narrative. 'What are you looking for?... Who are you looking for?' (John 1:35-37). A God lost in speculation, in dead legal and/or theological debate, or some self-satisfying or fear-ridden personal spirituality? Is our God someone hidden in a ritual that has become routine, but makes us feel good, because we are convinced that in this way God is pleased with us? A 'nice' Jesus that satisfies our hang-ups demanding a spiritual crutch to lean on as for our personal and agenda?

Where are we looking for this God revealed by Jesus, and where do we expect to find him? To what extent am I prepared to accept that my God walks along dusty roads and shares my dark thoughts, unbeknown to me and yet present in spite of me?' These are fundamental questions of faith, and unless we are prepared to abandon our own expectations of God and move away from our own personal concerns, then we will never experience resurrection from our pain, our brokenness, and our death. Then our claim to discipleship will be vain.

> We too, at times, are emptied of hope, wanting only a God who is fashioned to our own sketchy design, wishing to remain snuggled up on our cosy cocoon, pining for what is familiar and tried and comfortable, afraid of losing our security, or bogged down in the rut of routine or the heavy sands of

---

[55] Mitch Albon, *Tuesday with Morrie*, 65.

our problems, or blinded by our self-centredness, deafened by the strident sounds inside and around us. And, like the Emmaus couple, we are closed to the divine stranger, and he goes unrecognised.[56]

Memories along the Road

The encounter with Jesus does not take place in some spectacular theophany that would assuage the ego of those who thirst for extraordinary phenomena. Jesus is not the charlatan of the sideshows, because very early in his struggle to come to terms with his own identity and his mission, he had already refused the temptation of throwing himself down from the pinnacle of the temple to convince people of his divine mission (Luke 4:9-11). The encounter with Jesus happens at the point of intersection of two stories: our personal life story, and the God story as lived and revealed in Jesus of Nazareth.

> He walks with them along the twisting, dusty road. As they seize on his ignorance and eagerly tell it all over again, Jesus listens to their story and their angst, listens with compassion and understanding, lives with them their questioning bewilderment. He is content to wait, not rushing with blinding, instant solutions, just prompting them with a question or two to enable them to bear out their problem, to explain their grief; he does not force the pace. He walks their way with them, stopping and starting with their halting rhythm. It is such listening, waiting and empathy which frees them to be open and which creates space, eventually permitting a ray of light to probe and penetrate the gloom.[57]

When we are prepared to abandon our inward-looking monologue of self-pity and self-condemnation and begin instead to listen with the heart to the Word of God, then we encounter God in the Word.

---

[56] Michael T. Winstanley, *Come and See*, 113.
[57] Ibid., 112-113.

When Jesus becomes the Risen and Living Word of God enabling us to discover God's living and undying presence – the Shekinah of God – within the most secret recesses of our psyche, as well as through the most banal events of our daily routine, then we will experience Resurrection.

Jesus is the stranger who walks along on dusty roads and speaks words of reassurance and revelation precisely on those dusty and unexpected places.

> The risen Jesus is to be found walking by our side too, walking our way with us; he is the faithful companion, meeting us on our ground, on our terms, in the messy midst of our reality, present in our groping and our shadows. Frequently, his strengthening and liberating presence is mediated by others who, through their own suffering journeying, have learned how to 'be with', have learned the meaning of compassion.[58]

The encounter along the road to Emmaus, then, becomes a reminder of that primal relationship burning within the heart of God and struggling to spark up in the heart of those who dare claim fellowship in discipleship, and yet struggle with coming to terms with a reality that seems to overwhelm them. As they journey, leaden-footed, away from the place of salvation and Shekinah, the two disciples of Emmaus share the depth of their distress and disappointment and in so doing they call into play another powerful and foundational element of faith and discipleship: memory.

It is precisely through this call to remember that their eyes are eventually opened to the authentic message of Scriptures about the reality of God and the true meaning of what has just happened to them. It is through this revelation that they come to understand that the cross is not the ultimate tragedy that they had come to believe, but the necessary and ultimate instrument of salvation.

Memory, like journey, is one of the hallmarks of the biblical tradition. Memory of what Yahweh had done through the ages

---

[58] Ibid., 113.

informs the whole socio-cultural context of Jewish life and faith, as Jesus would have known it. Exodus was much more than just an event of long ago, spectacular and unimaginable though it may have been. The memory of that event became the focus of the whole of Jewish life, from sowing crops to worshipping in the temple. The faithful Jew would repeatedly pray, '*Shema Israel*, remember Israel' who you were and what God has done to you, through you, and in spite of you. It is precisely this need to remember that the Stranger taps into, recalling a story of a God faithful at all times, even and especially in the face of death, loss, and abandonment. As the Stranger's words unfold, the gloominess of their thoughts begin to dissipate, and the closeness of their heart begins to open up to new perspectives and new possibilities.

> As so often happens in situations of grief and bereavement, they recall what has taken place, retrace familiar contours, in an attempt to keep a person or a situation alive, clinging in tight gripped desperation to a past which had meaning and brought joy and love.[59]

If we are to encounter the Risen Lord as the living Presence of God in our life and not just look for a dead body in empty tomb, we must engage memory, and thus recall what God has done for us along our personal journey.

Eyes Wide Open

Through the words of the Stranger, the disciples come to recognise the ancient story not as a saga of long ago, but as their personal story, calling them to look beyond and through their own petty concerns and to see reality with the eyes of an ever-faithful God. Yahweh has never abandoned them in the past, and hence he will most surely not abandon them in the future, though their present is all anguish and

---

[59] Ibid., 112.

confusion, and they have no idea of what this future may hold. The Stranger is at pains to show the distraught and distrustful disciples, grieving over the loss of a good friend as well as the collapse of their expectations for the future, that nothing has gone wrong. Like the ancient stories about Moses and Exodus, these Jerusalem events are also experiences of death and resurrection, of life against all human possibilities, and seemingly against all human hope. Resurrection is an experience of life in spite of evil, mistakes, sufferings and deaths and our obsession with the signs of death in the end only inhibits any experience of life and resurrection.

As Saint Benedict would comment, suddenly the ears and eyes of their heart are opened. Now their hearts are burning within them, but no longer with anger. They are burning with newfound and unexpected meaning and joy. By looking back on their past, they are now able to see forward with optimism and hope. Such is the power of memory, to reveal the unseen of our past and to beckon us, with hope and courage, into the unknown of our future.

The experience of the stranger walking with them (*compassion*), the Word spoken and perceived as the Word of a God with us (*presence*), the memory and the re-enactment of what the Lord has done for them (*remembrance*), all these combine together to bring about a radical change, a conversion of heart and mind that invests the totality of the disciples' lives at the deepest level. Fear turns into courage, grief into joy, absence into presence, loss into hope, darkness into light, and distance becomes intimacy.

It all seems so utterly senseless and impossible, and they want to hold on to it all. Their hearts burning with desire to move from the distance of the Stranger to the intimacy of table fellowship, they invite him into their lives, to share the sacredness of their table and the intimacy of their home, to become part of their lives. That is the turning point of the story of Emmaus. That is also the turning point of our discipleship journey, the radical change from self to God as the focus of our lives.

As long as the disciples were concerned exclusively with their own problems and grief and disappointment, there was no possibility of their recognising the Lord; their horizons were shrouded in thick cloud. But when once they began to look outwards, to see the stranger's needs for food and rest, to think of him, to open their hearts to the other, then the clouds began to lift, and the sun filtered through.[60]

It is at this moment of intimacy that the Stranger, taking the initiative, breaks bread and shares drink in a gesture that was all too familiar to those people. Suddenly, that gesture – so familiar in the context of the bodily presence of the Master – takes on a totally new and unexpected meaning. *Enlightened by the Word, and strengthened by the companionship, the disciples see well beyond the ritual into total recognition of the living presence of God in their lives.* That casual encounter with the unknown, that painful retelling of their own deaths and brokenness, and that disclosure brought on by the Word uttered and listened to, all these have now reached the ultimate climax and fulfilment in the breaking of the bread. Now the Lord is truly part of the disciple's life beyond death and in spite of death.

Eucharist: Encounter, Revelation and Mission

The two disciples returning to Emmaus recognised Jesus at the breaking of bread. That is where it all happens: an encounter with the Lord alive in spite of death and beyond death, and an encounter with each other as a community gathered at Eucharist. Most Resurrection stories have one element in common, the Eucharistic community. *'Thomas was not with them, when Jesus came'*, but eventually he too experienced Resurrection in that Upper Room when they were all there together (John 20:24-29). Returning disheartened and despondent from a fruitless night fishing on the lake, but actually they too were just escaping memory and

---
[60] Ibid, 115-116.

Resurrection: A Journey into Self-Discovery (Emmaus)

pain of loss, the disciples meet a Stranger on the shore of the lake offering them breakfast, and in that improvised and unexpected table fellowship they encounter the Lord whom they grieve for as dead (John 21:1-19).

In Scripture, table fellowship speaks of eternity, of intimacy and of oneness. That is the message of the journey to Emmaus. Wherever our life journey may take us, God is with us in the totality of our being forever, oneness realised in the Resurrection of Jesus and expressed through Eucharist. Eucharist is precisely this sense of undying presence and total involvement of the Risen Lord in each banal and insignificant moment of the disciples' lives, an involvement and an intimacy brought on by our God journeying with us and sitting with us through it all.

> How often do we find that the demands of the Lord are too much for us? We too walk away from our Jerusalem, where the action of God can be difficult to cope with, especially as it sometimes runs contrary to our hopes. Reading the story of the breaking of the bread at Emmaus we are strengthened in our faltering faith. Jesus sets out to walk with his wandering disciples of all times. He instructs, and he breaks bread with us... and in this way he leads us home.[61]

Because of Easter, these words of memory, hope and consolation need to resonate again in our liturgy and in our life. Christ is present and reveals himself totally in the breaking of the bread. Only then, the disciples come to know the presence of the Lord and feel this presence pulsating through their lives, their hearts burning with an unexpected and vibrant knowing the Lord. This burning is uncontainable, an energy transforming radically the individual and setting the whole world afire. The discovery of a God-with-us beyond death and in spite of death becomes energy for mission, and others must know, or the news is not Good News at all. Eucharist is the ultimate sign of God's eternal presence in our individual and

---

[61] Francis J. Moloney, *This is the Gospel of the Lord* – Year A, 115.

collective life, but it must also become the energy that spurs us to spread the Good News that not even death can keep God away from us. And so the disciples race back to Jerusalem, the place they have turned their backs to in anger and disillusionment, the place of salvation through death, to tell the others, only to have their thunder stolen as they, in turn, are told that *'the Lord has risen indeed, and he has appeared to Simon!'* (Luke 24:34).

Witnessing is inescapable and foundational for the disciple. Having witnessed the living Presence of God in their own lives, the disciple in turn becomes a bearer of Good News to the world, while remaining open in faith and to the faith experience of others. The disciple lives and dies in a web of relationships and in a dynamics of give and take, energised by one ultimate truth, God is with us, walks with us and listens to us. *No matter what life affords, for the person of faith, God challenges us to remember, prods us to go beyond self-preoccupation into an entirely new way of seeing presence, because, in Jesus, not even death could keep God away from us.*

Conclusion

All our life-stories, both individual and collective, are dotted with incidents that reveal the active presence of God in our life. Often, however, such experiences remain forgotten, tucked away in the recesses of our memory, overgrown with concerns with our own agenda or with the pain that they may engender. At the same time, when looked at from a different perspective or revived in hindsight, for the person of faith these are glimpses of God walking by our side and revealing his presence in spite of brokenness or even death. Friendship, healing, courage, hope, love, compassion, forgiveness – these are but a few of the glimpses of God with us in spite of any opposite manifestation. Bringing these glimpses to consciousness must spur us on to future hope in spite of the pain of loss and darkness of tomb within us and all around us.

We need to change perspective and look at our story from the point of view of life and not of death because death has been conquered and subdued by life in Jesus' Paschal Mystery of death and resurrection. Having revealed himself as the Living One in spite of death on all sides, Jesus calls his doubtful disciples and this confused and fragmented world into the ultimate awareness of life, screaming to the universe and for all time that not even death could keep Jesus away from his disciples. Therefore we can face our future into eternity with courage and hope and have no fear of brokenness and personal darkness, because *not even death can ever keep God away from us. That is our destiny and an infallible source of peace and joy, come what may.*

Finally, having revealed himself as the Living One in spite of death on all sides, Jesus calls his doubtful and confused disciples into the *complete intimacy of table fellowship*. The *destiny* of the disciple is to enter into *a personal relationship of love and intimacy with one's God*, and nothing will frustrate this primordial dream of God.

That is why he is there, hidden but ever-present to each and every one, irrespective of who they are or what they have done. As Pope Francis pointed out in one of his Easter addresses,

> The word 'truly' in the Easter proclamation underscores that the Lord's resurrection is a reality, not just wishful thinking. And this means that humanity's journey has a sure footing in hope and therefore can move forward with confidence in facing the many challenges now and ahead. May we allow ourselves to experience amazement at the joyful proclamation of Easter, at the light that illumines the darkness and the gloom in which, all too often, our world finds itself enveloped.[62]

No matter what life may have in store for us, God wants to share fully every experience in a relationship so intimate and so eternal

---

[62] https://cathnews.com/2023/04/11/christ-is-truly-risen-giving-humanity-a-sure-footing-in... – (accessed 15/04/23)

that *not even death can break or nullify*. The God who lived fully and tragically our life experience to the ultimate extent of death, is the very God who will not allow us to be swallowed up in death and darkness ever again. *If not even death could keep Jesus away from his disciples, absolutely nothing will ever keep God away from us.*

Peace: the Gift of a Wounded and Risen Christ (Thomas)

John 20:19-29

SOME OF THE MOST POWERFUL ENERGIES and life-giving experiences can never be adequately expressed. They are so personal, so deep and all transforming that we simply lack the language to articulate them fully. Thus, we try to convey the experience of love through its manifestations of personal feelings, without ever conveying exactly what love is or fathoming its full depth. We speak of love in terms of time, place, feelings or processes, but, in the end, these often camouflage or even destroy love itself as the life-experience of a person with others. It is impossible to say what love is, without speaking of what love does, and in the end, we only see what love does and not necessarily what love really is. We need to experience love to understand love!

'Rationality' versus 'Experience'

The Christian understanding of Resurrection belongs precisely to this category of inexpressible energies and experiences. The disciples experienced the active living presence of Jesus after his death as a personal, communal and historical event that transformed not only the person of the Jesus they knew but changed radically and forever their own lives and history, their self-image and relationships, and their understanding of life and death. Such was the power of the experience that any attempt at finding rational answers to questions of what, how, where and when, created only further confusion.

That is why the Easter narratives just do not make sense – not logical sense, that is. If we seek common details or accurate information of place, time or even geography, the various accounts of Resurrection share many contradictions but offer few similarities or logical sequence. One moment Jesus is a gardener, next he is a casual stranger along a dusty and empty road. One version has Jesus revealing himself only to one or two people looking for a dead body inside an empty tomb, while at the same time he is bursting through locked doors to speak of peace and consolation to a group of distraught and terrified disciples. One minute he asks for a piece of bread in a room in Jerusalem; next, as if by some sort of transporter, both Jesus and his disciples are some one hundred kilometres further north, on the shore of the lake of Genezareth. There, the Unknown One is taking a leisurely morning stroll and chatting to some fishermen, tired and frustrated by a fruitless night on the water with nothing to show for their struggles.

Because of its lack of scientific and rational explanation, the natural tendency of scepticism and uncertainty nourished by our controlled and technological age would be to feel justified in rejecting the whole concept of resurrection as insulting to human rationality. However, resurrection is not about pure logical rationality or scientific proof alone, but about faith, challenging precisely a purely rational approach to life. I feel fully alive when I experience love, given and received, and no random conglomerate of physical, chemical or emotional energy will ever be able to create, deny or manipulate the experience that makes me alive, loved and loving. It all depends on one's understanding and on one's experience and mindset about life and love.

In the Christian understanding of reality, life is always *'more'*, *'further'* and *'much greater'* than its purely physical measurable expression, and Christianity takes up the challenge of this 'more' and 'beyond' precisely through the foundational event of the

Resurrection of Jesus. Resurrection is the fundamental truth of faith in life in its totality, embracing the human and the divine, the finite and the infinite, the here and now as well as the beyond and the eternal. Resurrection is not a rational explanation of some sort of resuscitation or re-incarnation. If we are to understand *Resurrection, we have to look beyond physical and scientific proof or accuracy of information. We have to speak the language of faith and the ultimate incomprehensibility of God in our human story.*

Resurrection as Encounter

When we look at the resurrection narratives, we cannot but notice the contradictory nature of the sensory evidence. The Risen Lord seems to be everywhere and nowhere at the same time, defying time, space and distances as far apart as Galilee and Jerusalem at once. He is breaking through locked doors or playing the unknown stranger, falling in step along the road or taking a stroll along the Sea of Galilee in the early morning and, against all fishing sense, telling professional and seasoned fishermen where the fish are biting.

One such fascinating post-Easter Gospel narrative story opens with Jesus' greeting his distraught and confused disciples by offering them the gift of peace (John 20:19-24), a deep peace of the heart that can only be authentic and healing if received and accepted as a gratuitous gift, from the very one they have betrayed and abandoned as dead. However, one of the Twelve,

> *Thomas was not with them when Jesus came. So the other disciples told him, 'We have seen the Lord' But he said to them, 'Unless I see the mark of the nails in his hands and put my finger in the mark of the nails and my hand in his side, I will not believe.'* (John 20:24-25)

As far as Thomas is concerned, Jesus is dead and buried, his world has collapsed, and he feels cheated in his faith and trust in the preacher from Nazareth. Like most of the other disciples, he has lost both faith and trust in Jesus, and while the others seek relief in leaving the place of their experience of Jesus and returning to the tried and true of their pre-call life, Thomas will only be at peace when *Thomas* has conquered his inner turmoil of anger, disappointment and victimhood by his own efforts and through physical confrontation with the pre-Easter Jesus. He is the ultimate paradigm of rationality, and for him Jesus is no longer one of us but the separate one, outside the realm of his own relationship. Thomas is heatedly and frustratingly seeking peace and healing not as a gift but as his own doing, a personal reassurance to ease the gnawing of his heart and quieten his mind. The very reassurance of his friends becomes a challenge to his faith that he cannot accept, cutting even more deeply into his pain and mistrust.

The one thing we know for sure about the Resurrection of Jesus is that it proved to be a radical encounter, transcending human categories of measurement and analysis, but powerful enough to transform people in a manner and at such a personal depth that, humanly speaking, there is no logical process or explanation. Precisely because such transformation belongs to the realm of deep personal experience of life, of love, and of faith, it transcends human measurement and data analysis. Like Thomas and the other disciples, we are so preoccupied with death and with looking for the signs of death that we fail to accept and to see the presence of the living God in our midst.

In a rather bizarre travesty of the Easter event, someone tried to point out that, unfortunately, Jesus missed the moment by some two thousand years. Had he chosen to come back from the dead in our electronically enslaved age, with its ubiquitous and all-seeing eyes and powerful paraphernalia, every instant of whatever happened inside and outside that tomb would have been recorded, exactly, and in real time, and then people would have believed in him. The presumption being that had Resurrection been subjected to our electronically enslaved age, with ubiquitous all-seeing eyes and powerful ultrasound, it would have been easy to believe in

Resurrection. Unfortunately, when it comes to Resurrection, all the electronic gimmickry in the world would have recorded nothing but emptiness, full of deadly silence, as Mary of Magdala found while desperately looking for a dead body in an empty tomb. There is only one possible answer to this fantasy-driven scenario; absolute emptiness, full of deadly silence, just as if Thomas-like 'we had not been there when he came back' to life from the darkness of the tomb.

Thomas 'the Twin' is seeking scientific and logical reassurance for the claim that the Lord has truly risen by demanding sensory evidence through touch, sight and sound. However, the real evidence came through a personal encounter and not through feeling and touching. The Jesus that stands before the disciples is the resurrected Jesus, alive and active in spite of going through death and lying in the tomb for three days, and by appealing to the evidence of some technological science fiction wizardry, often we speak of resurrection when all the time we look for a resuscitation, whereby a body in which all the vital functions appear to have ceased, regains the exact features and the self-same energies that it had before. Resurrection is not resuscitation. Christian resurrection implies *total, radical and universal transformation; an all-transforming experience that touches the lives of those who live through it so powerfully and so personally that their own weak and broken lives now exudes life out of death, giving in turn life to those trapped in the slavery and finality of death.*

A Call to Faith

Popular Christian tradition has not always been kind to Thomas, called the Twin, the one 'who was not with them when Jesus came" (John 20:24-25), so much so that the very name *'Doubting Thomas'* became the epitome of doubting unbelief. On reflection, however, we can all identify with Thomas, and maybe feel that, humanly speaking, such a reputation is not wholly justified, particularly when it applies to the realm of faith. *Christian belief means to stand constantly on the line of demarcation between doubt and faith, emptiness and fullness, insecurity and certitude, and ultimately positioning oneself between life and death.*

Although a fundamentalist perception would abhor the idea of doubt and insecurity in matters of faith, doubt can be healthy when it implies a search for truth or a personal journey for understanding. Indeed, doubt is necessary if we are to remain open to the self-revelation of God and of faith on God's terms. Unfortunately, it is precisely in this latter dimension of openness to the unconditional certainty of God that Thomas misses the point. With that double conditional *'unless I'*, Thomas makes it clear that he has nothing to do with searching and everything with rejecting, even the possibility that Jesus is alive.

Would we have reacted any differently under the circumstances? In the face of the tragedy that has unfolded, Thomas is as distraught and as broken as the other disciples cowering in the upper room, but he is the down-to-earth man of the land, of practical and immediate simplicity. Death is death and it is final, and any speculation about its absolute finality is precisely that – idle speculation that only an impossible physical experience of sensory seeing and touching can disprove.

Thomas was probably too busy focusing on his own personal misfortunes, grief and self-pity to be there when the Lord came. He was about his own death and not about the presence of Jesus alive. In this perspective, it makes good sense to seek scientific and logical reassurance, as Thomas demanded by calling upon sensory proof like touching and feeling, seeing and hearing, as evidence to justify our claim.

Christian Resurrection is an experience of presence perceived and accepted by faith, before and in spite of any sensory evidence to the contrary. Easter does not celebrate the resuscitation of a dead body, but the cosmic and revolutionary transformation that takes place when one accepts the presence of our living God through and in spite of having to grapple with ultimate evil and death itself. But such an acceptance is not easy, because the news is too good to be true. It demands that we put on hold the very finality of death in favour of a radical new perception of life, not only beyond death but also in spite of death. It requires that we convert from a culture of doubt and fear into one of hope and inner peace in spite of everything and anything. It enjoins on us that we suspend judgment on human frailty and hopelessness, because not death but fullness of life has the final say in our human-divine destiny.

Significantly, when confronted by Jesus who calls him by name and challenges him to satisfy his sensory curiosity and touch the wounds made by the nails, Thomas does not follow up on his doubting words, because there is no longer need of that anymore. Instead, he burst out in that cry of absolute joy fired by total abandonment in faith: *'My Lord, and my God!'* (John 20:28). Thomas' journey of faith from resuscitation to resurrection is now complete beyond personal expectations or conditions. The physical proofs are irrelevant now, because he has seen and accepted the Lord who has gone through death and is alive and invites him into his life. He has encountered and experienced resurrection, life in spite of death. Until then, Thomas was responding to his own agenda, holding on to a Saviour of his own making. Now, in that letting go of his own expectations, he moved into that faith that recognises the living presence of the Risen Lord beyond death and in his own life.

Resurrection is an experience of life in spite of evil, mistakes, suffering and death; and our obsession with the signs of death in the end inhibits any experience of life and resurrection. Resurrection is an invitation to allow the power of God to transform us into fullness of life and peace when all around us is destruction and death.

Peace – The Gift of Resurrection

After his resurrection, Jesus' first greeting was to offer his gift of peace to people whose hearts were entrapped by fear, mistrust and unbelief. That offer and recognition in the midst of death and turmoil becomes the catalyst for an explosion of trust, hope and uncontained joy; and of life in spite of death.

Do we dare to utter the word peace? Do we still believe in peace? The tragedy of 11 September 2001 will remain a turning point in world history, etched forever in the world's memory, a marker event that unleashed in this world as much as in our individual psyche an all-pervading and all-consuming culture of fear, mistrust and revenge. Most of all, 11 September 2001 has installed a distorted quest for peace no longer built on what binds humanity together but justified and stimulated by what separates us. In an all-out attempt at finding peace, we engage in an all-out never-ending war with each other, as nations, cultures or individuals. When we believe that peace has been violated on our side, then we canonise death as the ultimate and inevitable solution of life, and feel justified in challenging and destroying peace and bring death on the other side. In a frantic search for peace, we make war. In trying to build a world of unity and justice, we uphold what keeps us apart, we canonise differences, and we operate on an ethics of death–us against them. All the time, the world is ablaze, and the victims pile up by thousands every day in a twisted and paradoxical search for peace.

However, in spite of this tragic, misguided, frantic and frustrating search, the desire for peace is and will always be one of the deepest yearnings of the human heart – a yearning powerfully illustrated by the Word of God, where the term 'Peace' (Shalom) takes on a sacramental connotation as the active living presence of God with humanity. Peace is Yahweh's gift to his people and the sure sign of Emmanuel, God's self-gift to us as proclaimed by the angels at Bethlehem 'Peace on earth' (Luke 2:14). Facing betrayal and death in the intimacy and the struggle of the Upper Room, peace becomes Jesus' parting gift to his disciples:

> '*My peace I give you, my own peace I leave with you... This is my gift to you*' (John 14:27),

and after the Resurrection, by way of his welcome home gift, his first greeting was again,

> '*Peace be with you*' (John 20:19).

Paradoxically, the greater the absence or denial of peace, the more intense grows the desire and the yearning of the human heart. The proclamation of a unique presence of God through his gift of peace occurs mostly in the midst of turmoil, fear and death, and the Gospel narrative of Thomas 'the Twin' reflects well this inverse dynamism, highlighting two fundamental elements. First, peace is possible, individually and collectively, only when we acknowledge the presence of God in our lives and in our personal endeavours, at all levels of our human experience whatever the shape of this experience. Secondly, peace is possible when we accept it as a gift rather than as a conquest.

In international relationships as much as at the individual level of our own spiritual journey, when peace becomes something to be conquered or imposed, the result is precisely turmoil, destruction and death, right down in the deepest recesses of one's heart. For a long time, we have canonised a spirituality of conquest, of spiritual achievement, and of personal endeavour, at whatever cost. And so, peace becomes an unattainable mirage toward which to strive without ever reaching. On the contrary, the whole struggle becomes a paradox; the more one strives to achieve inner peace, the greater the inner turmoil generated, with consequent frustration, anger and hopelessness.

By contrast, Jesus comments declaring 'blessed are those who have not seen and yet have come to believe' (John 20:29) alerts us as much as the disciples that, because of Easter, the time has come to install a new economy of faith. The living presence of the risen Christ from now will be recognised and realised not through sensory or rational proofs but through Word and Sacrament expressed in the assembled community and energising the believer into the reality of his or her personal journey and story.

So long as peace remains a personal conquest, it will only enhance disquiet, tension and foster that sense of us and them that will engender fear, rejection and deep loneliness and mistrust. For Thomas, peace becomes a personal achievement to be obtained by personal efforts and though the sensory evidence of seeing and touching Jesus whose physical absence is the cause of all his turmoil, anger and unbelief. Only peace accepted as a gift flowing from the unconditional and gratuitous presence of God in my life will enable me to accept my brokenness and woundedness as the place of encounter with the Lord.

The salvation brought by Jesus is a far cry from that pie-in-the-sky-when-we-die sort of mentality, the result of personal achievements, superhuman struggle, or self-deprecation. The term salvation comes from the Latin word '*salus*', meaning health, wholeness and wellbeing, and that is what Jesus offers to the disciples as his homecoming and parting gifts. But a gift has to be accepted otherwise it becomes not only a refusal of relationship, but a rejection of love and an insult to the giver.

Wounded Peace

Faith in the resurrection is a seeing through death, a hearing through the silence deep in our hearts, a rejoicing when the world weighs heavily on our shoulders, an acknowledgment of presence when loneliness seems to enshroud us on all sides. Faith in the resurrection is embracing and being embraced by God precisely when physical, spiritual, emotional and psychological death is all around us.

Fittingly, Jesus' first post-Resurrection greeting to his disciples was to show them his wounds and offer them reassurance and deep inner peace through a wounded body for a broken people. For millions of men, women, and children on this earth today, such a greeting of healing through a broken body may sound as unbelievable and unacceptable as the announcement that Jesus was alive sounded to Thomas. Yet that is the gift that the Lord left to us at the Last Supper and the first fruit of the Resurrection after his earthly death.

The trouble is that often we forget that peace is a gift, and we waste our lives in futile and death-dealing efforts to make it happen according to our agenda and expectations. If we truly believe in Easter, we must convert to a faith-perception of reality as the place of a wounded humanity but an eternally living God. Even as broken and insecure we may be, Easter enjoins on us the need to accept that God chooses to break through death, enter our lives in spite of ourselves, and enliven the universal and collective yearning of the heart by offering us the gift of a life that breed joy, hope and life even in a wounded heart and a broken body. The resurrected Jesus bears the wounds of nails and spear for eternity. He does not hide brokenness; and challenges Thomas to have his wish and touch those wounds, as he had demanded.

With Thomas and like Thomas, the disciple must convert into accepting that the Jesus who stands there in a place of suffering, anger and frustration, with gaping wounds covering his physical body, is the one who alone can save us from ultimate death, restoring joy and transforming human inner and outer wars and turmoil into peace of heart and wholeness of life.

Thomas has no need to see the mark of the nails in his hands or put his finger on the mark of the nails, or his hand in his side (John 20:25). He simply accepts and acknowledges the living presence of his Lord in the one who stands before him marked with the signs of imperfection and brokenness, offering him heart-healing and inviting him to be at peace. In the end, the very wounds marking the human body of the Living One who had walked through and out of death become the catalyst not only of recognition but also of total acceptance of Jesus as the living and life-giving Lord and God in Thomas' life. In that acceptance, he not only discovered but experienced resurrection as Jesus' gift of life beyond death and in the presence of wounds and hurts. Having been called into it by name, Thomas' resurrection experience is now complete and personal, and now he is truly the disciple accepting the Lord and God in his life. The Risen yet Broken Jesus is a wounded Christ who brings healing, peace and hope in human brokenness.

There lies the saving power of Easter. Whether as individuals or as a church community, we will always be confronted by contradictions, brokenness and sinfulness; and our personal efforts to redeem such ills will often appear too daunting or even downright futile. Like Thomas, we may even protest our frustration at the irrationality and injustice deep within us and crushing us on all sides. Yes, often our church community carries painful wounds, self-inflicted by injustice and self-righteousness, pointing to inadequacy and challenging the world's credibility. But the wounded Christ stands there and by accepting God's life-giving presence in that woundedness, then we can journey with hope and courage even through pain and rejection. Then the wounded Christ will truly be salvation and our yearning hearts will overflow with peace in spite of whatever stands before us.

Wounded Healers

For us who celebrate the ancient memory, Easter is and must be this same everyday experience of discovering and accepting, because like Thomas we all struggle with doubt, fears, uncertainties, deceit and sinfulness. Not matter what our stories, through it all we know that we can be at peace, and live in joy and hope, because Jesus calls us by name and greets us with his living and active presence in the midst of all that is death dealing. Having experienced the living presence of Jesus in spite of and against all possibilities, now, like the disciples, we too are sent to become proclaimers and instruments of resurrection in spite of all the woundedness and brokenness that we carry, so that other wounded and broken ones may experience Easter peace in return.

Resurrection makes sense when we look back on our lives and wonder how we have possibly come through *that* situation and grown through it. Resurrection takes place when, in the face of a terminal verdict, we have the courage to journey into the future with strength and serenity. Resurrection takes place when the little child hugs the deserted mother and says, 'I love you, Mummy!' Resurrection takes place when sitting by the bedside of a dying parent we have the twofold courage to let go of them and invite them to let go of us as well and move into fullness of life. Resurrection takes place whenever and wherever good comes out of evil and we are ready to see in that transformation the living active and life-giving Presence of God, in whatever situation life may put before us. Easter is a commitment to accept God in our broken story and in our uncertain world, so that the whole world will know deep peace in spite of personal brokenness, doubt and the struggle to believe. Then we will be energised into journeying on in life with hope and joy, beyond human frailties, sinfulness, doubt and broken or false expectations.

Most Resurrection stories have one element in common, the Eucharistic community. Thomas was not with them when Jesus came, but he eventually experienced Resurrection in that Upper Room when they were all there together. The two disciples returning to Emmaus recognised Jesus at the breaking of bread, and Jesus himself invited the disciples to breakfast on the shores of the lake of Genezareth. That is where it all happens; an encounter with the Lord alive in spite of death and beyond death incarnated in the encounter with each other as a community gathered at Eucharist. The living presence of the risen Christ from now on will be recognised and realised not through sensory or rational proofs but through Word and Sacrament expressed in the assembled community and energising the believer into the reality of his or her personal journey and story.

Jesus' greeting of peace, then, becomes an injunction, bidding us to review and re-establish our relationship with ourselves, with God and with each other. Individually and collectively, we will enjoy peace when we stop looking at each other from the perspective of what divides us and begin to acknowledge what unites us. Peace will be possible when I go beyond my own personal weak, broken and confusing world and see the other, not as a competitor but as enrichment. Peace will be possible when I have the courage to accept that my imperfections and sinfulness are part of who I am, and trust that God is right there in the midst of it all. Peace will be possible when we trust that, in spite of all negativities that harbour deep within us and all around us, God is there greeting us with his gift of peace.

May we be such a community, a Eucharistic Community celebrating the Lord alive and active, individually and collectively! May we too hear those final words of today's Gospel, *'Happy are those who have not seen and yet believe'* (John 20:27), and may we have the faith to open our yearning hearts to the God whom not even death could keep away from us.

A Shepherd God

John 10:1-30

The Language of Images – The Language of Faith

WE LIVE IN A WORLD of images and symbols. As we drive along the road, we automatically stop when a bright red light appears in front of us, or we pull over at the sound of a screaming siren. We extend a hand in welcome and we hug a child in affection. We clap our hands in affirmation and approval and we say 'sorry' in support and sympathy. Our life is full of gestures, words and symbols whose meaning goes way beyond the immediate experience. Far more than their literal meaning, it is this message that we need to be able to perceive and act upon, beyond their symbolic representation, a message that often is too personal or too deep to be expressed in words or rational arguments.

Personal experiences are sometime difficult to express, and relationships can be experienced but never fully described. The more intense the emotion and the deeper the relationship, the more difficult it becomes to find the words to express adequately the experience. Consequently, a person becomes a ray of sunshine, a heavy downpour of rain has something to do with cats and dogs, and the heart transcends its anatomical structure to become a giving of oneself to another person in love. When we have difficulty in expressing the deeply personal reality of an event, we resort to images. By engaging our imagination, we overcome the limitations of head-language and enter the realm of heart-communication, and by going beyond the limitations of speculative language, we are projected into the realm of relationship.

That is why images and symbols drawn from daily life are the diamond drill of communication, dominating particularly throughout the whole biblical narrative, precisely because Scripture is trying to say something about ourselves and about God that transcends our daily experience. By tapping into daily reality, figurative language projects us into a totally other level of reality that cannot be expressed by sensory articulation – a world of depth, of meaning, and of a whole God-and-faith realm of people and events. The fundamental message that the Word of God tries to convey is to express the personal relationship between God and real people, and this kind of depth relationship is so intense that only the open-ended message of imagination can fathom or fully express. In this context, the parables of Jesus are a masterpiece not only of story-telling and of doctrine by a Master Storyteller, but they also represent a masterpiece on the use of images and symbols.

Within the rural culture of biblical times, we read of wheat and weeds, of shepherds and sheep, of farmers and vinedressers, of sowing and vine-tending, of food and drink, of wedding feasts and lost coins, of children leaving home and of women giving birth, of violence in the streets and poor widows giving their last penny in almsgiving, and of a myriad of other examples and life situations drawn from the immediate daily experience of both storyteller and listener.

> Images show us the unknown faces of our own souls and generate the energy needed for change... The point in not to portray or create anything so much as simply to let responses arise in and through our hands... Myths and images can help us to perceive inner spiritual reality, by speaking to truth that is greater than facts... Myth is so deep a dynamic, creative force that you can only tell stories about it.[63]

---

[63] Barbara Davis, *We Are Caught in this Mystery*, Sisters of the Good Shepherd, Australia, 2011, 8

However, precisely because biblical images are drawn from daily experience, they are often linked to specific time, place and cultures. They can be so heavily culturally conditioned that their message becomes unintelligible to us today, and it becomes essential that we unravel the husks of time and place so that we can unravel the pith of the message, telling us of that human-divine relationship which the Word of God is trying to convey to us.

One such image that I believe to be fundamental for understanding our relationship with God and God's relationship with each and every one of us is the image of the *Good Shepherd* (John 10). In a pastoral setting such as biblical Palestine, images of sheep and shepherds take on a unique but understandable dominance in conveying the fundamental message of faith-relationship that underscores both the Old and the New Testament, and the Liturgy highlights the same message especially during the post-Easter season.

Unwrapping the Husk

That dominance of the biblical image of the Good Shepherd overflows very early into the Christian iconography, and one of the first representations of Christ found in the ancient Catacombs of Rome is precisely a graphic representation of the Risen Jesus inspired by the parable of the Good Shepherd (John 10:1-6).[64]

However, I must confess to having been a very slow learner in reading the message conveyed by such imagery, and the rich biblical imagery has remained quite unappealing and unintelligible through many years of exposure to Scripture reading and of pastoral work. By contrast, precisely because of this cultural conditioning, another powerful post-Easter biblical image spoke to me and will always speak to me with far greater power as a central theme of Scripture,

---

[64] http://www.vatican.va/roman_curia/pontifical_commissions/archeo/inglese/documents/rc... (Accessed 20/02/2016)

namely the relationship God wants to establish with each of us individually and all of us collectively. I refer to the image-parable of the vine and the branches that Jesus adopted and left to us as his Last Will and Testament (John 15:1-4). To this day, the well-manicured garden-like vineyards of the Yarra Valley remind me a great deal of home, where the land was covered almost exclusively with luscious vines as far as the eye could stretch.

It was only a chance event in my late thirties that the powerful but hidden message of the shepherd as pointed out by Jesus, suddenly exploded into my awareness, linking and surpassing both my culture milieu and the millennial expression of Scripture.

For one thing, for a long time, the thought of being likened to a sheep did not really appeal to me. Secondly, as a youngster, I grew up in a part of the world where shepherds were looked upon as strange and aloof people who would appear in the middle of winter on the outskirts of town. In this scenario sheep and shepherd were almost unknown, except at the onset of winter as the land was preparing to fall asleep under the thick blanket of snow.

It was then that small flocks would sometime appear on the outskirts of the village, as a curious novelty for us children and as sign that winter had definitely set in. By now, heavy snow would have obliterated their pastures higher up the mountain regions driving these people to lower levels in search of greener grounds. They would lease some grazing paddocks from the local farmers, set up camp under tents and living, mostly away from the majority of the townsfolk during that time, and watch their locks forage for a few weeks. They rarely would come into the village, and the children were never known to mix with us. Then they would disappear, stealthily, almost overnight, not to be seen again for another twelve months. A short stay by strange people, living in a strange manner and never mixing with us – not even the children! An odd curiosity, harbinger of cold winter snow, we thought! Eventually, I came to this country, where I encountered quite an opposite scenario, so contrasting that to my mind sheep became identified with a valuable

A Shepherd God

economic proposition counted not by units but by thousands. Again, that did nothing for me to endear myself to the idea of being a sheep, even if led by a shepherd-God.

It was only in my late thirties that the energy of the image suddenly and unexpectedly made sense to me, and it did that in very powerful and unexpected manner. In the course of a trip to Palestine, one day a couple of friends invited me to visit a Bedouin camp, not far from historic Bethlehem. The official tourist guide who met us was very keen to make a serious impression on these 'American' visitors and taking us through heavily carpet laden tents and gathering spaces, enthusiastically set out to illustrate the life around the tent settlement.

After walking us through a variety of multi-shaped and multi-purpose tents and gathering spaces, heavily hung with richly embroidered tapestry, all the time the guide proudly enlightening us about their use and purpose, we came out into the open again, and immediately he pointed to a small rocky outcrop half-way up a gently sloping hillside. 'And there is the shepherd', he sentenced with conviction. Did he read that 'so-what-look' on our faces? He must have, as he immediately launched into an enthusiastic description of the Palestinian shepherd. 'Things haven't changed in three thousand years, you know!' – he started – 'because the shepherd is a shepherd forever, and that is all he can be', he explained. No, those sheep (about 20 goats, really!), did not belong to him, but they were entrusted to him by various families of the clan.

He was the trusted guardian of those animals and his whole life was totally immersed with their life and welfare, living with his flock, and sleeping out in the fields, under a tent with the sheep around him for mutual security and company. Yes, he had a name for each of them and they would respond to a personal unique pitch of his reed whistle, as they recognised their sound and their call. Yes, he would follow the brash one boldly wondering off, and gently prod on along the track the quiet and feeble. It was then that I found myself hearing again from the mouth of this simple but convinced Bedouin the same expressions that were now familiar from my years of repeated reading of Scripture, without ever confronting the pith of the message.

His enthusiasm was now an unrelenting crescendo. Our guide looked at us and sentenced with conviction, 'That man is a shepherd, and he can be nothing else. He is born a shepherd; he will die a shepherd and he cannot be anything else but a shepherd. *Take away those sheep from him, and he is nobody, he will no longer exist! His life is with those sheep, or he is nothing!*' Then the final authoritative revelation. '*Take away those sheep, and he has no reason for living, he becomes nobody*'.

Suddenly, I found myself hearing the live voice of the Gospel of John for the first time almost forty years later, with the same imagery, the same tone and most of all the message addressed to me and about me.

> *'I am the good shepherd. The good shepherd lays down his life for the sheep. The hired hand, who is not the shepherd and does not own the sheep... I am the good shepherd. I know my own and my own know me... And I lay down my life for the sheep. I have other sheep that do not belong to this fold. I must bring them also, and they will listen to my voice. So there will be one flock, one shepherd.*' (John 10:11-12.14-16)

For the first time in my life, I understood the meaning and the power of the shepherd-image: our God is a Shepherd-God, that One who can only be God in relation to us, and we are the reason for God's very existence. That is why God will stop at nothing to search and find me, not matter what I do or where I stray, and rejoices at bringing me back from my straying ways. I no longer resent being likened to a sheep following a God who wants to share his life with me to an extent that my life is God's life and God's life is my life in return. The relationship is total, life-giving and eternal, and we can only be thankful for such revelation.

The Biblical Image of the Good Shepherd

hat is why the image-parable of the shepherd runs unrestrained through the whole of Scripture, describing both the nature of God and that obsessive divine yearning and behaviour in reaching to the whole of humanity through his chosen people.

> The Scriptural image of the shepherd is certainly a window into the mystery of God and God's dealings with us. It illustrates God's provident care and healing love. It is also a symbol which captures so expressively the reality and role of Jesus. It captures his compassion, his teaching and revealing, his healing and solicitude, the life-giving and liberating intimacy of his relating, his faith protecting, and his commitment to us to the extent of dying for us. It is an image which beckons us to reflection and contemplation, and to a response of trusting love.[65]

In every culture down through the ages, faith and spirituality revolve around its socio-cultural context and reflect this pattern of daily life and draw expression and energy from that daily life. The original people of Israel was innately a nomadic people, and it is only through the dominant categories of that culture that they can understand their personal and national identity in relation to their God and express their beliefs and celebrate their rituals on the rhythm of seasons and place.

In the pastoral setting of first century Palestine, more than family heirlooms or expensive goods, the real riches lay outside the bounds of a dwelling, generally in the form of a small flock of sheep and goats, grazing about a rocky outcrop on the very edge of the village. Down through the centuries of its history, that was the precious treasure for the biblical family, a treasure that had to be jealously safeguarded from wild animals and nightly marauders. Encircled by a secure enclosure, the shepherd, that one trusted

---

[65] Michael T. Winstanley, *Don Bosco's Gospel Way*, Bolton: Don Bosco Publications 2002, 40

member of the clan, would diligently keep watch at the gate; indeed, he would sleep under the stars by that gate, surrounded by his flock.

Here was deep preciousness and a powerful significance at the same time. That flock was much more than an economic security or a means of livelihood. It assumed a sense of cultural identity expressing the intimate relationship between God and his people. From the very beginning of its millennial history, dying Jacob blessed Joseph and his brothers saying,

> *The God before whom my ancestors Abraham and Isaac walked, the God who has been my shepherd all my life to this day ... let them grow into a multitude on the earth.* (Genesis 48:15)

Over the centuries, this reminder of Israel's unique identity and of God's commitment to his promises became the mantra of the whole prophetic tradition. Reflecting on the national tragedy of the exile and the total destruction of Israel's very identity, he prophet Isaiah will remind the people of God's unfailing fidelity by likening the return from Babylon and the reconstruction of Israel to a coming home in the evening when

> *Yahweh will feed his flock like a shepherd, he will gather the lambs in his arms and carry them in his bosom, and gently lead them to the mother sheep.* (Isaiah 40:11)

The Old Testament thus is a millennial story of a rural and pastoral people whose very livelihood depended almost exclusively on nurturing and caring for their small but invaluable flocks.

> '*I myself will be the shepherd of my sheep, and I will make them lie down*', says the Lord God. (Ezekiel 34:15)

Psalm 23 (*'The Lord is my Shepherd'*) carries a bucolic feeling about it, as the pray-er stands in amazement, gazing on a peaceful and peace-filling scene of a shepherd looking on a flock grazing by a flowing stream in absolute security and abundant nourishment.

A Shepherd God

With Ezekiel, Isaiah and Jeremiah, we have a personification of the relationship between Israel as God's flock and Yahweh as the ever-nurturing and protecting Shepherd. Such was the relationship between shepherds and sheep that the flock became the symbol of their lifestyle and the expression of the social, political and religious culture of Israel. Such was the intensity and the power of the image that Yahweh himself identified with '*The Shepherd of Israel*', totally given over to the care and welfare of his chosen flock. The identification was thus sanctioned, complete and eternal. The Shepherd-God was the guarantor of safety and preciousness for Israel, and Israel was Yahweh's uniquely precious flock. Sung in the psalms and proclaimed by the prophets, through the oracle of Ezekiel, Yahweh declares,

> '*I myself will be the shepherd of my sheep, and I will make them lie down*', says the Lord God. (Ezekiel 34:15)

The prophetic literature leaves no doubt that God is not only *The Shepherd* who leads and protects his flock, but he delegates this precious task to the leaders of the people. In a way, the image of a Shepherd-God flows instinctively down to those who have been entrusted with the responsibility *to be shepherd* and to secure care of the flock. It is up to them, the leaders, to ensure that the human response to the relationship with God is fostered and the sheep are fed and looked after. The flock is too precious a treasure to be abandoned, and the same prophetic culture becomes unforgiving in denouncing those leaders who, called to be shepherds, fail to care for the God's precious possession.

> *Woe to the shepherds who destroy and scatter the sheep of my pasture*', says the Lord. *Therefore, thus says the Lord, the God of Israel, concerning the shepherds who shepherd my people. It is you who have scattered my flock, and have driven them away, and you have not attended to them. So I will attend to you for your evil doing... I myself will gather the remnant of my flock out of all the lands where I have driven them. I will bring them back to their fold and they shall be fruitful and multiply. I*

will raise up a shepherd over them who will shepherd them, and they shall not fear any longer, or be dismayed, nor shall any be missing. (Jeremiah 23:1-4)

Likewise, Ezekiel is fierce against the shepherds who have betrayed their call and abuse the treasure that is the flock entrusted to them.

> *'As I live' says the Lord God, because my sheep have become a prey, and my sheep have become food for all the wild animals, since there was no shepherd; and because my shepherds have not searched for my sheep, but the shepherds have fed themselves, and have not fed my sheep; therefore, you shepherds, hear the word of the Lord: Thus says the Lord God, I am against the shepherds; and I will demand my sheep at their hand, and put a stop to their feeding the sheep; no longer shall the shepherds feed themselves. I will rescue my sheep from their mouths, so that they may not be food for them.'* (Ezekiel 34:8-11)

Clearly, the image parable of the shepherd in the Old Testament has a clear double dimension, a personal dimension and a community commitment: the nature of the *mutual relationship* between us and God and the *mission* of the people of God, but particularly of the leaders, to nourish and ensure safety and growth for the whole flock.

True to his socio-religious culture, Jesus is familiar with the Old Testament image-parable of the Good Shepherd, and he readily taps into the same image highlighted strongly by John 10:1-18. The whole chapter is dominated by the symbolic language of sheep and shepherd as a catechesis of the central theme of Jesus' whole earthly life and mission.

> *'I came that they may have life and have it abundantly.'* (John 10:10)

Fullness of life is what God wants for us, and this gift is ours because Jesus, in total obedience to the Father, is the Shepherd who does not find laying down of his life for humanity too great a price to pay so that we may have life.

The allegory of Chapter 10 is as powerful in what it condemns as it is in what it affirms. It is an allegory in the sense that several aspects of one reality (sheep, shepherd, hired workers and gates to pasture) are used as metaphors to understand another reality (Jesus, believers and leaders).[66]

By contraposing a series of opposites, such as the gate versus the wall of the sheepfold, shepherd versus stranger, and the authentic shepherd versus the hireling, Jesus highlights the transformation that faith and abandonment into our Shepherd-God can bring about in our life. The Shepherd God is the God who knows us with a deep and personal knowing of the heart, offers us security if we but trust in him, and want at all costs to enter into a relationship so personal and so deep that it is all-embracing and life-giving, and nothing will frustrate that yearning of God, not even death itself.

'I am the good shepherd. I know my own and my own know me, just as the Father knows me and I know the Father. And I lay down my life for the sheep.' (John 10:14-15)

Each person ever created is worth more than all the world, and God is prepared to risk the whole world for each and every one. God is reckless when it comes to us and will do anything to bring us home from our wayward wonderings, seeking, pursuing and wasting energy for each of us.

The parable of the Lost Sheep is a classic illustration of this divine recklessness, expressed once again in terms of sheep and shepherds.

'Which one of you, having a hundred sheep and losing one of them, does not leave the ninety-nine in the wilderness and go after the one that is lost until he finds it? When he has found

---

[66] Barbara Davis, *We Are Caught Into This Mystery*, 59

it, he lays it on his shoulders and rejoices. And when he comes home, he calls together his friends and neighbours, saying to them, "Rejoice with me, for I have found my sheep that was lost". (Luke 15:4-7)

Here we have an unbelievable situation deliberately told in hyperbolic terms, as Jesus is sometimes inclined to do. Like for most parables aimed at shocking his audience into a direct challenge, this one also must have sounded shocking to Jesus' contemporaries. No one in Israel could claim possession to more than twenty to twenty-five sheep or goats, and these were entrusted to the care of the shepherd who would look after them even at the risk of his own life. A flock of one hundred sheep was an unimaginable and unattainable fortune that only an unbelievably rich person could dream of. Yet Jesus tells his hearers very bluntly and us that this shepherd was prepared to risk everything – his reputation, his livelihood and indeed his life – and do the unthinkable of abandoning an unattainable rich treasure of one hundred sheep for the sake of just that one, who after all had decided to go astray and leave the flock!

We can only surmise the response of Jesus' hearers to such a preposterous narrative, but to us, two millennia later, the pith of the story is unquestionable. The parable of the reckless God abandoning everything to go searching for me demands a conversion of both heart and mind by contraposing positive attitudes to negative experiences, expressed through joy even in a situation of loss and fear.

Rejoice with me, for I have found my sheep that was lost. (Luke 15:6)

Is such a revelation too good to be true? Well, Jesus persists in reassuring us that we are individually and collectively entrusted into his hands by the Father himself, because God thinks that we are worth more than anything in creation and *no one can steal us from the Father's obsessive possession* (John 10:29).

A Spirituality of 'The Good Shepherd'

As Pope Francis has been asserting to the whole world over a decade, the God of mercy and compassion is prepared to lose everything just for me, to meet all my needs whatever my needs or my faults may be.[67]

However, this realisation raises a double challenges for us as no doubt it did for Jesus' hearers. It seriously confronts both our God-image and our self-image. What does this divine recklessness do to my private cherished idea of God and to my God-image? What kind of God is my God? Likewise, who am I really, if this God considers me so precious and worth more than the whole world? Can I accept such confrontation and live accordingly, or is the news too good to be true, and so I prefer to wallow in self-pity, rather than accepting that God thinks that I am worth risking everything, and comes after me precisely when I prefer to wander away and live by my personal agenda?

When I am lost in confusion and anxiety, imprisoned by loneliness, fear and guilt, or I feel trapped by weakness, mistakes and sinfulness, if I believe in the Shepherd God, I can only respond through hope, courage and trust that come from knowing that my Shepherd God will come after me, embrace me in my uncleanliness and fears, put me on his shoulders and takes me home rejoicing. Whatever I think I am the unwilling sheep, I am God's most treasured possession and the reason for God being God. God's life is totally and integrally enmeshed with mine; and God's care, concern, presence, healing, and affection is completely focused on me! This God knows me by my name; indeed he has given me a name, and even if I do tend to be a wanderer, seeking personal interest and agenda, somehow I can never escape God's watchful eye calling me to safety, or his searching presence, bestowing safety, healing and security.

---

[67] Pope Francis, *The Name of God is Mercy*, Bluebird Books for Life, 2016

> *'Very truly, I tell you, I am the gate for the sheep... Whoever enters by me will be saved, and will come in and go out and find pasture... I came that they may have life, and have it abundantly... I am the good shepherd. The good shepherd lays down his life for the sheep... I am the good shepherd. I know my own and my own know me, just as the Father knows me and I know the Father. And I lay down my life for the sheep.'* (John 10:11-15)

Gates and doors are meant to give security and safety, preventing intruders and marauders from entering, and safeguarding the people and the property inside the house. Anybody who has been the victim of a housebreaking or of any unauthorised entry will know that nothing is more disturbing and disquieting than finding an unknown intruder in one's private dwelling or discovering the horror of a ransacked home. Then, beyond the pain of loss and damage of personal and precious property, one feels violated deep inside one's psyche where the trauma can leave scars for a lifetime with psychological syndromes of insecurity, anxiety and suspicion. Our life can be full of intruders disturbing our peace and creating anxiety for our future. Yet, the disciple can be at peace, protected inside the wall of God's love and safe with our God at the gate.

As human beings, we must be worth a great deal if our Shepherd-God commits himself to stand by us in order to secure our comings and goings, and to safeguard our wellbeing, not only as a faithful guard, but as the very gate into life itself. In this powerful rural image, Jesus identifies himself as the instrumental presence and energy that will give us fullness of life and make us who we are meant to be and to become. All too often, we waste a great deal of psychological and emotional energy in breast beating and wallowing in self-pity, nourishing that deep but unspoken sense of unworthiness and of being unloved, while all the time our God is there at the gate of our hearts, calling us into awareness that we are precious in God's eyes and loved as we are. Too often, we curse the darkness of the night, while not realising that our God is there as our security right through that night.

During the Year of Mercy, when God is identified with mercy personified, Pope Francis reminded us that

> There are no situations in life we cannot get out of, we are not condemned to sink into the quicksand, in which the more we move the deeper we sink. Jesus is there, his hand extended, ready to reach out to us and pull us out of the mud, out of sin, out of the abyss of evil into which we may have fallen. We need only be conscious of ourselves, and not lick our wounds.[68]

The all-pervading sense of unworthiness often breeds an equivalent and even more dangerous sense of fear, insecurity and hopelessness which we try to exorcise through compulsions, abuse, or escape into palliatives. But escape-palliatives bring no healing; they only conceal, distorting our perceptions, easing the pain inside and generating a twisted sense of reality through loss of life-meaning and of personal identity. For the believing disciple, the only security that will heal and generate life is the acceptance of our God, which is integral both to the exhilaration of full daylight as well as to the dark experiences of our lives. Ultimately, our claim to faith rests or falls on our readiness to trust God-presence at every turn and twist of our story, and to draw energy for individual and cosmic fulfilment by the awareness and acceptance of this Easter-centred, life-giving presence.

Significantly, Jesus did not say 'I am *like* a shepherd', but used an expression of ultimate authority and identification, *I am*, projecting us immediately into God's very self-disclosure to Moses and the people of Israel. '*I am who I am*' (Exodus 3:14) is the name of God in the Old Testament, bringing into play life and the deeply personal and freeing life-relationship between Yahweh and his people. This is the mantra of the liturgical texts of the Easter Season, where Jesus uses the same expression, *I am*, to identify himself with energy for life (bread), oneness of life between God and us (vine), total and

---

[68] Pope Francis, *The Name of God is Mercy*, Penguin, 2016, 85

absolute care even at the cost of one's life (shepherd), and personal intimate relationship (friends).

Maybe such a revelation sounds too good to be true, and we may even wonder if we are ever worthy or capable to receive such care from our God. Maybe, like the shepherds of my childhood, God can occasionally be the strange one just drifting on the outskirts of our daily reality. And yet whatever the straying on the rocky outcrop of our existence, God's choice is to be the shepherd-God, and God's name will never change. *I AM the Good Shepherd* who is prepared to lay down his life for you and has no reason for existing except for me and you.

Clearly, besides making a statement of self-revelation and pointing to the fundamental rationale of Jesus' life and mission, these words carry a triple intent. First, by identifying himself with the shepherd keeping watch at the gate of the sheepfold, *Jesus calls forth in the disciples a new awareness of their preciousness in the eyes of God*. Secondly, by making himself the guarantor of life-giving Good News, *he offers reassurance and peace, allaying fears and undue anxiety in the face of struggle and personal or collective negativity*. Thirdly, Jesus entrusts his mission of peace and of guardianship *to the believing disciples, wounded to become healers, called to be messengers and instruments of peace, joy and security for the whole world*. Secured by the Good Shepherd guiding our comings and goings through the various gates of our lives, now believers must in turn become shepherds to each other and to the whole world.

The Mission of Shepherding (John 21)

The reassurance of God's unconditional care and loving presence in our life must become energy for action because the Word of God addressed to us personally does not allow for privacy but carries always a universally social aspect enjoining on the disciples a missionary dimension. The dominant imagery of the flock going in and out of the gate of life led by the one shepherd necessarily implies not just one sheep but a multiplicity, precisely a whole flock. Faith in a God of love transcends any form of privatisation and individualism, detached or unaware of any other member of the flock. We are precious in God's eyes because we belong with others, and others will discover their preciousness to God through our life lived with them.

Gifted by God's loving and life-giving presence, in turn the disciples must each become a wounded healer, bearing such gifts to the whole world. Aware of being shepherded into safety and fulfilment by our God, now we have no option but to become shepherds and bearers of peace and salvation. Failing any awareness and commitment to community on our part, Jesus' life and death on our behalf becomes meaningless, and our claim to faith could well turn into that marauding action of betrayal, destruction, and death of the flock against which the prophets warned us centuries ago (Ezekiel 34:1-10), and Jesus pointed out with great realism (John 8:8.10).

John has absolutely no doubt that love is the key, both as a gift of being loved unconditionally by our God and by committing our life equally unconditionally to love of each other by incarnating the values and attitudes of the Good Shepherd towards his sheep spelt out in John 10.

At the end of John's narrative, we encounter Jesus appearing to a group of distraught and confused disciples returning to shore, their fishing net empty and their hearts and minds in turmoil after a fruitless and dark night on the lake (John 21). There, the 'Stranger' of the Resurrection stories meets them, and having turned into a Fisherman-God and provided an astonishing abundance of fish where and when none was meant to be, invites them into the intimacy of table fellowship. Within a scenario of intimate friendship mixed with darkness, uncertainty, confusion and denial, Jesus elicits from Peter that triple declaration of love. Yes, Peter, the broken and rough man who had denied his Lord, has not lost the love for his Lord, or a Pope Francis would say, 'sinner but never bad'.⁶⁹ To every repeated affirmation of love by Peter, Jesus responds enjoins on him to go and feed God's flock and look after God's sheep. *'Peter, do you love me?... feed my sheep!...'*, thus pointing out the indissoluble link between our relationship with God and the mission to foster and nurture this relationship to the whole world.

> *When they had finished breakfast, Jesus said to Simon Peter, 'Simon son of John, do you love me more than these?' He said to him, 'Yes, Lord; you know that I love you'. Jesus said to him, 'Feed my lambs'. A second time he said to him, 'Simon, son of John, do you love me?' He said to him, 'Yes, Lord; you know that I love you'. Jesus said to him, 'Tend my sheep'. He said to him the third time, 'Simon, son of John, do you love me?' Peter felt hurt because he said to him the third time, 'Do you love me?' And he said to him, 'Lord, you know everything; you know that I love you'. Jesus said to him, 'Feed my sheep'.* (John 21:15-17)

It is fascinating and significant that this is the first and only time that we encounter an explicit 'missioning' by Jesus in the Fourth Gospel, and it is a missioning that enjoins on Peter the divine expectation not only to become a shepherd, but, in doing so, to move away from a gatherer for himself that was Peter the fisherman to a caretaker and a nurturer of others. Peter knew nothing about shepherding, yet his protestation of faith in the Lord commits him to become Peter the shepherd minding sheep and lambs. It does not matter if Peter knows nothing about sheep. Now that he has experiences the care, love and healing presence of Jesus, he has no other option but to become a carer, a lover and a healing presence for others.

The Christian community is not a social, cultural, political, racial or any other form of ghetto, nor is it a conglomerate of gregarious individuals jealously guarding their private relationships with God, bearing a personally distinctive badge, and congregating under some artificial religious banner. Central to Christian faith

---

[69] Pope Francis, *The Name of God is Mercy*, 37-47.

is the absolute and active conviction of oneness, within a living integration of people who acknowledge, love and accept each other, energised by the Shepherd-God prepared to lay down his life for them, and leading them securely into personal and communal fulfilment of life and love.

As Christians, we cannot isolate ourselves at any level of our community, and Jesus himself has strong words of condemnation for the leadership that seeks personal fulfilment by destroying and marauding the Christian community. As a human reality, no church is perfect and we must own the truth that often individuals and indeed shepherds will wander and go astray, leaving the community to bear the scars and weaknesses of brokenness and infidelity.

The temptation to control is a powerful and destructive energy in all of us, choosing to break through the enclosure of community and love rather than following the shepherd through the gate of fidelity. However, if we are prepared to accept that our God stands by us, seeks us and secures us though any experience of day and night, then we can journey on and be shepherd to each other with courage and hope, secure that we are loved in our individual or collective unfaithfulness, strengthened in our weakness and brokenness, and enlightened in our darkness.

Conclusion

With God as the energy of our lives and with Jesus as the secure pathway to personal fulfilment, we know that at every heartbeat of our existence we are *embraced by the loving care of our God and we can truly face life with hope in uncertainty, courage in our setbacks and joy in our struggles.* As we wonder through the rocky outcrops of our stories and the uncertainties and darkness that may at times surround us like the disciples returning empty-handed after a fruitless night, we can claim with the Apostle Paul,

> *If God is for us... neither death, nor life... nor anything else in all creation, will be able to separate us from the love of God in Christ Jesus our Lord.* (Romans 8:31, 38-39)

As I look back at the shepherds of my younger years at the foot of the Alps, I will never again see strange people living a strange lives aloof from everybody and disappearing into the dead of winter. Now, the shepherd is the harbinger of deep and precious relationship, of overwhelming care and of eternal, life-giving presence. And all this is lavished on me. Though at times I may be an unwilling sheep, a wanderer often seeking personal adventures of my own, I am God's most treasured possession and the raison d'être for God being God. Totally and integrally enmeshed with my life, God's concern, presence and affection are focused completely on me! The drifter in me is forever searching for personal interests that take me away from the path set out by the Shepherd- God, or I may be lost among the briars deep in the crevasses of sinfulness and personal mistakes. Yet, I can never escape God's watchful eye calling me to safety, or his searching presence, bestowing on me unconditional care, compassion, healing and security.

> *If God is for us... neither death, nor life... nor anything else in all creation, will be able to separate us from the love of God in Christ Jesus our Lord.* (Romans 8:31, 38-39)

Vine: Obsessive Possessiveness (Self)

John 15:3-16

THROUGH A VARIETY AND DIVERSITY of threads, all four Gospel narratives converge on the last evening of Jesus' life, when – facing the climax of his life and ministry – he gathered his disciples in the Upper Room. There, in the deep intimacy of an ancient family meal, he entrusted to them his last will and testament, giving full vent to an explosion of unconditional love as one does with intimate and trusted friends.

However, while Mark, Matthew and Luke focus exclusively on Jesus' self-giving to humanity in Eucharist, John does not mention specifically the institution in the context of the drama of the Last Supper, substituting that last Will and Testament with the parable in action of the *Washing of the Feet* to express the fundamental truth that he wants to leave to us as his memory and for which he is about to lay down his life.

In a long conversation embracing a quarter of his Gospel narrative, mingling strong symbolic gestures like washing the disciples' feet and evocative figurative language such as shepherd, sheep, gate, vine and branches, woman in labour, Jesus articulates for all time that unique and eternal human-divine relationship binding together God to us and to each other in the one reality and one energy: 'Love'. In his last will and testament, Jesus is at pains to express the deep relationship that God longs to establish with all of us, individually and collectively, and in the image of the vine and branches, Jesus reveals the symbiosis of two elements undergirding dual intertwined and unchangeable relations of God and humanity.

Abiding or Rejection

In an attempt at giving expression to the inexpressible reality of God in human terms and drawing heavily on its agricultural tradition alongside the imagery of the shepherd, biblical language is rich in images of vines and vineyards. In the Old Testament, vines and vineyards came to be identified with the fulfilment of God's promises to his people, a symbol of the new reality where God would be Israel's God, and Israel would belong entirely to God (Isaiah 5:1-10); a mutuality of life and relationship promised and anticipated for centuries (Jeremiah 2:21; Ezekiel 28:26; Hosea 10:1; Psalm 80). Israel is the vine of God, God's very obsession as the psalmist prays:

> *You brought a vine out of Egypt; you drove out the nations and planted it.*
> *You cleared the ground for it; it took deep root and filled the land.*
> *The mountains were covered with its shade, the mighty cedars with its branches;*
> *it sent out its branches to the sea, and its shoots to the river.*
> *Why then have you broken down its walls,*
> *so that all who pass along the way pluck its fruit?*
> *The boar from the forest ravages it, and all that move in the field feed on it.*
> *Turn again, O God of hosts; look down from heaven, and see; have regard for this vine.*
> (Psalm 80)

By drawing our attention and reflecting on daily experiences, in all his teaching and preaching, Jesus constantly pushes our consciousness beyond the narrow limits of the daily and the personal, into a universal view of reality, where God is at work and the message becomes Good News. True to his own cultural and religious tradition, Jesus repeatedly likened the vineyard to the God's active and life-giving presence which he called 'the Kingdom', and some of his most dramatic parables are set precisely within this agricultural context (Matthew 19:26-20: 21:28-46; Mark 12:11-12:14; Luke 13:1-11; 20:4-21).

In Matthew 20:1-16, we encounter a generous but controversial landowner who invites labourers to work in his vineyard, and then rewards them not out of their personal merits or the hours they have laboured, but out of his gratuitous generosity, paying the last arrival the same wage as the first. Questionable as it may seem to our categories of retributive justice, Jesus is not about industrial relationships or labour laws. He is about the Kingdom, a reality which is not the result of conquest, personal achievements, or merits, but exclusively a gift offered to us by our God inviting us into his life out of his love for us, as we are, and on his generous terms.

A gift carries a strong connotation of mutual relationship between giver and receiver, and it can only be an expression of love between people when accepted with gratitude by the receiver. Conversely, refused or ignored, the gift becomes a statement of rejection of the relationship and an insult towards the giver. That is the only human condition attached to the Kingdom: God invites us into his life and love, but we must say 'yes' to the offer.

This tension between God's unconditional invitation on the one hand and, on the other, the human tendency to seek and adopt a personal satisfying and self-styled relationship by asserting one's own freedom of decision, is exemplified by a number of synoptic narratives unified under the one title of *'The Wicked Tenants'* (Matthew 21:33-46; Mark 12:1-11; Luke 20:9-17) joined together by one single theme; God's will do anything to draw us into his loving relationship, but he seems impotent against the human decision to refuse his advances. Matthew clearly stresses the love relationship between God and his people by placing the parable within the context of a discussion Jesus has with the leaders of the people, in which Jesus sternly points out that prostitutes and tax collectors can claim priority before God, ahead of God's very own chosen ones. This is because, unlike those who should know better, prostitutes and tax collectors have accepted the presence of God in their lives (Matthew 21:18-32).

God incessantly calls each of us into his own and as his own possession, drawing us to himself, and energising us by his own life-energy, but we must be prepared to say yes to this invitation, to accept his love, to let the flow of life-energy flow through us and so become active instruments of his vineyard. By contrast, as the parables tell us, any refusal to accept the flow of love between God and us will result in self-destruction. Any attempt at asserting one's individuality by refusing to be instruments of fruitfulness and goodness in the world blocks the flow of God-enriched love and energy and leads to total death. At the same time, when we accept the invitation into God's life-giving presence and abide in his presence, then there is no stopping the vitality and energy for goodness that is unleashed in our life, because then God will be fully at work in us and our life will be truly a source of fruitfulness and goodness for the whole world.

Oneness of Life and Love

This concept of allowing God's love to flow in us and energise us into life is repeatedly expressed in the Fourth Gospel by the word *'abide'* which, mantra-like, runs through John's narrative from the very beginning, and is emblematic of John's Gospel where, significantly, it occurs eleven times in John 15:4-16, twenty-three times in the short Johannine letters, and only five times in the rest of the New Testament. Following Jesus in discipleship means *to abide in his love* (John 15:4-16), to be caught passionately and obsessively in a love affair so intense that often it defies any human attempt at verbal expression, a love affair that can only be understood and experienced by two people madly in love with each other. The relationship between God and each one of us is so intense and so life-giving that it finds full expression in the life-giving sap that, human blood-like, floods every fibre of the vine, roots, trunks, canes and branches, seeping deep into the leaves and the tiniest shoots and tendrils, to bring life and abundant fruitfulness.

However, like in a network of interconnected channels, each dependent of the other for a constant rush of energy, all the elements need to ensure an uninterrupted flow, and even a single blockage paralyses the whole system of life course. In the same manner, in the discipleship, the life-energy that binds Jesus with the Father flowing through both of them as one life-sap, also binds Jesus to his disciples, and, in turn, the same life-giving sap is shared totally and equally by the disciples, binding them to one another. The same one vital sap flows through God, each of us individually and all of us collectively, and we are all sharers in the same Spirit-DNA. Anything else is death and destruction, *'because I live and you will live also'* (John 14:19-20). The sap-energy that enlivens God gives life to the disciples; and the love with which the Father loves Jesus is the same love that the Father has for the disciples. *'The Father himself loves you, because you have loved me'* (John 16:27). The rationale for this fundamental and yet almost inexpressible bond between God and us lies in the powerful dynamism of shared life and love expressed through the metaphor of the vine a metaphor that speaks of *vigorous vitality, of shared oneness of life, and of dramatic and painful stripping*, all at once.

Let us go down into the vineyard then, and let that parable speak to us, about us, and about God-with-us. Indeed, the image of the vine speaks to me of something greater than richness of life and abundance of fruitfulness, though born out of stripping and cutting and pruning. The image-memory of vines and vineyards and vinedressers brings me back to my childhood days in a small corner of the world tucked away between Italy, France and Switzerland, and it speak to me of obsessive love.

Obsessive Possessiveness

I grew up in one of the main vine-producing area of Northern Italy, and vines are a primordial element etched in my memory – a land teeming with exclusively luscious green and gold as far as the eye can stretch. I remember that as a child I was convinced that the whole world was made up of hills covered with vines, and – to my younger brother – the big industrial city of Turin was only 'the place where there are no vineyards'. With amusing and child-like honesty, he would ask my father how those people could live and what they were doing all day, if they had no vineyards to till and no vines to tend.

To own a plot of land planted with vines, carefully manicured in neat rows, meant far more than an economic proposition. It was part of the very identity of the old farmer of Piedmont, as even his parlance would reveal. Many years on, I still remember how the old folks in the small country village had a peculiar way to describe absolute poverty or destitution. Whenever a new family moved in the district in search of a future or some casual work, these new arrivals were called 'those without even two vines to bless themselves with!' People were identified by the location of their vineyard more than by their home address, and bankruptcy was called 'losing that last piece of vineyard'. Vines and vignerons seemed to be linked by a living relationship such that vines and vineyards specified the very identity of their owners and qualified their socio-economic status.

Recently, I had the opportunity not only of revisiting those memories, but of tramping through those perfectly manicured rows of freshness and vitality, and to breath in deep gulps the richness of memory and of goodness. It was during one of these strolls that I remembered one of those once-in-a-life-time experiences that open up a whole new vision of reality, and it revealed to me for the first time the full power of Jesus' words: *'I am the true vine, and my Father is the gardener.'* (John 15:1)

Vine: Obsessive Possessiveness (Self)

I was in my late middle age years, when, in trying to play the concerned son, I hurt my mother, and I hurt her deeply. Our family too had a small plot of land behind the old house where mum and dad tended a few vines more as a hobby and as cultural expression than for any economic value they may have engendered. Actually, those vines alongside the old family home had long borne the harsh and twisted markings of age. They had been there for as long as I could remember, and by then I had passed my fiftieth birthday. My father had died some years before, but mum kept tending those vines with passion and religious duty. No, it was not easy to climb the steep hill to which they clung, but mother would not abandon those small, twisted trunks, nor she would stop talking about them to anyone who happened to pass by. It was then that in my ignorance I tried to play the dutiful and concerned son by suggesting to her that, maybe just maybe, it was time to let go of those old vines, to rip them up and to save time and energy.

The reaction was immediate, shockingly passionate, and unforgettably emotional. Mother looked at me sternly, her eyes bulging with reproach and tears. 'So long as I live, those vines will remain there' – she sentenced with conviction. 'Don't you know that those were our first vines, our first possession? Your father and I planted them one by one, carefully sowing the dreams of our life, when you were barely two years old, and I was carrying your brother yet unborn?' – And to think that by then both of us were in our late fifties!). She caught her breath and wiped a tear, but the passion did not subside. 'Don't you know that every one of those vines carries a million memories, laughter, anxiety, plans, and experiences of intense togetherness with your father and with us all?' Then the final plea: 'No, please, don't deprive me of those memories! My life is there! Our life is there!'

I felt guilty in my efficiency-focused narrow-mindedness. No, I never mentioned those vines again, and one of my most enduring memories is of mum standing in the midst of those old vines, just looking at them, still being energised by the memories, even if by then she could no longer tend them from wild noxious weeds all around.

Mum was obsessively possessive of those vines, and those words of Jesus will never sound the same again to me: *'I am the vine and you are the branches, and my Father is the vine dresser'* (John 15:5).

Love Calls for Sharing

Ours is a God longing and yearning to enter into intimate and eternal relationship with each of us, sharing life to the full, and transforming our very selves in spite of ourselves. Our call is to accept this unique, personal and eternal relationship with our God, obsessively possessive or me and you. We are God's fruitfulness, work of divine-human labours and dreams, energised and nurtured by the sap of life of an obsessively possessive Life Giver God (John 10:10).

> *'This is to my Father's glory, that you bear much fruit, showing yourselves to be my disciples.'* (John 18:8)

Nurtured by the energy of its sap flowing into every fibre and hidden bud, the vine explodes into life, bearing fruit and shelter and freshness all around it. Somehow, it cannot contain the vitality with which it is gifted. Paradoxically, unless it bears fruit, the vine will die, choked by its own sap of life. It is the same with the love lavished on the disciple: unless this love is shared in turn among one another, then love is wasted.

Energised by the same divine energy, this powerful dynamic of love becomes the only and unequivocal yardstick of the love the disciples must have for one another. The two imperatives of *abiding in God's love* and of *loving one another* are not sequential but consequential as two sides of the same coin. When the love-sap of God becomes the energy of our daily life expressed in deeply human and concrete mutual relationships, we will be true disciples of Jesus, called to witness and proclaim God's fruitful, life-giving presence, energising the world. If the life we live is the life of love for one another, then people will 'know' the God of love who longs to embrace them and share life and love into complete fruitfulness (John 14:31; 17:20-24).

Painful Fruitfulness

Only by accepting the love of the vinedresser who calls me friend (John 15:14-15) and yet strips me bare, we will truly discover the God of life and freedom and we will truly experience fruitfulness beyond belief or any human expectation. This is the stunning revelation that Jesus left us as his parting gift: God loves us with 'a love beyond all telling'. However, Jesus was also a great realist, and the image of the vine is as much a stunning disclosure of God relationship with humanity as it is a challenging prospect (John 15:1-8).

The explosive power of the vine's richness and abundance of life and fruitfulness is born of stripping and cutting and pruning. The whole life cycle of the vine from bud to fruit is conditional to obsessive tearing and stripping away. Indeed, the greater the expression of vitality the more drastic is the cutting away, to the point that growth seems to be inversely proportional to the savagery of the vignerons. At the very peak of its explosive potential, right through the summer season and into early autumn, the vine is deprived of its ultimate richness.

> *'I am the true vine, and my Father is the gardener. He cuts off every branch in me that bears no fruit, while every branch that does bear fruit he prunes so that it will be even more fruitful.'*
> (John 15:1-2)

I have seen it happen for a lifetime. Week after week, and long before the first signs of the fruit appear, scissors, bare hands, secateurs and powerful clippers attack the vine in a relentless and violent activity of stripping off its explosive growth. From late spring and throughout the full vitality of summer, when the vine is at its most majestic, vigorous branches are cut down and its superb foliage thinned and rarefied, as if some relentless destructive force was trying violently to subdue the power of growth and vitality, exploding uncontrollably into life and self-giving. And the process continued, repeated again and again, many time over the summer period with the alleged rationale of enabling the vine to direct its energy to almost insignificant tendrils that will eventually bear the longed-for fruitfulness.

Finally, at the very peak of its explosive potential the vine is deprived of its ultimate richness and of the very rationale of that long process of cutting and pruning and stripping. It is vintage time, and the vinedresser rejoices as he gathers the ultimate self-giving of the vine: the gift of its abundance and fruitfulness. Yes, the vinedresser knows the time, the vintage time, and this is the time to strip the vine of its very ultimate abundance and richness, giving up its own self-realisation and achievement, until there is nothing left on its red and amber coloured branches but tired and crumpled leaves dying abandoned in the fading autumn sun and dulling morning mist.

Now, bare and abandoned, the vine is left to die, by itself in dank and cold earth shrouded in mists and winter chill. But it will not die, in spite of further pain being in store, because the vine is too precious a gift to be thrown away. I have seen what happens to vines once their rich fruit has been stripped and taken away! At the onset of winter, when cold mist and dense fog begin to obliterate the last traces of sunlight, the vinedresser sets to work again. Secateurs, rusty clippers, and sharply filed saws set to work, tearing, cutting, stripping bare that vine, only recently exploding with richness of life and lavish fruitfulness. That obsessive possessiveness that had nurtured that vine for months now seems to have turned into fearsome ruthlessness, as rich foliage and intricate twines are torn asunder, gathered into bundles on the dank earth.

Yet, with some strange inner vision, the eye of the artist seems to guide the apparent savage hand of the vinedresser. Yes, the vinedresser knows the single strand that needs to be set free and then, apparently, abandoned to the coldness and darkness of the winter. That single strand attached to the old gnarly vine, and that ten centimetres strand alone bare and stripped of all beauty, will be the one that will blossom at the first cold rays of the springtime sun.

That is the promise and the power of Jesus' 'I-am-statement'. Its very nature is to be a source of life, and so long as the tiniest remnant of cane remains attached to the old and twisted trunk and stock – thus allowing the flow of life sap – the vine will never die. Though barren, twisted and apparently abandoned, by clinging to the mother trunk and roots, the vine becomes the ultimate source of life. So long as we cling to him, even if tired, twisted or empty, we will experience life in full and never taste death or annihilation, whatever our human story may be. Our life will have its challenges, its stripping, and its barrenness, but we will not die. This is precisely the story of the vine: *life through stripping away and apparent abandonment* even of its power and fretfulness.

I have seen the cutting and the stripping, and I have seen the glow of joy and hope on the face of the vinedresser as his keen eye discovers that small, fragile and almost insignificant 'speck', breaking out of that single strand left abandoned to the rigours of winter. That 'They are breaking!' is the exited mutual call of the old vignerons still ringing in my ears as the cold paleness of the early spring sun thaws out the frozen soil, and the small, almost invisible dot-like bud appears on that lonely strand left abandoned through the winter months. The paradox of the vine's life cycle is now complete. The vine stripped of its energy, beauty and most of all of its fruitfulness, is now ready for a new burst of vitality. All that abandonment, struggle and pain now heralds a completely new explosion of life and fruitfulness and deep love. Life begins again, and the dance of joy, hope and excitement goes on.

Pruning for Life

'I am the true vine, and my Father is the gardener. He cuts off every branch in me that bears no fruit, while every branch that does bear fruit he prunes so that it will be even more fruitful.'
(John 15:1-2)

As Christians, we are not about canonising suffering as some good to be pursued and fostered, a springboard into an otherworldly or after-life reward directly proportional to the degree or amount of suffering one has to endure throughout one's earthly experience. God's possessive love truly embraces us across, in, and through the full gamut of human experiences, and even through the painful pruning of the winter of suffering and death. Sometime this flow may have its pains and deprivations, and it may well be that at times pruning and cutting may seem overwhelming, mist and cold may envelop us on all sides, and we feel destitute and abandoned, deprived of all energy and of future possibilities and achievements.

The winters of the vine invite us to trust and to let God into our pain, abandoning our false images and our false expectations and securities into God's hands. When we have the courage and strength to do that, then truly pain becomes redemptive and life-giving, and God's pruning will only revitalise us into new possibilities and release the life sap of more vigorous and more fruitful,. Then God's presence will truly become a reality in our life and in our world because God's energy will truly course in our life in all seasons and under every imaginable circumstance. When our life is reduced to an insignificant twig with nothing to hold on to of our own making, only God can then make us into what God has always wanted us to be.

Only in this perspective can we speak of abundant fruitfulness through suffering and death. Then suffering will not be in vain, but it will become a witness of trust and love in God. Then our life will become a revelation of the God of life and love, and of trust in God actively present in our human story. The struggle and pain will truly be heralds of more abundant fruitfulness and deeper love. *Only by accepting the love of the vinedresser who calls me friend and yet strips me bare, we will truly discover the God of life and freedom and will truly experience fruitfulness beyond belief or human expectations.*

The vinedresser knows the time and patiently waits for the smallest bud to break the delicate skin of that short stump left in the snow. Then he rejoices because the vital flow of divine sap will surely and inevitably burst out into a new explosion of life and rich fruitfulness. With the Vinedresser–God, we too will be able to rejoice because fullness of life is inevitably our destiny if we but accept that we are the branches that the Father tends with obsession and possessive and love.

> *'I am the vine you are the branches.* A pruned vine does not look beautiful, but during harvest time it produces much fruit. The greatest challenge is to continue to recognise God's pruning hand in my life. Then I can avoid resentment and depression and become even more grateful that I am called upon to bear even more fruit than I thought I could. Suffering then becomes a way of purification and allows me to rejoice in its fruits with deep gratitude and without pride.[70]

Conclusion

Jesus is very explicit. *'I am the vine, and my Father is the vinedresser'* (John 15:1), and if we are to live fully, we have no choice but to accept the flow of life and love that binds us to our God and to each other. Sometimes this flow may have its pains and deprivations. It may well seem that, at times, pruning and cutting are overwhelming; mist and cold may envelop us on all sides, and we feel destitute and abandoned, deprived of all energy and dreams. Like the disciples we may occasionally feel confused, bewildered and afraid, as we may not like to own what the message reveals to us or about us. Like the

---

[70] Henri. J. Nouwen, *'The Farewell Discourse'*, in Michael O'Loughlin (ed.), *Henri Nouwen – Jesus: A Gospel*, (Maryknoll NY: Orbis Books, 2001), 91-92

fragile vine of our own self, we will often feel stripped, pruned, cut and left bare. Yes, we may feel that the news is too good to be true and we do not quite measure up to our own expectations. We may hear the call to let go of our fears and anxieties and walk through brokenness in trust. We may be touched at the very core of our being with a mixture of joy and pain, hope and sadness, energy and fragility. That will be the transforming moment, the pain of deep love born out of the stripping and tearing that heralds the passing from winter into spring. That will be the decisive moment revealing our authenticity and calling us to enter more deeply into intimacy with God.

In those moments of pain, let us resist the temptation to rush for immediate solutions, a set of prayers, or some devotional practice. Let us simply accept the challenge to stay with God-the-Vinedresser, longing to be in friendship and in intimate union of life and love with each of us and all of us. The Vinedresser knows the time and patiently waits for the smallest bud to break the delicate skin of that short stump abandoned to the winter rigours. Then he rejoices because the vital flow of divine sap will burst surely and inevitably out into a new explosion of life and rich fruitfulness. Then, with the Vinedresser God, we too can rejoice in fullness of life and inevitable our destiny, if we but accept that we are the branches that the Father tends with obsessive and possessive love.

'I am the true vine, you are the branches, and my Father is the vinedresser' (John 15:1, 5).

Goodbyes Among Friends

John 15:14-15

THE WRITTEN GOSPELS are not biographical accounts, as we understand such a definition, but communal reflections about Jesus circulating throughout the diverse, early Christian communities and reflecting various historical traditions. As such, they clearly portray a Jewish understanding of Jesus and the memory of those particular communities reported by four evangelists. Consequently, the events of Jesus' life and mission are always told from the perspective of a specific cultural and religious perspective of each particular community reading those events from the standpoint of its need, and its social, religious and historical demographics.

The four narratives of Jesus' Last Supper on the night before he died is a classic example of this cultural, social and religious diversity. Traditionally, we generally equate the Last Supper in the Upper Room as the moment when Jesus, having gathered his disciples, instituted the Eucharist. But while this is the memory of Jesus for Mark, Matthew and Luke, John, while devoting five chapters of his narrative to that particular gathering, never once refers to the Eucharist as the central event of that evening then celebrated throughout the last twenty Christian centuries.

On the contrary, unique and most insightful of the four evangelists, John operates from a very personal and much deeper understanding of Jesus by focusing not on information about faith but on transformation into faith. For John, belief involves acceptance of Jesus' revelation of the Father and a personal and collective awareness of being drawn into a unique relationship of love and life with the God Jesus revealed. John does this by shaping that fundamental event of the Last Supper around a long conversation of Jesus with his disciples, almost a monologue that will remain forever his last will and testament. Clearly struggling to find the right words and the adequate images to convey his feelings for his disciples, Jesus tells them who he really is for them, and who they are in the eyes of God. In the end, he sums it all up by calling repeatedly upon the word 'Love' and on the image of deep friendship.

'I Call You Friends'

The very term *'friendship'* conjures up a whole gamut of emotions and energies, of deep personal experiences, of life challenges, value systems, and intense personal relationships.

Perhaps, a certain line of spirituality has twisted the very concept of friendship into negative connotations; but to shun friendship is to deny our humanity and to condemn ourselves to loneliness, aridity and self-destruction, as I painfully discovered while ministering as a school chaplain when one day a young teenager asked to see me. Invited to initiate the conversation, after an uneasy silence, she blurted out with icy cold expression but with a firm tone, 'I hate myself!'" Surprised as much by the self-revelation as by the strong conviction in her voice, before I could either comment or gather some inner composure, without waiting or expecting any answer from me, she voluntarily continued, 'I hate myself, because I have no friends in this school!' She was a newly enrolled student, the only one from her previous grade class, and her lack of friends had sadly turned into self-hatred. Fortunately, like all good stories of friendship, this one was easily solved leading to *'and they all lived happily ever after'*.

Some years later, as I was meeting a group of senior students for a day's event, one of them approached me with an inquisitive smile and asked me if I remembered her. No, I did not remember her, I confessed, and she proceeded to refresh my memory. 'I was the one who hated herself'', she said, with a satisfied look and the confident self-assurance of a class leaders who was determined to help younger ones to feel at home in the group.

Friendship is supportive, affirming, healing and life-giving. Friends hold no secrets from each other, no fear, and no pretence. Friends long to be together and they feel their mutual presence even in sensory absence, in physical distance and beyond time and space, spending large amounts of each day on the social media to each other. Idealistic, friends can be naïve and blind to each other's weaknesses, yet quick at discovering and upholding giftedness and idealising the other. Friends are simply there, and live and grow because of that unique relationship that binds them—precisely, a relationship of *love*.

That is the kind of relationship Jesus revealed to his disciples on that fateful night when he reassured them with the words, '*You are my friends!*'. Ultimately, our response to Jesus in faith can never be measured in terms of what we do, but only in terms of who we are by accepting that we are God's very own friends, people whose integrity and authenticity lie in being open and transparent to the transforming presence of God; frail, reconciled and uniquely precious but always aware of him being there beyond and, in spite of physical absence, ready and available to journey together with others in compassion and community.

Bonded Together by Love

Jesus shuns rational and abstract philosophical language. Instead, he addresses his disciples and us with very direct personal prepositions, 'I, you, my, we, us, yours', to express who God is for us and who we are for God. For the believer, faith is not a matter of pleasing God or achieving salvation by our human efforts or personal merits. As Jesus reassured us, we are chosen to be loved unconditionally by our God, and our side of the mutual relationship consists in receiving and accepting God's love, as he himself spelt it all out in the word Love (John 15:16-17).

As believers, we are held in a three-way mutuality of life-relationship – Jesus, the Father and the disciples, *bonded into one, energised by love, and vivified by love.* Love is the leitmotif of the long conversation in the Upper Room the night before Jesus died, a night heavy with emotions, ranging from fear to intimacy, and in that setting he told us that love is the ultimate and only rationale of God being God and of God relating to each of us without distinction or condition (John 15:9-17). Love is the energy that makes us who we are, and love is both our destiny and the focus of our relatedness to God and to each other. 'You are my friend(s)'.

We are the objects of an eternal, incredible love affair of God with us, the ones who have words of love addressed to them in an outpouring of emotions that only two people madly in love with each other can understand.

> *In this is love, not that we loved God but that he loved us (1 John 4:10) (because) he chose us in Christ before the foundation of the world to be holy and blameless before him in love.* (Ephesians 1:4)

We need not be afraid or sceptical of the word 'love' by reducing it to shallow sentimentality, shunning any form of human emotion and love relationship as if it were the ultimate and all-destructive temptation from the evil one. A spirituality advocating a platonic otherworldly construct of love can only enslave to fear and guilt, destroying its energy and power for life gifted to us by God.

Love as Jesus left to his disciples at the Last Supper is the human experience of God, and unless one can truly love someone and be loved by another person in return, we will never really know God. On the same occasion, Jesus reminds his disciples that love born of intimate friendship is the harbinger of peace, joy and trust; and he leaves these as his parting gifts for those who accept his love and share it in return with each other. If we accept God's love for us then we will experience peace and joy, and our hearts will never again know fear and guilt, because we are God's very intimate ones, regardless of who we may be or what we may think.

This is our reality and our identity revealed to us by Jesus on the night of his earthly goodbye. We are the ones with whom God longs to share the intimacy of table fellowship, carrying all the brokenness, shortcomings and infidelities personified by that motley crew that Jesus was addressing that night, those very ones whom he called friends and would soon betray him, abandoning him to the most ignominious and horrid of deaths.. We are the ones who are reassured that from all time and for all time he will never leave us orphans or fearful or alone. We are God's passionate obsession, loved and embraced passionately by our God, intimate friends for whom Jesus prayed, entrusting us into the hands of the Father before walking to his own earthly goodbyes in death (John 17) and enjoining on us the task of taking up his mission.

Caught up in this explosive dynamic of divine love-energy, now we are both object and instruments of God's obsessive love-dream; objects of his loving choice and on whom he depends for the establishing of his gifts of peace and joy in a world of disfigured and twisted love and servile fear. This is the destiny God calls us to in Jesus' earthly goodbye. Embraced by love we have no choice but to be instruments of love.

Going Home

God is both passionate and obsessive in his love for you and me, but he needs our human love and our friendship towards each other in order to reveal his passionate love for the whole world and for all time. That is why the post Easter liturgy – while celebrating the living presence of Jesus with his disciples – carries a strong undertone of incompleteness of the present and of promise of a future reality that speaks of absence and yet is teeming with presence. In the Upper Room Jesus' words of reassurance of an eternal love relationship in spite of and beyond death carry a clear *present intentionality* and a *future projection* at the same time, rendering Easter-Pentecost an in-between time, a template for the now and the not yet of our journey of faith.

All the Resurrection narratives exhibit a clear tension brought on by the interaction and intertwining of opposites; a beyond in the here and now, a sightless seeing, a presence in absence, fullness of life in the finality of death, a divine dynamic operating in the concrete human experience of each person. As a prelude to the unfolding of Jesus' human story when his would-be followers would betray him, scatter and run away, Jesus speaks of the inevitable destiny of his mission in terms of going away and of leaving. Although the message would have been quite incomprehensible to those around the table in the Upper Room, Jesus persistently speaks of a reality 'beyond', of loss, absence, departure, and separation – experiences that would soon leave his disciples confused, bewildered, and shattered.

Unbeknown to them, his disciples would never again encounter the Jesus of Nazareth they knew, and they would completely lose sight of his physical presence. However, in the same breath he reassures them that they need not fear. Yes, they will be lonely, know rejection and struggle with suffering, but they will never be orphaned, forgotten or alone. Precisely because God holds them in his love and care, though hidden from sensory perception or cerebral grasp, for the believing disciples this sense of caring presence invests the totality of life experience 'now', while leading to a 'beyond' full of promise and of expectancy, pregnant with accomplishment and with wholeness of life.

However, more than departure and separation, the dominant tone is one of gathering together into oneness, of newness, and of fullness of life. He tells them that he will be 'going to the Father' (John 14:28) and yet he continually reassures them that they will still see him, and he will be with them. Jesus' repeated reference to his going away is always accompanied and counterbalanced by the reassurance of a 'coming', a coming of someone who would continue his mission and bring to fulfilment the destiny of his disciples; but a coming that is conditional to him 'going away' and sending the Advocate. Jesus' 'going to the Father' is a '*going home*', and home is where we belong, where we are fully ourselves and share unconditionally the richness of love and life gifted to us and making us who we are; and those are Jesus' parting gifts to his disciples of all time:

> '*I tell you the truth: it is to your advantage that I go away, for if I do not go away, the Advocate will not come to you; but if I go, I will send him to you.*' (John 16:7)

This is the revelation and promise of Jesus at the last supper; his gift and his promise before his final earthly act which he called 'going to the Father' – a promise that he personified and called the Paraclete.

The 'Advocate'

This is the core revelation and promise of Jesus at the Last Supper; his parting gift before going to the Father and the promise which he personified and called '*the Advocate*', *who in his physical absence* '*will speak-to-the-world*' *for him through us,* whereby the totality and newness of life beyond the death of Jesus becomes the on-going experience of the disciple. For the believer caught in the dualism and contradictions of life, the new presence of Jesus through his Spirit impregnating our very DNA is the energy for the journey of life, and love is the concrete expression that makes this presence real and active in the reality of each day.

Belief in God's presence in human affairs proclaimed and witnessed by Jesus demands both awareness and acceptance of this living and ongoing presence in the real and concrete '*now*' beyond or in spite of contrary sensory evidence and in the most diverse and even death-dealing situations we may become entangled in. Once Jesus' physical presence is no longer accessible through the human senses, the power of his resurrection does not die but becomes the human experience of life 'beyond' and 'within' through the active and life-giving presence of the Spirit. The truth of the presence and action of the Spirit in each of us is not only a memory of having been signed with a sacramental ritual such as Confirmation. What makes God's presence alive and active is our readiness to live out the reality that is ours, totally impregnated with the creative power of God in us, constantly energising us into life and urging us to bring life and love around us. For the believer, 'life in spite of death' is both destiny and energy informing the concrete reality now.

That is why Jesus urges us to rejoice and hope; we have no need or reason to feel orphaned, abandoned or afraid, whatever our personal or collective stories. The Spirit of God is the Spirit of Life that brought Jesus through the experience of death and into the fullness of life. The Spirit promised by Jesus as his ultimate and absolute gift to us is the same breath of God of the first instant of creation, and the energy for truth and love that will enliven our earthly journey. The Spirit is the power of life that comes from and leads to love: love of God for us flowing into real and concrete love for each other on the journey of life, transforming the believer into living proof of God's active and loving presence in people's lives and on the roads of our world.

> *'If you love me, you will keep my commandments... They who have my commandments and keep them are those who love me; and those who love me will be loved by my Father, and I will love them and reveal myself to them.'* (John 14:15, 21)

Love is the ultimate sign of God's presence in the reality of everyday, and love is the one absolute commandment enjoined on the followers of Jesus called to *'advocate'* and *'speak-to-the-world' for him*, allowing for no exception under any circumstance. Jesus always equates the commandments with love because the urging of the Spirit to bring life and love is not a legal imposition, but a necessary outflow of a personal awareness of being caught up in the power of God alive and active in us. As Christians, we do not act out of legalism but out of love, and if we accept the presence of

God through the power of the Spirit in our lives, we leave ourselves no option but to bring life and love to others unconditionally and absolutely.

Energised by the Spirit, we must each become an energiser for the whole world. Whoever and wherever these others may be, every human being is caught up in a spiral of divine presence and love, and everyone is destined for fullness of life. But this vortex of creative and life-giving power can only become a reality if our lives are symbols and instruments of resurrection, exuding life and love into the world and its history.

When the world sees us hopeful in the midst of uncertainty, compassionate in the presence of suffering, active when all around is helpless apathy, loving in the face of rejection and personal hurts, joyful when darkness is deep and frightening, peace-filled through personal struggles, comforting to the lonely and rejected – then the world will know the meaning of Jesus' reassurance that he will not leave us orphan people; and the world will experience the truth of the living and loving presence of God. Then the whole world will be transformed by the touch of God and the power of the Spirit, yes through us and in spite of us.

Presence in Absence (Ascension)

Mark 16:15-20 / Matthew 28:1-10

Confusion and Promises Fulfilled

AS WE COME TO THE END of the liturgical cycle of Easter centred on Jesus' appearances to his disciples after his resurrection, the liturgy puts before us the last such encounter in what Christian tradition has come to know as the Ascension of Jesus to the Father.

On the last evening of his earthly life, Jesus gathered his disciples in the upper room, the place that was to become the hub of the followers of Jesus. In an atmosphere of intense emotion and in the intimacy of a ritual meal, Jesus engaged in a long conversation mixing expressions of deep emotions in a mantra-like persistence on the theme of love, together with down-to-earth realism. Warning his followers of what lay ahead, making no secret about the fact that very soon, he would no longer be with them, and they would be looking for him in vain. Engaging at length about his leaving them, he persisted on advising them that he would be going home, '*to prepare a place for them*', while at the same time repeatedly reassuring them that he would not leave them orphan or alone.

Not that such reassurance contributed in any way to ease their pain when events precipitated rapidly both for Jesus and for his disciples who, within a few hours, saw him hanging dead on a cross, and his body entombed in a grave. Yes, he did come back to them after the Resurrection, but soon after he left them for the second time, and this time definitively, when he returned to his Father and

Presence in Absence (Ascension)

our Father, to his God and to our God, as he had told them many times before that he would (John 20:17).

This hide and seek sequence of Jesus dying and rising, appearing and disappearing, sharing a meal and vanishing from their eyes only threw the disciples into deeper confusion, a roller coaster of contradictory emotions, a bewilderment of cosmic proportion. As he had warned them, the disciples are truly lost, not knowing what to make of him, of his dying and of his being with them again. Yet through it all, they are gripped by the power of an experience that has no human rationale beyond the fact that only God could pull this off. They had seen Jesus dead and buried and yet there he was, inside a locked room, asking them for a piece of fish to eat. As they stood, their minds numb with confusion and fear, he greeted them with the gift of peace, the one element that really ran at a very low level of priority in their hearts and in that environment.. They were running away, trying to forget and pretend it had never happened, and he falls in step with them on the road, sharing their pain and enlivening their hope. He is back from the dead, totally himself, and yet they will never be able to hold on to him as they did before (John 20:17).

During that central revelatory conversation at the Last Supper (John 14:12.28), Jesus had already primed his disciples for the pain of separation, repeatedly foreshadowing the fact that he would leave them and go away. Likewise, after his Resurrection, in the encounter with Mary, distraught for the loss of her Master and searching for him as a dead body in an empty tomb, the risen Jesus reassures her of his living presence beyond death, but points beyond the here and now, telling her

> 'Do not hold on to me, because I have not yet ascended to the Father. But go to my brothers and say to them, "I am ascending to my Father and your Father, to my God and your God".' (John 20:18)

Such a strange mix of reassurance and warning will remain obscure to the disciples for a time; but to us, with the hindsight of two thousand years of Christian tradition, it has the flavour of a preamble to some momentous event representing the climax of the Gospel narrative, and the final fulfilment of Jesus' life and mission. Clearly, Jesus is saying goodbye to his disciples, but in that mix of events more like an au revoir and a goodbye full of promise.

In the Gospel narratives, eventually Jesus leaves the disciples not once but twice, the second time definitely and forever, telling us that he must return to the Father in that unique and mysterious event we call the Ascension, the event which in many ways reproposes the same pre-resurrection scenario. Each time the disciples face the confusion of extremes, and all the transforming consequences, and each time they are called to make sense of unexplained and unexpected loss, abandonment and confusion (Acts 1:6-11). In both cases, the disciples have to deal with a situation of immeasurable loss and of hopeless emptiness. At the same time, in both cases, the disciples are caught up in an event that becomes a turning point in their individual stories, as well as in the community story. In both cases, in the end, the deep sense of loss somehow explodes into a sense of wonder and joy that defies human words, and transposes those who lived through it into a totally new level of reality and self-understanding.

The post-Resurrection disciples and believers of all times will always be trapped in a confusion of extremes, an interplay of presence in absence, of intimacy without possessiveness, of fullness of life when all the evidence is of death. *Jesus is there, but he is no longer theirs.* No longer can the disciples hold on to the Lord as their possession, but precisely when they reach out to him as they knew him, the Risen Lord constantly distances himself from them, as the end of the Emmaus event beautifully illustrates (Luke 24:13-35). That is the dominant constant of the biblical narrative highlighting the twin event of Resurrection and Ascension as the one experience of the Lord without any personally sensory experience of his physical presence. This is also *the call for all of us when we claim faith in Jesus, dead and risen and forever the living revelation of God with us.*

Endings and Beginnings

Ascension celebrates the fulfilment of those anticipated predictions, although the disciples will be forever caught in the dilemma of opposites. As John says in his narrative of the Ascension, those first eyewitnesses to the end failed spectacularly to understand the meaning of Jesus' words and of his whole life and death: 'On that mountain some doubted' (John 20:17).

As such, the context of today's celebration carries a significant element of closure. Together with the celebration of Pentecost, this gathering on the mountain of Galilee brings to conclusion not only the liturgical cycle of Easter, but the earthly story and mission of Jesus. *Jesus' Ascension* to the Father is more than just a physical hovering in the sky, but *a revelation that the Lord has now ascended to a totally other level of reality, a level that defies time and space, nearness or distance, physical absence or personal presence. Jesus' Ascension is both the fulfilment of a promise and the confirmation of a destiny.*

At the same time, the final words of Jesus clearly declare the very opposite of any departure or conclusion but speak of new beginnings and of presence now and in the future. The closing line of Matthew's Gospel,

'I am with you always, to the end of the age.' (Matthew 28:20)

was Jesus' welcome greeting into a totally new reality for those who stood by him on the mountain, wondering and confused at what was happening to them and around them. Once again, we have that interface of beginnings and endings, of future and past, and of presence and absence which is so dominant throughout the Easter narratives and during the post-Easter liturgical season.

Just as the Resurrection had been the supreme proclamation revealing the eternal, unfailing and life-giving presence of the Lord beyond and in spite of the finality of death in the human story, the final earthly goodbye of Jesus to those who followed him is the absolute reassurance of this eternal presence beyond and in spite of his physical absence in their future story. *Ascension celebrates the continuity of God's eternal presence-in-absence in our lives and in our world, in life and in death.*

While Matthew (28:16-20) and Mark (16:19-20) only hint at this duality of perspective, Luke clearly highlights both dimensions of ending and beginning by giving us two diverse narratives of the event, each throwing a different light on a story of past and future at the same time. At the end of his Gospel, Luke tells us that

> *While (Jesus) was blessing them, he withdrew from them and was carried up into heaven.* (Luke 24:51)

However, things do not end there, because the third evangelist picks up the same story as the opening lines of Acts with an obvious forward intentionality and perspective, centred on those very same disciples still doubt-full and fear-full, who are repeatedly told that they are now to be his witnesses and his instruments in the Galilees of this world and for all time.

> *'You will receive power when the Holy Spirit has come upon you; and you will be my witnesses in Jerusalem, in all Judea and Samaria, and to the ends of the earth.' When he had said this, as they were watching, he was lifted up, and a cloud took him out of their sight.'* (Acts 1:8-9)

Going Home

The final and definitive physical appearance of Jesus to his disciples taps directly into that perennial and natural yearning of the human heart which seeks to be at home, tending unceasingly to reach beyond purely sensory evidence and the limitations of time and space, beyond the measurable and foreseeable.

On the mountain, he is true to his word, fulfilling the promise made to his immediate followers in the Upper Room, and to all believers for all time. In that raising to a new level of being by Jesus in the midst of confusion of extremes, as believers are given *a glimpse of our own destiny in the future, and a commitment to live by in the present*.

In Jesus' mind, leaving his disciples was never meant to be a separation from the present but a projection into a future of total union with the Father, for himself and for all those who claimed fellowship and discipleship. Jesus' persistence about going to the Father to prepare a place for his disciples speaks clearly of home and homecoming, and never of closure and abandonment. The pain of leaving is a function of the joy of embracing home.

Ascension celebrates yearning for fulfilment, for homecoming and for oneness, as well as celebrating our roots and our destiny at the same time. At the Last Supper, Jesus spoke at length to his disciples about his leaving them, telling them persistently that he would be '*going home, to prepare a place*' for them, while at the same time repeatedly reassuring them that he would not leave them orphans or alone, with his promise that he would come back and take us home with him (John 14:1-3).

> "*I go to prepare a place for you. And if I go and prepare a place for you, I will come again and will take you to myself, so that where I am, there you may be also.*" (John 14:2-3)

That is Jesus' going-away promise and a reassurance of our inalienable destiny in an eternal oneness of togetherness where he is and where we are all meant to be with each other and with our God, the life-giving Father whose heart yearns just as much for our return to him as ours longs to go back home where we belong.

Allow me to share a cherished personal memory. On the last day of one of my last visits to my elderly mother, the day before my departure that would take me across half the world to the opposite end of the globe, she gave me a precious going away gift, one that I will treasure for the rest of my life. In the course of a casual conversation, she commented with a glint in her eyes and a wavering in her voice: 'I would love you to stay a little longer, but I know that in order for both of us to enjoy your next visit home, you must go away now'. That insight of an over ninety year old seemed to echo strongly the words of Jesus when he told his disciples that it was necessary for him to go away so that they might have fullness of life, peace and joy in the power of the Spirit. *Jesus went home so that we too may be at home.*

Home is where the heart belongs, and one of the most powerful yearnings of the human heart is 'to *find* a home', 'to *be* at home', or 'to *go* home'. In our normal parlance, home does not refer exclusively to geographical or temporal categories but carries strong connotations beyond time and place. All of us have experienced moments when *'we feel at home'*, while thousands of kilometres away from our place of residence. *Home is where one belongs in freedom and peace, where affections are expressed and lived out in mutual joy, where one is welcomed and where encounters and relationships blossom and are re-energised.*

Ascension celebrates our destiny on the blueprint of Jesus' homecoming, the final and eternal union with the Father. Today we are reminded that *our destiny is total union with God and with each other*, precisely the kind of union which our heart yearns for and which God has destined for each of us, from eternity and for eternity (Ephesians 1). Jesus' Ascension is more than just a physical hovering in the sky before disappearing from human sight, but a revelation that *the Lord has now ascended to a totally other level of reality* – a level that defies time and space, nearness or distance, physical absence or personal presence. In that raising to a new level of reality by Jesus, we are all given a glimpse of our own destiny in the future and of a commitment to live by for the rest of our living years.

Presence in Absence (Ascension)

At the end of that long conversation with those he calls 'children' and 'friends', after repeatedly reassuring us not to be afraid and to trust him, he places us into the hands of the Father in one of the most emotional and stirring prayers on our behalf and for all time. In a sudden and spectacular change of mood while still speaking to his disciples but returning to the Father, Jesus prays:

> *'They were yours... I am asking on their behalf; I am not asking on behalf of the world, but on behalf of those whom you gave me, because they are yours... I am no longer in the world, but they are in the world... I am not asking you to take them out of the world, but I ask you to protect them from the evil one... Sanctify them in the truth;... so that they also may be sanctified in truth. Holy Father, protect them in your name... so that they may be one, as we are one... so that they may have my joy made complete in themselves.'* (John 17:1-14)

Wherever we may be and whatever our hearts may yearn to embrace and to hold, we rest on one absolute security: with his last human breath, Jesus placed us in the hands of the Father for the rest of our journey towards home with him and one with each other. As Jesus is with the Father, so we will be with God and in eternal 'common-unity' forever. In these terms, the celebration of Jesus' return to the Father – rather than a departure – becomes the fulfilment of his ultimate wish and a mission for us to live his presence in togetherness with one another, in the sure knowledge that in Jesus' physical absence we are safe and at peace in the hands of the Father and energised by the Spirit. That is our destiny but is also a commitment for us who are left with the memory of his presence and a promise of hope now, commitment to joy now, and unconditional love now.

The presence-absence of Jesus in the life of the disciples exudes the flavour of a call to a spectacular transformation and new beginnings into a world of hope, of energy and a renewed sense of presence, because transformation and new beginnings are the very raison d'être of the Easter-Ascension-Pentecost liturgical season.

Because of Ascension, the disciple is called to live through the struggles and dilemmas of making sense of the words, actions and promises of Jesus on the one hand, and on the other, of dealing with experiences, full of questions and the confusion and uncertainties the first followers of Jesus went through in the immediate before and after the Resurrection experience.

After the Ascension and Jesus of Nazareth was no longer with them, the early disciples had only the memory of Jesus, of what he did and of what he said, but a memory of an extraordinary, all-transforming experience, and a deep sense of having been chosen, befriended, called by name by Jesus, as well as of having been repeatedly left orphaned. Are we such people of transformation, of new beginnings, of renewed energy and of fresh awareness? Alternatively, do we just celebrate a series of empty rituals, perhaps gazing at events of the past, like the disciples looking up into an empty sky, with no significance and even less bearing on our daily lives?

Not Passive Spectators but Committed Actors

While the return of Jesus to the Father marks the end of his human story, at the same time it makes us not just passive spectators of God's action in the world, but primary actors in the story of humanity – a humanity now and forever impregnated with the energy of God who totally shared our human condition, from birth to death.

From this perspective of presence-in-absence, Ascension takes on a totally new meaning and becomes a pivotal event in the ongoing Christian story, intertwining into one past, present and future. The critical message of the whole Easter liturgical season is not about loss and loneliness, but about intertwining our way of life here and now with our perspective on a future, projecting us into a future reality of love, peace and joy. Ascension is not a looking up into an empty sky, but a commitment to becoming ever more grounded on this earth and instruments of that future of eternal love, peace and joy lived and witnessed now in our daily reality.

The three synoptics (Matthew 28:16-20; Mark 16:19-20; Luke 24:50-53) come to a sudden, abrupt and virtually stark conclusion of their narrative, with only Luke's explicitly mentioning in yet a different context that

> *as they were watching, (Jesus) was lifted up and a cloud took him out of their sight.* (Acts 1:10)

and the disciples standing gazing into the heavens, worrying about the destiny of Jesus, wondering, once again, about the absurdity of another good-bye, of more unanswered questions, and of further loss and loneliness. Occasionally, we encounter experiences where the sense of loss can be so chronic and all-pervading, that even idle wondering and speculation seem to relieve the boredom of asking questions of 'why' or 'where is your God'. On such occasions, questions and disillusionment cut deeply into the sameness and practicality of our lives and, like a fiery sword of light, challenge and reshape our praxis and our perspective.

As the disciples stood bewildered, confused and some 'still doubting' to the end looking at the sky (Matthew 28:17) the final au revoir greets them with words of *promise, companionship, mission.*

> '*Go therefore and make disciples of all nations, baptising them in the name of the Father and of the Son and of the Holy Spirit, and teaching them to obey everything that I have commanded you. And remember, I am with you always, to the end of the age.*' (Matthew 28:18-20)

All of us today and forever, like the first disciples, need to hear those words challenging us and heed the injunction spoken by the messengers of God.

> '*Men of Galilee, why do you stand looking up towards heaven? This Jesus, who has been taken up from you into heaven, will*

come in the same way as you saw him go into heaven.' (Acts 1:11)

There is a strong sense of earthiness in the message to

'Go into all the world and proclaim the good news to the whole creation.' (Mark 16:15)

– a message projecting the disciple into a future presence and action that will bring presence in absence and peace in turmoil precisely in the earthiness of everyday life.

While leaving us to till the earth we stand on, the absence-presence of Jesus who ascends to the heavens to prepare a place for his disciples is not some other-worldly, pie-in-the-sky dream, but a *'presence in spite of physical absence'*. This is the presence that only the heart knows and yearns for, a presence that makes us feel at home and radiates *'at-homeness'* all around us. In the end, *the physical absence of Jesus in our world will only be redeemed by our presence to each other, as people embracing home and committing ourselves to the Jerusalem and Galilees of our daily lives.* Wherever we may be and whatever our hearts may yearn to embrace and to hold, we rest on one absolute security of resting in the heart and hands of our Father where Jesus, with his last human breath, placed us a few hours before his death and resurrection.

Ascension is a commitment to the present and future energised by memory of the past. Any attempt at holding on to the sensory and visible meets with the same injunction of the angels to the women at the empty tomb.

'Go quickly and tell his disciples, "He has been raised from the dead, and indeed he is going ahead of you in Galilee; there you will see him"' (Matthew 28:7)

when Jesus himself greeted the grieving women at the tomb by reassuring them with the words and telling them,

'Go and tell my brothers to go to Galilee; there they will see me.'
(Matthew 28:10)

Galilee is the place of realistic practicalities, of down-to-earth simplicity, of ordinariness and commonality, of heart-people with little regard for the strict Judaic observances or the legalistic convolutions of Jerusalem. Galilee is 'the Galilee of the Gentiles',, the potpourri of cultures, ethnicity and traditions where reality is what you see, and what you see is never quite perfect, or what you expect to find. Galilee is the place where Jesus is to be encountered, and where our presence as disciples must witness to his presence in absence.

The ordinary, the everyday, the unexpected and limited Galilee of our lives and of the life around us is both the place of encounter and of mission for the disciple. The disciples are to stop gazing into the sky. They must look for and realise concretely God's living and active presence where they are, and there find the Lord, as much as bring the Lord to others. The presence of Jesus in the Spirit is not some other-worldly, pie-in-the-sky fantasy, but a presence in spite of physical absence. enabling us to assume a new self-awareness of who we are and a new vision as to what we do, both as individual believing disciples.

Sometimes, this presence and mission may appear to us as inadequate or even as terrifying as handling snakes and drinking poison (Mark 16:18). In the end, however, *the physical absence of Jesus in our world will only be redeemed by our presence to each other*, as people who know the presence of God in their lives and are committed to the Kingdom right here and now.

No Looking Up to Heaven

The Fourth Gospel has no official missioning in its story. And yet all the Easter narratives are pregnant with the injunction to go and proclaim what the disciples have witnessed (John 20:17). The missionary dimension is not an optional extra for the Easter-person. On the contrary, discipleship cannot be genuine unless the Good News is proclaimed by those who claim belief in the resurrection beyond any sensory proof.

The disciple is a missionary by their very nature, but the mission is not their own. Each is entrusted with the mission and can lay no entitlement to the mission except the claim to being a mediator and an instrument. The message proclaimed is not of one's own making, nor do we possess the Risen Lord that we proclaim. To Mary of Magdala who was trying to hold the Risen Lord as her own, Jesus said,

> *'Do not hold on to me, because I have not yet ascended to the Father. But go to my brothers and say to them, "I am ascending to my Father and your Father, to my God and your God". Mary Magdalene went and announced to the disciples, 'I have seen the Lord'; and she told them that he had said these things to her.* (John 20-17-18)

'Go and tell my brothers and sisters' is not just an invitation but a challenge to our authenticity as believing disciples in whatever life-journey we embrace. The drive to mission must stem from deep inside the heart of the one who claims to have seen the Lord, as an energy that comes from the Lord and leads to the Lord. The disciple never possesses the Risen Lord as an exclusively private personal relationship, but simply proclaims to the whole world the Lord each has seen and experienced in their own life.

Anything short of this theological understanding of mission makes for personal advancement or professional expertise, but not necessarily for evangelising discipleship. The disciple is to go and proclaim to the whole world that *'the Lord is risen'* (Matthew 27:40; Mark 14:58; John 2:19), even if all sensory evidence or human rationality seem to deny that presence. Our faith in the Risen Lord becomes authentic and credible only when we live by the spirit of joy and hope embedded in the Easter event, and others experience that joy and peace in us and through us.

Presence in Absence (Ascension)

Ascension challenges us to understand Church as 'Ecclesia' (ἐκκλησία), the reality where *belonging implies the absolute imperative to be visible evidence of this eternal and life-giving presence*, and never a consumer of ritual legalism or a number in a sectarian club. First century Palestine spoke of the 'Galilee of the nations', not as a geographical identification but as a way of being and living. Like Church for us, Galilee had a universal and people-centred connotation, linking together people of the most diverse backgrounds, social status, economic, and religious persuasions. Galilee meant life lived in the full gamut of daily experiences of work and family, struggles and success, relationships, and beliefs. There Jesus sent his disciples to carry on his mission of healing and salvation.

In the potpourri of our busy suburban streets and tenement houses, in our family struggles, in our exhilarating encounters, in the boredom and difficulties of making ends meet, in giving life and in sharing love – there, we must proclaim the living, healing, and affirming presence of God, and *we must do it*. Unless this happens, we will be those people standing with our feet on the ground and looking into an empty sky, without understanding and without hope. Unless we become responsible instruments of peace and concrete down-to-earth committed love, the Ascension of the Lord will only degenerate into the ultimate act of separation of God from our world, and his work, life and death, a meaningless sophism, lost in some old dusty history books. If we do not become actors of presence and instruments of life and love, not only will the world be poorer, but we will have betrayed our personal protestation of faith, and indeed we will never be able to recognise or find the very God in which we claim to believe.

In a world driven by efficient organisations and structures based on hierarchical systems of operation to ensure success as the ultimate and exclusive value, we may be tempted to point to the Church as the institution chosen by Christ to ensure efficiency and success in proclaiming Good News and continuing his work through time and space. However, if we as individuals do not feel personally responsible for the mission that is but a life-long realisation of our Baptismal claim, no institution will ever touch and transform the life of people or make God's saving presence a reality in this world. Individually and collectively, we are responsible in our time and our space, and we are weak, and sinful, and broken. This Church – called to incarnate the mission left by Jesus – carries all the frailty and weakness of humanity, and cannot make any claim to absolute perfection, nor give any guarantee of success. As someone facetiously put it, 'if you want a perfect Church, please join it; but just remember that from that moment onwards, your chosen Church will no longer be perfect'.

Our efforts may often appear insignificant, our vision may be blurred and our resolve weakened. Our witness will know rejection and attract contradiction. But in Jesus, God is there, yes, to the end of time and on that one certainty we commit ourselves to the world that stands uncertain, broken, and searching for a meaning in the emptiness of sky and tomb. Human frailty, weakness, misunderstandings and shortcomings will always make heavy demands on our commitment and our witnessing, often obscuring the vision and weakening the resolve. But there, in that weakness and in those heavy personal demands, also lies the greatest challenge to authenticity and the stimulus to that fruitfulness which Jesus refers to and which is inherent to the metaphor of the vine (John 15:1-5).

Jesus reminded us very clearly: *'You did not choose me but I chose you. And I appointed you go and bear fruit, fruit that will last'* (John 15:16); and in that one choice of his lies our greatest challenge, both in terms of commitment and of trust on our part. Only when we are prepared to stop looking into the empty sky of speculation and theory but enter completely into the reality of the Galilees of our lives and there become presence to each other through serving without imposition or control, and through receiving service with openness and trust, only then will the vine be abundantly fruitful;

only then we will be truly disciples sent out to meet the Lord in the many Galilees of this world.

When our commitment to human promotion, to justice, and peace has become the lived reality for everyone in the world, then we will have finally understood Ascension; we will have listened for the first time to the parting words of Jesus and become leaven of life and love for our world and our time. Only then will God become present and visible once again amidst the confusion and darkness that may surround us, and we will have become true disciples committed to the God with us here, and we will be journeying on towards our destiny of fullness that is life and love together as a community and with our God.

The Energy of God in our Hands (The Spirit)

Acts 2:1-12

At the Break of Morning

ALL OF US HAVE OUR LITTLE PET HATES – small, niggling little things that annoy and irritate us: food that we avoid because of its colour, positioning of papers and clips on our desks, people exhibiting a certain mannerism. But while such 'pet hates' undoubtedly irritate us, they also raise our awareness of differences and diverse reaction to the beauty and richness in us and around us. Indeed, those very annoying peculiarities can sometime be the source of rich and deep insights and, occasionally, of dramatic awareness stimulating change and transformations. That is what happened to me that early morning.

I dislike the wind intensely. It makes me particularly up-tight, unbearable to myself and others, and that had been a particularly wild night – swishing, howling, creaking of boards and rattling of windows, crashing of branches and swirling of dead autumn leaves against my door. I had slept in fits and starts as the haphazard yet unrelenting upsurge of that invisible fury kept me awake all night, thus adding to my frustration and tiredness. How foolish to be angry at the wind, but I did feel a strong surge of anger spurred on by that subconscious certainty that I had absolutely no control either over the elements or over my unreasonable though self-justified reactions. The flickering electric clock said 6.00 AM and I peeped through the curtains, unconvinced that the new day would somehow relieve the restlessness of a sleepless night. It was so intensely dark out there, and I double-checked the time.

Suddenly and most unexplainably, heavy boots on my feet and the thick coat wrapped tightly round my body, I was halfway up that track affectionately but for no particular reason called Mount Tabor, winding through sparse clumps of trees and green pastures dotted with cattle grazing unconcerned by the vagaries of the wind or the moodiness of the unusual morning visitor. I had been up that semi-barren hill many times before when the sun was warm and the three-hundred-and-sixty-degrees vista was breathtaking; but never before had I trudged my way up the that rocky outcrop at six in the morning, challenging a fierce, early winter storm.

This was a unique climb, strange in its unplanned timing and spontaneity. 'Sheer madness brought on by the frustrations of a sleepless night and a howling wind!' I thought. 'There is no other reason why I should be walking up this track at this time of morning', I mused, almost as self-justification for my uncharacteristic and, deep down, unwanted morning hike.

It was then that I saw it. I stopped short, just before the brow of Tabor, my eyes fixed on the dark outline of the near hills to the East. A bright red and orange sheath of light was tearing the black sky apart, ripping away large chunks of clouds in a spectacular and awesome dance of colours and shapes, almost angrily revealing life bursting forth from the dark womb of a stormy night. Even the howling wind had taken on a new role now, rising and falling in unison and creative harmony with the symphony of a new day exploding in the morning sky. Crimson, orange, yellow and blue spread and danced across the sky as the darker fragments of the heavy night clouds raced recklessly into some magical dissolution towards the Northeast.

Eyes fixed on the kaleidoscopic revelry, I reached the brow of the hill just as the explosion of light and colour had overtaken me, and it was now bathing the valley below, spreading a myriad of hues on the vast expanse of the city and across to distant Mount Macedon, that soft, bluish outline marking out the western horizon, sparkling clear but mostly unnoticed over years.

Day had broken through, and the onrush of light and warmth had overcome the wildness of the night wind. A new sense of life, and peace and harmony seemed to take over, soothing my moods and my limbs and bringing into relief objects and details seen a thousand times yet never captured before. As I gazed into the distant horizon, now swept clean, washed by the fury of the night and brought to life by the warmth of the new light, I felt a new vision awakening and a new perspective come into relief. Distant and faint objects came into focus with astonishing sharpness and clarity, as if they were now at arm's length. The dullness of the city sky, shrouded in weeks-long smog, was now crystal clear, revealing a unique richness of shapes and forms. The autumn colours of the nearby hills at my back breathed a sense of wonder and of growth that no Michelangelo will ever portray.

In a majestic all-transforming explosion of light and life. suddenly I became aware of a powerful stillness. Yes, the wind stood still... and the kookaburra laughed... and the hawk hovered silently overhead... and all because of that irritating and stormy night! It was then that the final and sudden realisation overwhelmed me: it was Pentecost Sunday morning. Any wonder then that the early Christians, in trying to express the experience that had overwhelmed them on that first Pentecost morning, could only articulate it precisely through the imagery of wind and fire (Acts 2:1-12).

Like for the creation story, the event of Pentecost proved of such cosmic dimensions that only images and the language of metaphors could adequately express its manifestations and consequences.

> *When Pentecost day came round, they had all met in one room, when suddenly they heard what sounded like a powerful wind from heaven, the noise of which filled the entire house in which they were sitting; and something appeared to them that seemed like tongues of fire; these separated and came to rest on the head*

> *of each of them. They were all filled with the Holy Spirit and began to speak foreign languages as the Spirit gave them the gift of speech. Now there were devout people living in Jerusalem from every nation under heaven, and at this sound they all assembled, each one bewildered to hear these men speaking their own language. They were amazed and astonished.... Everyone was amazed and unable to explain it.* (Acts 2:1-12)

Pentecost: Death and Re-birth

The narrative of the Pentecost event carries a strong sense of deja vu, immersing the reader into the powerful cosmic events of God's creative act of Genesis 1, when

> *the earth was a formless void, there was darkness over the deep, and God's spirit hovered over the water* (Genesis 1:2)

and because of this breath of God, chaos was redeemed and life exploded into being. The primordial elements of fire and wind speak of total transformation not only of the cosmic world, but all living creatures at their deepest and most authentic psychic and spiritual level, affecting in a radical way the lives, and indeed the very being of those who lived through it. For the disciples gathered in the Upper Room, grieving the loss of Jesus of Nazareth and all that this loss meant for their lives, Pentecost re-interpreted and reincarnated a moment of crucial transformation of their life story and a new beginning, totally unexpected, unplanned and unexplainable. It was as if an irresistible energy had invested those people upturning every dimension of their life and propelling them into a totally new and surprising way of being. Pentecost recalls both the saving historical event of Jesus' Resurrection and, most importantly, the disciples' personal experience of Resurrection.

Taking a chronological view of the events, John Shea makes the interesting point that the disciples experience twice the loss of Jesus. The first time when he walked out of the Upper Room into the darkness of the night and eventually into his death and burial, and then again when he leaves them staring into the sky as he finally 'goes to the Father'. Between these two events, the powerful, all-transforming experience of Resurrection shatters fear and death itself, only to be shattered in return by the final 'going away'. As Diarmuid McGann comments:

> Absence and presence seem to be a rhythm all through the Gospel... Each moment of absence seems to be followed by a more intense moment of presence. When he has been with them for a while they begin to take him for granted and create an illusion about themselves... (*and*) heir identity becomes inflated. In the moment of darkness there is a reversal, and in the experience of absence they are invited into a new awareness.[71]

From a literal perspective, one cannot but notice the strong parallelism between the Easter stories of the gospels and the Pentecost narrative of Acts 2. In both cases, the disciples are in a state of shock, withdrawal and denial, searching for a meaning in the world-shattering upheaval they have just experienced. In both cases, the scenario is one of 'loss of immeasurable consequence', of emptiness, and of hopeless waiting for the furore to simmer down, before returning each to their fields and their nets, in the hope maybe of obliterating the tragic and unfortunate events that brought them to this point.

In both events, there is a definitive turning point that has neither rhyme nor reason in human terms, but an event of such magnitude that only a direct intervention of God in human history could have brought it about. In both events, the deep sense of loss somehow explodes into a sense of wonder and joy that defies human words and propels those who lived through it not only to proclaim a revolutionary message, but to live in a totally new way.

---

[71] Diarmuid McGann, *The Journeying Self. The Gospel of Mark through a Jungian Perspective*, New York NJ: Paulist Press, 1985, 159

Jesus' reassurance to his disciples at the Last Supper that he would not leave them orphans because the Father would *'send another advocate to be with them forever'* (John 14:16) must have sounded hollow and quite unintelligible on that tragic day of execution and burial or when they stood staring into the sky where the Lord seemed to have disappeared. But as they cowered once again in the Upper Room, waiting for the furore to calm down before returning each to their fields and their nets, trying to put it all out of their mind, suddenly it all made sense. Indeed, that strong wind and that wildfire that filled the place not only reminded them of the promise Jesus had left them but touched their heart and soul, transforming them totally into new creatures. Only then they understood Jesus' words and the story they had become caught into, a story now spoken in wind and fire. Then they remembered! (John 14:26-27).

The experience of Jesus is foundational for the Christian believer of all times. Historically, however the physical experience of Jesus' presence is short-lived, limited in time to a few individuals and, from a human perspective, unbelievably tragic in its ultimate solution. Once Jesus of Nazareth was no longer with them, the early Christians had only the memory of Jesus, of what he did and of what he said. But the memory could not just remain a nostalgic recall of past events, an empty ritual to be performed, or a sentimental and arrogant claim denying the stormy night. The memory of Jesus in the Church of all time can only be real to the extent that it becomes a realistic and critical evaluation of the present reality in the light of Jesus' life and death. without sweeteners or alibis, possessiveness or exclusivity. That *'Memory'*, celebrated in word and table fellowship became a celebration of the radical and dramatic transformation from death to life, pre-figured in Jesus' very life and mission, and engendered in their own lives by the onrush of the power promised to his disciples by Jesus at the Last Supper as his Last Will and Testament and as his parting gift.

> *'Do not let your hearts be troubled... You shall receive power when the Holy Spirit has come upon you; and you shall be my witnesses... and remember, I will be with you always, to the end of the age!'* (John 14:1;16:13; Matthew 28:20).

These are not just nice words from some ancient text, at best recalling an event of the distant past and probably irrelevant to our life and in our history. The believer of all time is nothing but the incarnator of the disciples of Jesus in real terms in our own time. For the first disciples, the Resurrection was only subsequent to Good Friday, and the early Christians had to come to terms with the absence of Jesus before they could proclaim him in faith as *'Jesus the Lord'*. They had to experience death before they could announce resurrection. They had to go through the eye of the storm before they came to the full self-realisation of being intimately linked with Jesus through the power of the Advocate whom Jesus would send from the Father (John 16:5-15). They had to go through the painful, but cleansing and transforming power of fire and storm so that the new life they proclaimed could be really seen as the power of God's Spirit at work in the lives of real men and women.

Just as the Resurrection event proclaimed what God worked in Jesus through the power of the Spirit, so the Pentecost event proclaimed the presence and the action of the same Divine Spirit in the life of people and in the whole of human history.

The one firm conviction of the early Christians was the certainty of the active presence of Jesus in their midst in a unique and all-transforming manner, a presence so powerful and so real that it could only be described in metaphors of fire and wind. Pentecost is precisely the celebration of this God-empowered transformation from death to life, from fear to hope, from sadness to joy, from absence to presence... not just for a handful of people hiding in a house for fear of the Jews, but for all believers and for all times. Reflecting on our personal and collective response to Pentecost in our own life experience, Francis J. Moloney comments:

Pentecost puts an end to fear. The gift of the Spirit must give us the courage to open doors we lock around us. The Christian Church must take a serious look at itself and its performance. How are we coping with the increasing complicated and godless world into which Jesus sends us? Have we closed the doors around us, forming an elite, happy that we have all the answers? We need to be transformed at Pentecost. Our fear must be turned into joy, the disciple must become the missionary, opening door that we have shut. Repeating the mission of Jesus himself, we have now been sent, not to judge the world, but to save it (see John 3:16).[72]

The Spirit: Presence and Destiny

As I came down from the mountain, now aglow in the morning sun, I became distinctly aware of being caught up in a process of transformation, far beyond my power of comprehension or my ability to express it. Light-footed and boisterous of mind and body, now I was no longer a mere spectator of a meteorological marvel. I knew that, by my standing there on that mountain, I had become an integral part of a re-creation which no human power could ever call into being. This was no mere passage of time from night to daylight, heralded by a spectacular sunrise. Here was much more than the beginning of a new day. This was a moment of passage from the warm apathy of a long summer to the wild but pregnant fruitfulness of autumn.

The fury of the nightly elements had ushered in a new season. The hot dry summer was coming to an end and the symphony of colour and sounds around me spoke of calm and gathering time just around the corner. A new presence impregnated the cosmos, and all around me a new energy was stirring. New gifts were in store, new energies groaned and waited to be released (Romans 8:22-24), new perspectives pushed beyond a horizon so clear now but probably

---

[72] Francis J. Moloney (1992), *This is the Gospel of the Lord. Year A*, (Homebush NSW: St Paul Publications, 1992, 125.

soon to be dulled by forgetfulness and self-interest, new visions and dreams gave meaning and worth both to the storm and to the untimely mountain climb. This was truly a transforming moment. And now, energised by both experience and memory of wind and fire, it was my turn to tell the story. My life had to tell that story.

The seasonal transformation and the natural rites of passage are inexorable and teeming with possibilities. Likewise, our liturgical cycle is calling us out of Easter and into Pentecost, the season of fire and wind, of transformation and new beginnings, of energy and renewed sense of presence. Are we such people of transformation, of new beginnings, of renewed energy and of fresh awareness? Or are we just gazing at an event of the past with no significance and even less bearing on our daily life?

The words spoken by God's messenger to the disciples gazing beyond the clouds, lost in unspoken speculation and anxiety, reveal a deep sensation of concrete earthiness and practicality in the present and future.

> Pentecost is not an abstract mystery. We are asked to accept the spirit of our actual lives. When we do this, then we no longer belittle our own lives but know that even with all our inferiorities and frustrations, just by ourselves, we are something.[73]

The Presence of Jesus in the Spirit is not an otherworldly pie-in-the-sky, but a Power in our life and in our hands enabling *a new self-awareness* of who we are and *a new missionary visualisation* of what we do, both as individual believers/disciples and as a Church community.

> *'Why are you men from Galilee standing here looking into the sky? Jesus who has been taken up from you into heaven, this same Jesus will come back in the same way as you have seen him go there.'* (Acts 1:11)

---

[73] Ronald Rolheiser, *Forgotten Among the Lilies. Learning to Love Beyond Our Fears*, New York NY: Doubleday, 2005, 195.

Pentecost is a celebration both of God's ongoing presence and of our own personal destiny as disciples. The sense of *presence* calls us to accept that the power of God's Spirit is forever at work in our life, whatever the vagaries of our human story. On the other hand, the sense of *destiny* challenges us to nourish our awareness that this active power of God at work is a power for *transformation* with a precise, uniquely personal and eternal intentionality of intimacy with God from all eternity and for all eternity (Ephesians 1:3-12).

There is no doubt in Paul's mind as to who we are once we accept the 'ruah of God' in our life. The Spirit promised by Jesus and sent by the Father establishes a total and intimate relationship between us and God, the relationship of child and life-giver (Romans 8:14-17). The believing disciples is forever a child of God, and God is forever our *'Abba'*, and the Spirit is the spirit of wholeness within ourselves, with each other, and with our God.

> *For all who are led by the Spirit of God are children of God. For you did not receive the spirit of slavery to fall back into fear, but you have received the spirit of adoption. When we cry, 'Abba! Father!' it is the Spirit himself bearing witness with our spirit that we are children of God, and if children, then heirs, heirs of God and fellow heirs with Christ, provided we suffer with him in order that we may also be glorified with him,* (Romans 8:14-17)

The disciples had to stop looking up to the heavens and start focusing on the earth where they stood and where they had been sent by the Lord. Are we people who have grown and been transformed, or have we been more concerned with maintaining our own perspectives and our securities? Are we people who have the courage to climb the mountain of self-discovery and allow ourselves to change our perspective on God, on ourselves and on others, or are we people who lock themselves in their own private spirituality, cursing the wind of change and of insecurity? Are we truly convinced of such a human-divine identity beyond some shallow sentimentality, ritual correctness, or academic assent? When the unexpected, the unplanned and the unwanted shatters all our well-laid plans, do we wallow in self-pity or do we become people of silent joy, of active hope and of down-to-earth commitment?

Hope is never waiting for things to happen to us. Hope is making things happen in spite of ourselves, and allowing God to make things happen through us, on the one surety that the Spirit-Advocate groans within us (Romans 8:26) and walks the darkness with us. Hope is seeing the smile of God in the smile of the child and the pain of God in the loneliness of the aged and/or abandoned person. Hope is remaining open to the revelation of God, wherever and however God reveals himself in our daily commonality and drudgery, in our success and laughter, in our living and in our dying as Paul reminded us.

> *If you are guided by the Spirit, you will be in no danger of yielding to self-indulgence, since self-indulgence is the opposite of the Spirit, the Spirit is totally against such a thing, and it is precisely because the two are so opposed that you do not always carry out your good intentions. If you are led by the Spirit, no law can touch you.... What the Spirit brings is... love, joy, peace, patience, kindness, goodness, trustfulness, gentleness and self-control... Since the Spirit is our life, let us be directed by the Spirit.* (Galatians 5:16-25)

Although at times we may wonder whether (Jesus') promises are true, Pentecost reminds us of the richness of the gifts of the Spirit. It should fill us with courage and encourage us to respond to those unsolicited acts of faith, love and hope which rise up within us. They are the evidence of the Spirit within us, leading us forward into the wholeness of the truth, and into the wholeness of ourselves, as we realise our dreams.[74]

This is the kind of transformation that we celebrate at Pentecost and to which we re-commit ourselves each time we say we believe

---

[74] Francis J. Moloney, *This is the Gospel of the Lord. Year B*, Homebush NSW: St Paul Publications, 1993, 131.

in God-with-us. However, unless this transformation becomes incarnated in every fibre of our being, we may hold on to the memory of a distant and unintelligible event for the sake of human traditions, but we will never celebrate the Memory of Jesus, the Risen Lord who left us with the assurance that he is with us always – *yes, to the end of time.* (Matthew 28:20). Awareness of this power of God in our hands must stimulate and energise us into a personal and communal action for joy, peace and hope.

Encounter in Galilee

As if impelled by a force beyond their control, recklessly and fearlessly, the disciples became proclaimers of hope and bearers of joy, hope and peace to the whole world,. Suddenly, those frightened disciples, buried behind locked doors, could no longer hold that power for themselves. Unafraid and free, they had to shout it to the whole world, because the whole world had to become unafraid and free in the power of the Spirit.

Pentecost carries both transformation and commitment to become transformers and energisers of divine presence in the lived reality of our world, each time we say we believe in God with us (Resurrection) and beyond us (Pentecost). A person who has been touched and transformed by the power of God can no longer be satisfied with an individualistic me-and-God-alone type of faith. Touched and transformed by the power of the Spirit, the disciples cannot hide the secret any longer, the family business has to be carried on and the secret revealed to energise the whole world into transformation. Profession of belief demands that this energy of God in our hands becomes Good News and energy of transformed life for the whole world.

Reflecting on our personal and collective response to Pentecost in our own life experience, Francis J. Moloney comments:

> Pentecost puts an end to fear. The gift of the Spirit must give us the courage to open doors we lock around us. Christian

Church must take a serious look at itself and its performance. How are we coping with the increasing complicated and godless world into which Jesus sends us? Have we closed the doors around us, forming an elite, happy that we have all the answers? We need to be transformed at Pentecost. Our fear must be turned into joy, the disciple must become the missionary, opening door that we have shut. Repeating the mission of Jesus himself, we have now been sent, not to judge the world, but to save it (see John 3:16).[75]

Pentecost carries both transformation and commitment to become transformers and energisers of divine presence in the lived reality of our world, each time we say we believe in God with us (Resurrection) and beyond us (Pentecost). What happened to the apostolic community, against all odds and in spite of human struggle to come to self-consciousness as a community, gathered and enlightened by the Spirit, must take place again today in our ecclesial assemblies, in our family gatherings, in our work-places and playgrounds, and in our tenement houses and down the street. The self-awareness of the Good News of a God whom we know as life-giver and energiser has to transform the world and radically change people in the way they think, they speak, and they act, or it is not Good News at all. Witness and commitment to joy, hope, peace and unity are not optional extras for the believer but the necessary outpouring of our faith in the power of God in our hands. Failing in this missionary dimension means our Christian story is not Good News at all.

Reflecting on our personal and collective response to Pentecost in our own life experience, Francis J. Moloney comments:

> Pentecost puts an end to fear. The gift of the Spirit must give us the courage to open doors we lock around us. Christian Church must take a serious look at itself and its performance. How are we coping with the increasing complicated and

---

[75] Francis J. Moloney (1992), *This is the Gospel of the Lord. Year A*, (Homebush NSW: St Paul Publications, 1992, 125.

godless world into which Jesus sends us? Have we closed the doors around us, forming an elite, happy that we have all the answers? We need to be transformed at Pentecost. Our fear must be turned into joy, the disciple must become the missionary, opening door that we have shut. Repeating the mission of Jesus himself, we have now been sent, not to judge the world, but to save it (see John 3:16).[76]

Today and for all time, God's Spirit hovers in the Church and, through their need and silent call for help, the poor are the unrecognised messengers of his presence, urging us to capture their call to be instruments of the Spirit. More than ever before, the poor today have a right to demand of us a commitment for justice that goes beyond some vague sense of solidarity or an in-principle declaration. In the Beatitudes, Jesus proclaimed *blessed the poor in spirit* (Matthew 5:3), and Spirit-energised transformation is a constant concrete intervention in human promotion, respect and fostering of life and its dignity at all levels, and practical sharing with the poor and needy in their daily journey of struggle, dependency and active hope.

When people see us joyful in the face of tribulations, hopeful in our daily struggles, at peace with questions and uncertainties, and loving in our mutual relationships beyond differences of personalities or roles, cultures or mores, then people will take notice and wonder. Then we would have proclaimed the action of the Spirit in us and started the conflagration of the presence of God's Spirit in our world. And then people will take notice and wonder and be transformed, and the world will know that peace and love that our hearts yearn for and groans from within, a peace and love put into our hands and heart by the living Power of God at work in us for eternity.

Every time we come together at worship, it is the Spirit that gathers us, that same Spirit that has given us life and love and has

---

[76] Ibid.

worked wonders in us, through us and, mostly, in spite of us. Let us acknowledge and give thanks for such gifts. Let us abide in his Presence in our lives and in our Christians assemblies. But let us also allow ourselves to be challenged by such Presence energising us on our life-journeys and sending us into an active transformation of our world.

Love is his Name
(Trinity)

John 3:16-18

The Inexpressible Question

THE PARADOX FASCINATES ME. 4 July 2012 marked a breakthrough of astronomical proportions in the scientific era. The Hedron collider at Cern (Switzerland) pushed our vision to the very edge of birthing of the universe and named it 'the God particle'. No, the scientists at Cern did not set out to prove or disprove the existence of God and their discovery has nothing to do with the debate on the relationship between faith and science. However, I propose that the naming itself is both revealing and paradoxical. The most sophisticated scientific research lacks the language to describe the most primordial and most powerful expression of the universe beyond introducing the term '*God*' as the foundational principle of reality. As someone said, 'it is possible to live without God, but it is not possible to avoid the question of God'.

The message is clear and very apt to any liturgical celebration where we are confronted with the fundamental question of God and with the meaning of our claim to belief in a God whom we describe as 'Trinity', a 'Triune God'. The answer to the question will always be partial, conditional to human liminality and unsatisfactory; but whether it is shaped by cultural categories, cosmic events, or deeply personal spiritual experiences, the question of God is timeless and absolutely unavoidable. Indeed, the very statement claiming absolute denial of God demands that we confront the question, at least as an academic pursuit or as an emotional response so that – according to Richard Dawkins – we can then reject it as an absurdity. Sixteen centuries ago, Augustine of Hippo already proclaimed this unavoidable timelessness deeply rooted into our human psyche by declaring that 'our hearts are restless until they rest in God'.

Every age and every culture throughout history has sought its own expression of God, an expression that will both shape and give meaning to the social values, creedal statements, moral stance and lifestyles, as well as a full gamut of traditions and forms of belief within that particular time and culture. At the same time, this cultural and timeless mix also demands an ongoing re-expression of the God-concept in language that will resonate as life-giving in each specific time and place, communities, and individuals, social mores and traditions, diverse cultures or particular needs of specific times and places. That is why the answer to 'who is your God' lies not so much in universal and unchanging creedal statements or philosophical-theological categories, but in the language of images and symbols delivering a message that is both concrete and universal, individual and collective at the same time.

Each of us holds a very personal and cherished image or expression of God, an image that will shape our worldview, justify our lifestyle and give meaning to our relationships. Unfortunately, a culturally conditioned image can also carry a heavy freight of negativity, of guilt, fear, and distant aloofness, as well as a maze of speculations, theological definitions or moral assumptions obfuscating completely the face of our God. God is one in three or three in one, God is up-there, or out-there, or somewhere else; a devotional idol or a moral club, aloof and distant from me and my life experience. Such a God will always remain judgmental, fearsome and unrecognised, more akin to a demanding despot than to the loving Life-Giver revealed by Jesus when he called him '*my Father and your Father*' (John 20:17).

Experience of Relationship

After centuries of theological and philosophical speculation, we tend to forget that Jesus never speculated about God. Instead, tapping into the ancient biblical language of personal experience and images, he challenged his contemporaries to look at their ordinary daily experience and there discover both the nature of God and God's presence in their life. What Jesus did was to coin a term that expressed the deepest and most authentic human relationship possible, and thus invited us to project our understanding of natural fatherhood on the nature and action of God. As Christians, if we are to understand the meaning of Jesus' life and death, we must look at his understanding of God as '*Abba-Father*'. Because he was not prepared to reduce God either to a sensory representation or to an abstract concept, Jesus challenged any idealised or idolatrous concept of God, to the point that it cost him his life. It would be much easier to speculate about a God in his heaven, a dispenser of goodies on request, or some idol-god controllable with performance and ritual. But Jesus went to his death in order to subvert any misconception that would distance God from us and isolate him into silent and distant loneliness.

Biblical language shuns philosophical speculation, and instead always implies interaction and relatedness. For Jesus, there is only one image that expresses fully such relatedness and interaction: God is *Abba* (Father), the name used by the young child addressing their father, probably for the first time. Very early in the Johannine narrative, Jesus' conversation with Nicodemus (John 3:16-18.21) revolves entirely around life exuding from the love of fatherhood and sonship.

> God so loved the world that he gave his only Son, so that everyone... may have eternal life... in order that the world might be saved through him. (John 3:16-18).

Our God is essentially relationship and any denial of this relationship between Father, Son and Absolute Love called the Spirit reduces God to an idol, a distant despot sitting alone in judgment and acting according to personal whims. On the contrary, nothing is more intimate and more life-giving than the relationship of parent and child and, even in the face of death, Jesus remained unwavering in his mission to reveal that this is precisely the kind of relationship that God seeks to enter into with each of us. God is Abba, the life-giver totally enmeshed for eternity with every human being in their personal and individual story with such bonds that nothing not even death will ever obliterate.

In this fatherhood-sonship perspective, Jesus simply reflects the original biblical concept of God as a pure and absolute relationship. If we have a father then we must posit a son that speaks of interaction, of multiplicity and of complementariness. But most of all it speaks of a deep, eternal, and unbreakable relationship. A son enjoys fullness of life because of the father's love, and a father can only be such because he has a son. A father and a son can only be who they are to the extent that at the deepest level of their being they share life and love and know that they are connected by mutually shared life and love.

The very use of terms like father and son speaks of a fundamental, eternal and undeniable relationship, a bond that is both life-giving and life-shaping energised by love. Long beyond and before any organic perspective, I am a living person because of a primordial love shared by my life-givers, a love so intense and so deep, that it materialised in me as a living person. Fathers and mothers, sons and daughters, the very terms speak of multiplicity, diversity, and of relationship to another, the very antithesis of a solitary being, aloof and distant, incapable of giving and sharing life and love. By implication, I can only speak of fatherhood/motherhood by reference to their power of sharing love and life, and through this sharing, giving life and love to others. Jesus is telling us today that the love between God, whom unequivocally he addresses as Father, and himself as the Son is so intense and so deep that it emerges into a living person, whom Christian Tradition calls the Spirit.

This Trinitarian dynamic refutes the very concept of separation, singularity and aloneness, while highlighting sharing in individuality and life-giving connections. God does not demand we unravel mathematical impossibilities or undertake flights of unreality. A superficial and purely speculative sense of God will readily marry the term Trinity with the term mystery, thus devaluing both realities into the realm of impossibilities rationalised by convoluted philosophical arguments. Etymologically, the term *mystery* (μυστήριον) has nothing to do with the unknown or the unexplainable, because in its original scriptural meaning the term describes a living and active presence of God here and now. This active presence redeems God from a domineering idol in the sky, a control freak interfering at whim with human affairs. Trinity points to an outward movement, to otherness, multiplicity and diversity as opposed to isolation and loneliness. Trinity implies plurality, but a plurality that is so powerful as to bind its characters into a unity of life and love.

Trinity Sunday not only confronts us with the question of 'Who is our God' but, more importantly, it gives the answer not in terms of time or place, of rational speculation or of imaginative flights of fantasy, but in terms of deep and personal human relationships. The very concept of 'Trinity' is not meant to entangle the mind in speculative or mathematical impossibilities. Rather, it wants to highlight relationship within a multiplicity, each element intimately related to one another, while each maintains its own personal individuality.

Living the Mystery

The greatest challenges in living out our faith lies is taking Jesus seriously, not because his message is too difficult to comprehend, or because it makes unreasonable demands of us, but because the message at times sounds just too good to be true. We are the objects of an unconditional movement of love between God and each individual person. The same relationship between Jesus and his

Father is the relationship that the Father seeks to establish with each of us from all eternity and for all eternity. In God's plan, we are meant to be caught in a divine-human love affair between God and each of us individually and collectively. It is the very nature of our God to seek a personal relationship with every human being.

Relationship binding diversity and plurality into oneness represents the very nature of God, and interpersonal relationships in our ordinary daily routines are the human expressions of this human-divine relationship of God with us and among each and every one of us which Jesus expressed as *love* shared and accepted. His words spell this out clearly and give us the key to understanding both God and self as a mutual abiding in love.

'As the Father has loved me, so I have loved you; abide in my love.' (John 15:9)

Love is the essence of who God is and of what God does. Perhaps that is why sometimes it is difficult to take Jesus seriously. The sense of being unloved often lurks deep and dangerous in our psyche, and the notion of a God who loves each human being individually and unconditionally appears not only foreign but truly unbelievable. The reality is that if we are to take Jesus' words seriously then we must accept that each and all of us as human beings are the object of this love affair, a relationship so deep and personal that nothing will ever frustrate it or obliterate it. Such deep and personal human-divine relationship is not the result of any particular merit or achievement on our parts, or of spiritual double-backward somersaults. God loves us simply and solely because that is the nature of God, and that is the way God operates.

Love is the essence of who God is and of what God does. Perhaps that is why sometimes it is difficult to take Jesus seriously. The sense of being unloved often lurks deep and dangerous in our psyche, and the notion of a God who loves each human being individually and unconditionally appears not only foreign but truly unbelievable. The reality is that if we are to take Jesus' words seriously then we must accept that each and all of us as human beings are the object of this love affair, a relationship so deep and personal that nothing will ever frustrate it or obliterate it. Such deep and personal human-divine relationship is not the result of any particular merit or achievement on our parts, or of spiritual double-backward somersaults. God loves us simply and solely because that is the nature of God, and that is the way God operates.

God can only be God in the here and now of life and love and the very concept of *Trinity* means *Love*. I see this Trinity-love in the smiling face of a child or of the elderly person who knows intuitively their dependence on the other and is grateful for the care and love lavished on them. I see this Trinity-love in every human family striving to develop strong mutual relationships and grow in reciprocal acknowledgment of individual giftedness in spite of individual diversity and personal differences. I see this Trinity-love in the face of every person who will not give up hope in the search for unity and love-engendered peace in this world, spurred on by the unshakeable belief in the goodness and dignity of a God-energised humanity.

For centuries, theological debate has put us on guard against any assumption of some multiplicity of gods that would deny the fundamental tenet of monotheistic biblical faith. Rather than being about a performance-like activity or cultic veneration of a distant and fearsome idol-god, biblical faith is about a fundamental life-giving love relationship of God with each and every human being, reflecting the kind of *total-love relationship – (Spirit) –* of *Father* and *Son* as preached and lived by Jesus towards his Abba-Father. The Trinitarian blessing *'in the name of the Father, the Son and the Holy Spirit'* more than making a theological statement is a proclamation of the outpouring of God's love into our life and the active presence of the Spirit in our hands. May we be people of courage and faith to move beyond rationality and allow ourselves to be embraced unconditionally by this love-energised, active presence of our God whose name is *Love*!

Food for the Poor from the Poor (The Body and Blood of the Lord)

John 6:51-58 / Luke 9:11-17

Revealed at the Table

IT MAY SOUND LIKE A TRIVIA QUESTION, but have you ever noticed how often the Gospel narrative seems to link significant events within the context of a meal.[77] This is particularly significant in relation to the Resurrection stories encompassed by two meal-centred bookends where Jesus reveals himself to the disciples for who he really is beyond all personal agenda: the Last Supper (Matthew 26:17-30; Mark 14:12-16; Luke 22:7-30), and Jesus' self-revelation at the end of the Emmaus journey, with two disciples who, in a futile attempt at obliterating forever the memory of their tragic lot (Luke 24:13-35). Likewise, John ends his Gospel with some tired and distraught disciples vainly attempting to escape the reality of their pain and loss by returning fruitlessly to their tried and true life of fishing (John 21:1-16). In their frustration, they fail to recognise the Lord who meets them and, against all fishing sense and their professional expertise, the stranger volunteers fishing instructions while tending to some bread cooking on a charcoal fire and inviting them to come and have breakfast out of the very

---

[77] Matthew 9:9-12; 14:13-21; 15:32-39; 26:6-13, 17-29; Mark 1:29-31; 2:15-17; 6:30-44; 8:1-10; 14:12-21; 16:14-16; Luke 4:38-39; 5:29-32; 9:10-17; 10:38-42; 19:1-10; 22:14-23; 24:13-35. 38-43; John 2:1-11; 6:1-14, 22-70; 12:1-8; chapters 13 to 17; 21:9-14.

abundance of the catch that they were not supposed to have dragged into their boat.

An immediate perusal of these and similar narratives of such meal-events may well be a doubtful apologetic argument as proof of the resurrection of Jesus. However, these meal-centred Resurrection stories are a call and a challenge for us today to re-interpret the relationship between us and God as revealed and established by the event.

Resurrection is as much a radical experience of presence and new life brought on by Jesus's life and ministry about us today as it was an historical event for the disciples two thousand years ago. However, such presence transpiring a powerful sense of *intimacy* and energising Jesus and his disciples through the medium of food and drink is not exclusive to the Paschal Mystery, but also throughout several key events interspersed throughout the four Gospel narrative. The Judeo-Christian tradition in the *New Revised Standard Version* of the Bible refers to *banquet* forty-four times, ten of which in the gospels alone. Adding then terms as *eating* and/or *drinking*, we are looking at more than six hundred occurrences, eighty-five of which only in the four Gospels.

In the Old Testament, the banquet is the ultimate expression of the fidelity of Yahweh, who will never forget his people, but will always keep his promises in spite of the infidelity and rejection of Israel, and of the apparent punishment for such infidelity. Likewise, in the New Testament, the banquet takes on the identification of the fulfilment of Yahweh' promises of *'preparing a banquet on the highest of mountains'*. Through Jesus, the banquet is the symbolic realisation of the active and living presence of God in human history, both here and now as, and not yet, but fully realised in the Parousia (Matthew's 22:2-10; Luke 14:8-13).

In the Gospels, Jesus' shared meal goes beyond the image of the beyond and the within but becomes an instrument of self-revelation of God as the energy and self-giving, reaching out to people, as well as challenging those around him to reach out to one another as exemplified by John 6:1-71.

While the three synoptics and Paul focus on the celebration of Passover and the handing over of the Eucharistic injunction on the disciples, John has a totally different understanding of the Last Supper as the self-handing over of himself to his disciples as their life-giving energy. He does not discuss formally any form of institution of the Eucharist during that last earthly evening of Jesus, but he deals intensely and profoundly with the Eucharistic theme in another incident involving food: the multiplication of the loaves and fishes (John 6). In a way, this is the first of a long list of experiences where the *Eucharist* becomes *a critical challenge and a discriminatory element of faith for the disciple.*

Message Beyond Appearance

The miracle of the multiplication of bread and fishes must have held a very particular significance for the early Church, if we consider that the four gospels retell the same event six times, with Mark and Matthew reporting it twice (Matthew 14:13-21 and 15:32-39; Mark 6:31-44 and 8:1-10; Luke 9:12-17; John 6:1-14), The details vary slightly, but all the narratives share the same intent.

On his journey, Jesus has just given his disciples one of the most spectacular signs of the loving and caring presence of God in their midst, by feeding thousands of people on five loaves and two fish (John 6:1-4). Jesus and the disciples have a problem, although both the nature of the problem and the proposed solution are diametrically opposite to each other, highlighting the tension of senselessness between human rationality and divine imperative, when it comes to accepting God in our life and in our mutual relationships. For Jesus, it is a personal problem demanding personal involvement and self-giving. The plight of a large group of tired and starving people arouses compassion in Jesus, and the question of 'how are we to meet the needs of these sheep without a shepherd?' (Mark 6:34) needs addressing because faith in the God revealed by Jesus demands that needs and suffering around us are an injunction to incarnate God's compassion and personal involvement. On the other hand, however, true to form, the disciples fail to see the sign and remain blind and almost unimpressed by it all, and the same plight of a hungry and lost crowd of people is someone else's problem, and this 'someone else' had better do something about it.

There is no self-giving nor even a hint of concern in such a 'common sense solution'. It is very much a matter of 'It is not my problem and I do not really want to get involved in something that I cannot do anything about anyway!' To their human prudence, this is a big social problem, to be resolved with a dismissal before it becomes a personal problem. Concerned about their personal needs and blinded by their own agenda, they cannot look beyond the real needs and the bare elements of food and all that this means for them. They fail to see the message or read the significance and the challenge of what Jesus is about.

The narrative opens with a dialogue between Jesus and his disciples, the latter being all intent on convincing the Master to adopt a quick, practical solution to the problem by dismissing the crowds. After all, it was getting late, and the place was a semi-barren desert.

> *'Where are we to get enough bread in the desert to feed so great a crowd?'* (Matthew 15:33),

question the disciples. It was only 'wise' to

> *'send the crowd away so that they may go into the surrounding villages and countryside, to lodge and get provisions; for we are here in a deserted place'* (Luke 9:12).

Even if rather dismissive and probably mirroring our efficiency and achievement-drunk culture, the disciples' advice sounds so familiar. Let them solve their own problems.

'We have no more than five loaves and two fish — unless we are to go and buy food for all these people.' (Luke 9:12-13)

Philip is also a very competent and practical accountant, and he quickly worked out that

'six months wages would not buy enough bread for each of them to get a little' (John 6:7).

However, Jesus is not that worldly wise. He is the compassionate one, and he immediately challenges his followers to compassion and service in their turn.

'You give them something to eat' (Mark 6:37).

Bewilderment, annoyance, questions! How preposterous! 'How could we?' No, it does not make sense! It is all right to follow the Master when he works spectacular miracles, when he speaks his affirming parables, when we are up the mountain of personal devotion and fervour, our hearts warmed at the thought that we are the special ones, or when we feel fired into rushing off to a social awareness program for a couple of months. Now he is asking the impossible! It defies all human rationality! Yes, God's call to his followers then and to us now may well sound devoid of human rationality and of immediate solutions.

Consequently, as is his wont, Jesus promptly takes the cue from the situation at hand. Tapping into their chronic misunderstanding, he pushes them and us beyond the bare elements into perceiving the active and life-giving presence of God in each insignificant skerrick of our story, in every fibre of our bodily frame, and in the deepest recesses of heart and psyche. The consequence of this looking beyond and within finds full expression in Jesus' great Eucharistic discourse that follows the narrative of the miracle in John which represents the living and dynamic core of eucharist, both in its message and in its transforming potency.

Paradoxically, while waxing eloquent for five chapters about the events of the Last Supper, the Fourth Gospel never once makes any direct reference to the Eucharist as such. The evangelist brings it all powerfully together – in Chapter 6, where Jesus moves away from a material perspective – centred on the elements of food – to a relational one between each of us and God.

From the very beginning, we are confronted with a clear challenge to our understanding of God and of humanity. The passage is not just about a difference of opinion between Jesus and his disciples, but an illustration of the distance that often exists in real terms between our declaration of faith and the concrete lived response of each day. Through the discourse about bread, Jesus confronts us with the reality of the relationship between himself and his disciples as the living expression of the relationship between us and God. However, in trying to identify Jesus as the energy which gives and fosters fullness of life and stressing the life interaction between God and humanity, John has Jesus using very confronting language.

> *'I am the living bread that came down from heaven. Whoever eats of this bread will live for ever; and the bread that I will give for the life of the world is my flesh... Very truly, I tell you, unless you eat the flesh of the Son of Man and drink his blood, you have no life in you.'* (John 6:51)

With that absolute authority and total integrity that marked all his life and ministry, he tells us to eat his flesh and drink his blood.

> *'Very truly, I tell you, unless you eat the flesh of the Son of Man and drink his blood, you have no life in you. Those who eat my flesh and drink my blood have eternal life.'* (John 6:53-54)

Stunningly shocking words, really! Yes, the words of Jesus in today's Gospel sound quite shocking and almost crude to the point that, confronted with such in-your-face realism, many of his hearers could not accept the intolerable language and turned their backs on him. Yet, unconcerned by the horrified reaction of his followers, he repeats the injunction, as if to stress the absolute necessity of taking his words seriously, Jesus pulls no punches, nor does he mince words.

> *'Unless you eat the flesh of the Son of Man and drink his blood, you have no life in you. Those who eat my flesh and drink my blood have eternal life, and I will raise them up on the last day; for my flesh is true food and my blood is true drink.'* (John 6:55-56).

That is the key to it all. Yes, the words of Jesus sound quite shocking and almost crude to the point that, confronted with such in-your-face realism, many of his hearers could not accept the intolerable language and turned their backs on him. Only a God madly in love with human beings could have set up such a dramatic scenario as to make himself food, in order to create that total, even physical and personal intimacy with every human being who is prepared to accept his word and enter into the human-divine relationship.

Those early followers turned their backs on him and 'no longer went about with him' (John 6:66) because they could not accept a God so intimately immersed in our human reality as to become our flesh and blood, the very energy of our daily life, the very essence of our humanity. God's longing for total immersion with intimacy can only be expressed with the energy and identification of the elements of food and drink becoming 'flesh and blood'. For the Semitic mind, the expression 'flesh and blood', rather than two separate elements of a living body, implies the whole person, a totality of body and soul, as much as of mind and heart. In this perspective, Jesus is inviting us to total imbibing for total identification with him as the living principle of human life and of the Father's love for every individual person who accepts such an invitation.

Eucharist is not a 'ritual doing', a performance or a re-enactment recalling something far away in time and space, even less a private devotion tugging at the emotional chords of the heart.

Nowhere in the Gospels does Jesus tell his disciples to adore him. Rather, he directs our attention to his Father. Adoring Jesus in Benediction is OK, but it is not what the Mass is about... the Eucharist is not about me and Jesus; it is about us in the Christian community, about us being transformed into the body of Christ, about us joining in the mission of Jesus in the world.[78]

Eucharist is an event in everyone's life experience, a mutual immersion of God into our personal lives and, in turn, of each of us into the energy of God, giving and sustaining our whole being in life and in death.

You Give Them Something to Eat

But the Christian Story does not stop with Jesus. It must never stop there, to a distant historical event. The Christian Story is living and it has to be written in flesh and blood, our flesh and blood, by those who accept the energy and presence of God's life-giving energy. Jesus' self-giving must become the stimulus and energy for the mission of the disciple who on the blueprint of the Master is called to give freely and unconditionally, so that the poor may hear Good News, captives may be set free, and blind people may rejoice in their sight restored (Luke 4:18).

Having unsuccessfully challenged his disciples to provide food for the crowds, Jesus presses the point by intimating clearly that it is really up to them to take up the responsibility for the situation with a peremptory '*You give them something to eat*' (Matthew 14:15-16). He not only takes control and feeds the hungry crowds,

> *Taking the five loaves and the two fish, he looked up to heaven, and blessed and broke the loaves, and gave them to his disciples*

---

[78] Christine Schenk, 'Is the Eucharistic Revival an Exercise in Cheap Grace?', in *National Catholic Reporter*, (NCR). (Accessed 29/06/2023).

to set before the people; and he divided the two fish among them all. (Mark 6:41)

In a strange twist to the story, one very significant element runs through all the six narratives of the miracle of the loaves and fishes, binding them all into one challenging call for us. While Jesus takes the initiative to feed the thousands out of some miserly loaves and fishes, it is the disciples who are called to action and asked to distribute the lavishness of God to the hungry, lost and tired crowds.

> *Then he ordered the crowd to sit down on the ground; and he took the seven loaves, and after giving thanks he broke them and gave them to his disciples to distribute; and they distributed them to the crowd.* (Mark 8:6).

In the end, Jesus depends on those insensitive, unwilling or incapable disciples to distribute the bread and fishes to the thousands they were desperately trying to ignore and 'send away'. Truly, God has no hands but those of the disciple and the disciple just cannot deny responsibility to become involved in doing what Jesus did: to feed the hungry and to journey in compassion with those very ones who originally were unwilling to become involved. Eucharist is the inescapable responsibility of the believer. Nourished and energised by God, we have no choice but to be and become nourishes and energisers for the whole world.

Both of Matthew's versions of this miracle give us an interesting insight by highlighting the fact that *'those who ate were about five thousand men, besides women and children'* (Matthew 14:21). At the same time, John identifies specifically a boy as the owner of the five barley loaves and two fish (John 6:8-9). Thus, after informing the reader that women and children did not count in the social structure of the time (Matthew 14:21), a small boy who is not even worth considering in the final count is the one who makes the five loaves and two fish available to Jesus. A small boy, as the writer of the Fourth Gospel tells us, with five barley loaves and two fish (John 6:9) is hardly the premise for a sumptuous feast to be shared among five thousand people. Yet the readiness of a child and a social outcast to share the poverty of those means worked the miracle and it became a feast for the hungry and the weary. *'And they all ate and were filled'* (Mark 6:42) and there was still some left over for the next day.

'And the disciples distributed them among the crowd.' The challenge however does not end with the generosity of a small boy. As if to prove a point, having given thanks for the abundance of God's gifts, Jesus asks the disciples to distribute the bread and fish to the crowds. Those very disciples who were seeking the sensible solution of dismissing the crowd and claiming destitution on all counts become the instruments of God's generous presence. With a truly compassionate practicality, Jesus addressed the immediate needs of those around him, wherever these needs were, and however they may have arisen.

In spite of their futile attempts at avoiding the challenge on the grounds of poverty or inadequacy, in the end, the disciples become the instrument of God's initiative and compassionate self-giving. Jesus not only asks us to feed the poor but he depends on us to distribute his giftedness to the crowds. In one of the many ironical twists of this story, *in the end the poor are the very one who distribute God's abundant riches to the poor out of their own poverty and destitution.*

The same claim is made of us when we sit at the Eucharistic table; we must become instruments at the hands of God for those who hunger for a word of thanks and of encouragement, those who seek understanding and compassion, and those who yearn for a hand reaching out to them in friendship and companionship. Precisely because we sit at the table of the Lord, we do not allow ourselves any option but to be people sent out to feed the hungry who stand around us. Imbibing the energy of God challenges and energises into action on behalf of others, while failing to accept the challenge, is to make a mockery of the Eucharist, because then we would conveniently ignore the injunction 'eat my flesh and drink my blood' (John 6:54).

In our poverty and liminality, we might question the possibility of this total, free, unconditional self-giving ever becoming a reality in any relationship, or at whatever level of commitment or stage of life we may be. Yes, it is possible to give of oneself totally. Indeed, it is not only possible, but it is an absolute imperative of discipleship, unless we want our life to become pretentious, and our claim to discipleship simply a veneer of personal devotions.

True biblical faith is not 'a doing for God', but 'a freeing God' to do with me and through me. I have nothing to contribute to the mission except my nothingness and destitution. It is relatively easy to feel compassion from the comfort of our lounge rooms and even to contribute of our surplus to starving children in the thousands of refugee camps around the world. It can feed our ego and nourish self-righteousness. It is much more challenging to address the real problems of addressing the diverse manifestations of hunger and abandonment of those who stand around us or reach out to those we would rather not see or would willingly send away.

All this makes heavy demands of time and energy; it frustrates and tires us out; it hurts and leaves us shattered. That is why the Fathers of the Church spoke of *becoming bread*. Not only we must feed the world out of our own poverty and limitations, but we must also become 'bread for the hungry' – bread that is broken, cut, torn, chewed up and transformed. All this hurts, and it hurts very deeply and intensely! Yet, that is the only way that the energy of God which we have imbibed at Eucharist is set free to energise the world.

Our contribution may be small and probably insignificant to world wisdom. Five loaves and two fishes among five thousand men is not exactly the most sumptuous of meals! Yet, 'All ate and were filled' (Matthew 14:20). They even gathered twelve baskets of broken pieces left over! Moreover, all this happened because the readiness and availability of 'a poor one' to share the poverty of his means revealed the active presence of God in a world of hungry and tired humanity. Only when our poverty becomes bread for those who stand around us will we truly be able to claim discipleship.

Our understanding of God's presence in the Eucharist cannot be disengaged from our understanding of what it means to be close, to be unified, *to be with* somebody and to give oneself as gift. It is in this context that Eucharist becomes truly 'a dangerous memory'. I can no longer ignore need and human suffering. I must become compassionate to those who wander with me through desert places.

Responsibility, affirmation, brotherly/sisterly love, forgiveness, equality, support, compassion, mutuality, empathy – these are not just nice words, or even life attitudes. They are radical demands stemming directly from Jesus' injunction *'you give them something to eat'*.

Eucharist commits me to openness beyond liking, and to friendship without self-protective boundaries.

Eucharist commits me to journey through my daily life together with everyone I meet, in the knowledge that each other's journey will be affected precisely by this 'being together'.

Eucharist commits me to availability without imposition; and sensitivity without manipulation.

Eucharist commits me to personal responsibility into whatever is life-giving, beyond the call of duty or the demands of a religious rule.

Eucharist commits me to recognition and affirmation as opposed to any form of stereotyping.

Eucharist commits me to become light and warmth to others, perhaps even when I may find myself groping in the dark, alone and cold.

Eucharist commits me to become that 'instrument of peace' that Francis of Assisi prayed for and sang about, without even a thought of expecting to be the recipient of God's gift of peace, 'for it is in giving that we receive, it is in pardoning that we are pardoned, and it is in dying that we are born to eternal life'.

The call to discipleship expressed in the self-gift Eucharist may at times appear far beyond human unaided capabilities. But Jesus, who invites us to become bread for the hungry and instruments of his compassion, energises us beyond our own expectations and empowers us to bear much fruit (John 15:5). On that one guarantee, let us recommit ourselves to be Eucharist to each other and instruments of God's self-giving to all.

Then, our gathering at Eucharist will make sense both as energy for our growth as disciples and as a stimulus to reach out to the brothers and sisters that God sets in our way each day of our lives. Then, truly, the Eucharist would have become *food for the poor from the poor* in a God-enriched world.

www.ingramcontent.com/pod-product-compliance
Lightning Source LLC
Chambersburg PA
CBHW012002090526
44590CB00026B/3843